ERITREA

Even The Stones Are Burning

New and Revised Edition

ERITREA
Even The Stones Are Burning
New and Revised Edition

Roy Pateman

The Red Sea Press, Inc.
Publishers & Distributors of Third World Books

11-D Princess Road
Lawrenceville, NJ 08648  P. O. Box 48
Asmara, ERITREA

The Red Sea Press, Inc.

Publishers & Distributors of Third World Books

11-D Princess Road
Lawrenceville, NJ 08648

P. O. Box 48
Asmara, ERITREA

Copyright © 1990 Roy Pateman

First Edition 1990
Second Edition 1998

Book design: Krystal Jackson
Cover design: Jonathan Gullery
Cover photograph from *Eritrea: Revolution at Dusk* (pp.86-87)
    by Robert Papstein (Red Sea Press, 1991) copyright © Robert Papstein, 1991

Library of Congress Cataloging-in-Publication Data

Pateman, Roy.
    Eritrea : even the stones are burning / Roy Pateman. -- 2nd, new &
rev. ed.
        p.   cm.
    Includes bibliographical references and index.
    ISBN 1-56902-057-4 (paper)
    1. Eritrea--Politics and government--1962-1993. 2. Eritrea-
-History--1962-1993. I. Title.
DT397.P38   19970
963.5--dc21   97-15405
                                                                CIP

For Carole

Contents

Preface to the Second Edition

Lorries come behind the tank carrying young men (and women) the fighters of the EPLF. They are dirty, battlestained and very tired. A dream—"Hilmee"—they are HERE in Asmara, the city they fought to free, to return to—this brave little city subjected to so much humiliation, to so much suffering, to so much death: this little city which has waited for thirty years.

—Thomas Johnston, *Hilmee*[1]

I am very pleased that *Eritrea: Even the Stones are Burning*, having already sold over 2,000 copies, is now appearing in its second edition. I am particularly glad that Eritreans almost universally like the book, and appreciate their many encouraging comments. My great thanks are also due to Thomas Keneally for his characteristically generous remarks on launching the book in Australia's Parliament House on 17 April 1991. The late Fred Hollows was also robustly supportive.

For this second edition, I have written an entirely new afterword, a piece that analyzes developments since 1990 and considers the many challenges that face independent Eritrea. It grew out of exercises I conducted with students at UCLA and from papers

I presented to the New York African Studies Association in April 1995 and to a faculty Seminar at the University of Melbourne, Australia in November 1995. I conclude that Eritreans will meet these challenges with the same determination and resourcefulness that characterized their long struggle for international recognition as a sovereign nation.

I have also used this opportunity to correct the few typographical errors that escaped the proofreaders of the first edition and to amend the text where absolutely necessary. I have not otherwise altered the text, as I think that it still holds up pretty well and will serve as an adequate explanation (at least for the moment) of why the Eritrean revolution was successful against such overwhelming odds. It is also a record of some extraordinary achievements.

The Ethiopian centralists, of course, conducted their battle against the Eritreans not just with bullets, but marshalled to their defense most of the academics who wrote on the subject. This war of words was waged with just as much vigor. Of those who bothered to notice the publication of the first edition of my book in 1990-1991—at an unfortunate time for them as the Dergue lurched from one military disaster to another—little need be said, but to re-emphasize that I shall not attempt to emulate their tone of sour grapes, bile, and hysteria. They have lost the intellectual battle, just as they lost the physical battle, and it is time for us to be generous in victory.

I am grateful for the many helpful and positive reviews I have received from scholars. Amare Tekle said that it was a "perceptive study of the essence of Eritrean nationalism and the historical development of the Eritrean nation."[2] Alex de Waal says that it "contains original scholarship, notably the discussion of Eritrean resistance to Italian rule, and the analysis of the role of the Arabs and Israelis in the conflict."[3]

Bob Papstein said "he has written the best introductory book on the subject."[4] Forrest Colburn, in the course of a long review article in *World Politics*, called it "well researched, well reasoned."[5] And Tom Killion "the best single text available for understanding contemporary Eritrea."[6] (This latter review was submitted to the journal *North-east African Studies*, but unaccountably did not appear!)

Little that has been published since 1990 has added much to our knowledge of the period I cover. Paul Henze's *The Horn of Africa: From War to Peace*, was out of date even before it appeared in 1991. It is very much Ethiopia-centric history as before, and starts off with the extraordinary assumption that a federation would solve all problems. However, I agree with him on the malevolent role of the former USSR in prolonging the war and encouraging misguided agricultural policies.[7]

Robert Patman's *The Soviet Union in the Horn of Africa* was published in 1990 but nevertheless draws mainly on research completed in 1986. It is now of interest as an historical curiosity.[8] John Markakis' chapter, "Ethnic Conflict and the State in the Horn of Africa," published in 1994 admits (belatedly) that a national Eritrean "consciousness was forged in a bloody struggle that lasted three decades."[9]

However, Okbazghi Yohannes' *Eritrea, A Pawn in World Politics* is very thorough and adds a great deal to our understanding of the external dimensions of the Eritrean conflict; an area which, apart from the role of the Middle Eastern powers, I deliberately did not cover in detail.[10]

We all owe a big debt to Dan Connell for his vivid and pioneering reportage from the field. *Against all Odds: a Chronicle of the Eritrean Revolution*, is a fine, readable account of his involvement in the struggle and is very useful on developments in the village of Zagr. His account of the way the EPLF waged the war is a valuable supplement to Chapter Seven of my book.[11]

We know that a number of the leading EPLF figures kept detailed personal diaries of the many years they spent in the field. So far one, by Al-Amin Mohammed Said, has come out in Arabic and Tigrinya.[12] All such personal accounts will be of great value when someone comes to write a comprehensive account of the war.

Ruth Iyob's *The Eritrean Struggle for Independence*, which grew out of her dissertation, is helpful on the ELM and the conflict between the liberation fronts in the 1961-1981 period; once again, I chose not to research this aspect in detail, but she gives further support for my general thesis.[13]

The Norwegian anthropologist, Kjetil Tronvoll spent two years in Eritrea, immediately after the liberation of Asmara, carrying out M.A. research in a highland village. He has proved to be a most original scholar.[14] John Young's work on the TPLF (soon to be published by Cambridge University Press) and over which we had many discussions, in Vancouver and Eritrea, is good on the comparison between the EPLF and TPLF.

John Sorenson's *Imagining Ethiopia* contains a very eloquent and convincing demolition of the myth of the Great Tradition. He shows again that this is an invention propagated by incoherent and inconsistent writers. I like particularly the description of three of the writers in the Great Tradition, Henze, Erlich and Clapham, as forming a "mutual confirmation" society.[15]

During the past seven years, I have visited Eritrea on five occasions. The most notable field trips were in 1990, 1991, 1993 and 1997. On the first occasion I traveled, again with Fisseha as guide and Daniel as driver—both superb professionals—for many hundred of miles behind the Ethiopian lines. Along with Richard Leonard, I was fortunate enough to be the first foreigner to visit the newly liberated southern highland towns of Adi Keih and Senafé.

I was privileged to be able to interview *Blatta* Mohamed Omar and *Grazmatch* Salam Mohammed Idris, members of the Eritrean Assembly; the latter was present on 14 November 1962 when it was announced that the Emperor had unilaterally dissolved the federation. He affirmed that no vote was taken and that some members of the assembly expressed their opposition "in low voices."[16]

In 1991, I visited Asmara for the first time. I was one of the first post-liberation foreigners to fly in from Addis Ababa and, thanks to the kindness of Cpt. Haile Gebre, Manager of Flying Operations for Ethiopian Airlines, spent the flight in the cockpit of a 727 jet. In Asmara, I had the great privilege to interview Wolde-ab Woldemarian, the father of Eritrean nationalism, who was back in Eritrea for the first time in thirty years.

The second particularly memorable occasion was the sovereignty referendum of 1993, when I was able to observe the process in Barentu, an area I had last visited in 1985 in very different circumstances when Ethiopian artillery was closing in on the town. I had the most congenial traveling companions in Yohannes Daniel (from the Evangelical Church of Barentu), Asmerom, Lou Witherite and Dick Scobie (from the Unitarian Universalist Service Committee).

The experience was a highly charged emotional experience for everyone involved. It is difficult to express sufficient admiration for the efficient and democratic way in which the exercise was conducted. The only reservation I had was the discovery, in all of the polling stations we visited in Gash province, of twice the number of official ballot papers and other supplies than was necessary for the poll. I am prepared to accept the Referendum Commissioner's explanation, that the excess was due to fears of the loss or damage of papers en route to the very remote polling stations. But if the poll had been conducted by unscrupulous people, such actions could be construed very differently and could certainly have affected the outcome.

That the most spectacular thunderstorm I have ever seen struck Barentu after the polls had closed on the third day, bringing vitally needed rain to much of the country, convinced everyone that God had finally decided to relieve the suffering of Eritrea.

I visited Eritrea again in 1997, when I very much enjoyed teaching for a semester at the University of Asmara. I managed to establish a degree program in political science, and hope that my connections with the University and the new Eritrea will last for as long as I draw breath. As a small token of my esteem for the people of Eritrea, all royalties from this edition will be invested in the Nacfa Corporation for the future of Eritrea.

During the past seven years, I have also benefited greatly from conversations and correspondence with H.E. Fessehaie Abraham (formerly Eritrean Ambassador to Australia), H.E. Raphael Walden (Ambassador of Israel to Eritrea), Tekie Beyene, Gebre Michael (Lelo), Issayas Tesfa Mariam, Nu Nu Kidane, Abraham Kidane, Dick Sklar, Petros Sebahtu, Wolde-ab Issak, Kjetil Tronvoll, Richard Greenfield, Ed Keller, Scott Jones, John Sorenson, John Young, Ararat and Salome Iyob, Tewolde Zerom, John DiStefano, Craig Calhoun, Pamela Delargy, Glenn Anders and Richard Leonard. I would like to thank all the other people I have talked to and interviewed in Eritrea, Sudan, and Ethiopia over the past fourteen years—in particular, President Isaias Afwerki.

All views are of course mine. I would like to pay a special tribute to Kassahun Checole, whose drive, vision, and enterprise has made such a success of the Red Sea Press and his other publishing companies.

I acknowledge, with gratitude, the continuing support from the Department of Political Science and the James S. Coleman African Studies Center at UCLA, which has enabled me to travel and do research on the Horn of Africa. My thanks also to the University of North Carolina and USAID who sponsored my last visit to Eritrea.

And Carole, as always, for her unfailing support and love. She has given this new edition the benefit of her unrivaled critical and analytical skills.

—Roy Pateman
Los Angeles
September, 1997

Notes

1. Thomas Johnston, "Hilmee," *University Notes*, 2, 2 (Asmara: University of Asmara, 1991), p. 45.
2. Amare Tekle, *Africa Today*, 38, 2 (1991):71.
3. Alex de Waal, *Canadian Journal of African Studies*, 26, 2 (1992):374.
4. Robert Papstein, *Journal of African History*, 33, 2 (1992):344.
5. Forrest Colburn, *World Politics*, 43 (July 1991):579.
6. Tom Killion, "Book Review," Submitted to *Northeast African Studies*, 2 April, 1992, p. 7.
7. Paul Henze, *The Horn of Africa: From War to Peace* (New York: St. Martin's Press, 1991.)
8. Robert G. Patman, *The Soviet Union in the Horn of Africa* (Cambridge: Cambridge University Press, 1990.)
9. John Markakis, "Ethnic Conflict and the State in the Horn of Africa," in K. Fukui and J. Markakis, eds. *Ethnicity and Conflict in the Horn of Africa* (London: James Currey, 1994), p.229.
10. Okbazghi Yohannes, *Eritrea, a Pawn in World Politics* (Gainesville: University of Florida Press, 1991).
11. Dan Connell, *Against All Odds: a Chronicle of the Eritrean Revolution* (Lawrenceville, N.J.: Red Sea Press, 1993.) In 1997, the book was reprinted with an afterword on the postwar transition.
12. Al-Amin Mohammed Said, *Sawra Eritra—Misiguamn Minqulqualin:Mesrih Wishtawi Mfihfah Sawra Eritra* (The Eritrean Revolution—Advances and Pitfalls: The Process and Internal Dynamics of the Eritrean Revolution) (Asmara: Red Sea Press, 1994.)
13. Ruth Iyob, *The Eritrean Struggle for Independence* (Cambridge: Cambridge University Press, 1995.)
14. Kjetil Tronvoll, "The Eritrean Referendum: Peasant Voices," *Eritrean Studies Review*, 1, 1 (1996):23-67. His work is also to be published in book from by Red Sea Press in 1997 as: *Mai Weini—A Small Village in the Highlands of Eritrea*.
15. John Sorenson, *Imagining Ethiopia* (New Brunswick, N.J.: Rutgers University Press, 1993):140.
16. *Blatta* Mohamed Omar and *Grazmatch* Salam Mohamed Idris, *Interviews with Author*, 13 August 1990.

Preface

For all students of human society; sympathy with the victims of historical processes and skepticism about the victor's claims provide essential safeguards against being taken in by the dominant mythology.

—Barrington Moore Jr., *Social Origins of Dictatorship and Democracy: Lord and Peasant in the Making of the Modern World[1]*

Thinking back about the reasons for my interest in Eritrea, it seems that while a very young man of fifteen, I must first have read articles sympathetic to the Eritrean cause in British leftist journals written before the USSR decided to support Ethiopia's annexation of the country. In 1960, while working with Army Intelligence in Nairobi I saw a number of reports emanating from the British embassy in Addis Ababa and consuls in Asmara that many Eritreans were getting increasingly restless over the impending end of federation with Ethiopia, and were preparing for an armed independence struggle. I also recollect that among the many foreign contingents marching on the anti-H Bomb demonstrations of the early 1960s were a number of Eritreans who had been forced into exile because of their opposition to Ethiopia's annexation of their country in 1962.

Over the years I read the anarchist-pacifist journal *Peace News*, one of the few reliable sources of information on the opposition to Ethiopia. Later, while working at the London headquarters of the National Farmers Union in the early 1970s, I once again came across a number of very able and articulate Eritrean and Ethiopian labor organizers and socialists, many of whom, regrettably, have perished in the bloody struggles that have convulsed the Horn of Africa.

But the most important reason for my recent interest is the friendship and inspiration of many committed and persuasive members of the Eritrean People's Liberation Front, with whom I have talked and occasionally argued over the years; my good friend, Fessehaie Abraham, coordinator of the Eritrean Relief Association in Australia, was the first of these. My debt to him and a generation of Eritreans is incalculable. I have tried to repay a small portion of that debt by sharing with others my understanding of why the Eritreans have been waging such a long and fierce fight for independence.

Eritrea is the site of Africa's longest running war—the twenty-eight-year-old struggle of the Eritrean people against their Ethiopian colonizers. Few people are aware of the complexities and contradictions which bedevil the search for the roots of this struggle—let alone the search for peace—in a conflict which has directly or indirectly led to the deaths of one million people. The struggle for independence also involves a struggle over history and the interpretation of the past. Eritreans have not been well served by historians; the bulk of history continues to be written by carriers of the "Great Tradition," people who believe (or at least promulgate the view) that "for 4,000 years Eritrea and Ethiopia have been identical in their origins, identical in their historical development, identical in the defense of the Ethiopian region."[2] Such views, uncritically promulgated, have allowed the Eritrean past to be abrogated and used in the service of a dominant mythology which is of increasingly dubious value.

In Chapter Two, I examine numerous primary and secondary materials to show that for most of recorded history, the ancestors of the present-day Eritreans carried on their lives free of Ethiopian rule. At many times in their history, they took up arms and opposed foreign invaders, Turks, Egyptians, Italians—and Ethiopians. I am aware that the term Eritrea did not come into use until the Italians named their nascent colony such in 1886; however, I shall use it to refer to the area of what is now in many observer's eyes, if not mine, legally, the fourteenth province of Ethiopia. Also, following historian Donald Crummey's lead, I shall use the term "Abyssinia" to refer to that part of modern Ethiopia lying northwest of Addis Ababa and roughly comprising the present provinces of Gojjam, Gondar, Showa, and parts of Tigray and Wollo.[3] I use the term "Ethiopia" to characterize the expanded empire after Menelik's conquests in the nineteenth century.

Chapter Three deals with a specific feature of the colonial period—Eritrean resistance to Italian rule. This is a very neglected area of research and scholars have only recently begun to deal with it. In the following chapter, I briefly summarize the argument that it is by no means certain that in the period from 1941 to 1952 the majority of Christian Eritreans wanted union with Ethiopia. This is a particularly frustrating area in which to work; even though some thirty-seven years have elapsed since the United Nations Commission for Eritrea met in Eritrea, Cairo and Geneva, some vital documents are still restricted by the UN and hence unavailable to researchers. However, I make use of evidence uncovered recently by other researchers who have taken advantage of the United States Freedom of Information Act to ascertain what highlanders really felt in the period up to 1962.

My fifth chapter deals with Ethiopian accounts of life in Eritrea after the 1974 revolution. Although I have visited much of the considerable area of Eritrea controlled by the EPLF, the Ethiopian Government has not allowed me into those towns and villages which it controls. For this chapter I have, therefore, been forced to rely upon Ethiopian Government sources and accounts by visitors allowed in by the Dergue, as the Ethiopian government is commonly known.

Part Two is devoted to what Bereket Habte Selassie has called "the human dimension of a fighting and suffering people determined to win its right to live as a free nation."[4] It discusses the

EPLF's attempts to create a new society and the impact upon the Eritrean people of successive cycles of drought and famine. This section also deals with some of the current debates on Eritrea and Ethiopia, including the argument that the success or failure of the Eritrean struggle is largely dependent upon the support of the Arab powers (Chapter Six), concerns over the viability of an independent Eritrea (Chapter Ten) and a history of the armed conflict.

The twenty-eight year war of liberation has received very little attention from scholars and spasmodic treatment from journalists. In Chapter Seven I have relied mainly on Eritrean material for primary sources. I endeavored to cross check accounts with eye witness reports, *Africa Confidential, Indian Ocean Newsletter*, and Ethiopian sources—the latter are most unreliable, while it has been said "EPLF communiques [are] generally reliable."[5] However, the EPLF does not publish casualty figures (presumably for reasons of morale). For obvious intelligence reasons it does not publish information on, for example, its strengths and order of battle. I am satisfied, however, after three visits to EPLF-held territory (the field) where I spent some time on various sections of the front line talking to commanders, and a reasonably exhaustive search of the available literature, of the substantial truth of EPLF claims. It is well though to remember the words of Carl von Clausewitz, the greatest of military historians, that "the returns made up on each side of losses in killed and wounded, are never exact, seldom truthful, and in most cases, full of intentional misrepresentations."[6]

Despite the lack of attention to the military dimensions of the liberation struggle, the literature on Eritrea is larger than one might expect for such a small country. Of living authors to whom I owe a debt, I would like to mention: Araia Tseggai, Basil Davidson, Lionel Cliffe, Dawit Wolde Giorgis, Haggai Erlich, James Firebrace, Richard Greenfield, Jordan Gebre-Medhin, Kassahun Checole, Richard Leonard, Richard Sherman, Tekeste Negash, and in particular, Bereket Habte Selassie. I would also like to express my thanks to the many Eritreans and Ethiopians I have interviewed in the field and in particular, Isaias Afwerki. It almost goes without saying that none of the above bear any responsibility for the interpretation I have made of their views and scholarship.

My first thoughts about the roots of Eritrean national liberation were voiced at staff colloquia held at the Department of Government, The University of Sydney, and the Sociology Department, Macquarie University, in 1983. My views were enhanced by a seminar I gave the Department of Cultural Anthropology at Uppsala University in 1988. Chapter Three grew out of the article "Eritrean Resistance During the Italian Occupation" published in 1989 in the *The Journal of Eritrean Studies.* Chapter Five originated in a paper presented in 1985 to the Fifth Annual Conference of the Joint Stanford-Berkeley Center for African Studies and also published in *The Journal of Eritrean Studies*, 1, 2, Winter 1987. An earlier version of Chapter Six, was given in New Orleans at the Twenty-eighth Annual Meeting of the African Studies Association and subsequently published in *Northeast African Studies*. Chapter Seven was originally given to the Twenty-ninth Annual Meeting of the African Studies Association and subsequently revised for publication in *Armed Forces and Society* 17, 1. Chapter Nine grew out of a chapter I contributed to *The Long Struggle of Eritrea for Independence and Constructive Peace*, published by Spokesman Press in 1988, and commissioned by The Research and Information Centre on Eritrea to commemorate the twenty-fifth anniversary of the start of the armed struggle in Eritrea. This chapter also formed the basis of papers delivered to the Annual Conference of the African Studies Association of Australasia and the Pacific in Adelaide, August 1987, and the Institute for Development Studies at Helsinki University in 1989. I have also drawn upon two of my unpublished papers. "Prospects for Peace in the Horn of Africa" was delivered to the African Studies Association Meeting in Chicago in 1988, and to a joint seminar organized by the Departments of Political Science and Peace and Conflict Studies at the University of Gothenburg in 1989. "How Libertarian is the EPLF?" was given to the History Workshop Conference at Brighton, England in 1988. My thanks to all contributors to the discussions which accompanied and followed these presentations, and also to Forrest Colburn and Donald Rothchild, former colleagues of mine in the Center for International Studies at Princeton University, for many illuminating conversations. I am also indebted to Ruth Iyob for her incisive comments and encouragement. The librarians at the Hoover Institution at Stanford, the Scandinavian Institute of African Studies in Uppsala, Northwestern University, and the Firestone Library at Princeton were invariably helpful in tracking down recondite materials. I wish to acknowledge with gratitude that I received partial funding for a trip to Eritrea in 1987 from the Center for International Studies and the Center for Regional Studies at Princeton University.

I would like to thank especially the countless number of Eritreans who have shown me such splendid hospitality in Australia, England, Italy, Sudan, Scandinavia and the USA, as well as in Eritrea. It is probably invidious to single out individuals, but I would like to express my appreciation to the men and women of the Protocol Department of the EPLF who have hosted me on three visits to the field, and to express my profound admiration to the members of the Eritrean Relief Association (ERA) who manage to run the world's best aid, rehabilitation and development outfit, amid appalling difficulties. All royalties from this book will go to ERA.

My greatest debt (for over 30 years) is acknowledged in the dedication.

—Roy Pateman
Los Angeles, 1990

Notes

1. Barrington Moore Jr., *Social Origins of Dictatorship and Democracy: Lord and Peasant in the Making of the Modern World.*
2. Akilou Abte-Wold, *Statement*, to Forty-third meeting of the United Nations Commission on Eritrea (1950) p. 46.
3. Donald Crummey, 'Abyssinian Feudalism,' *Past and Present*, 89, (1980) p.19.
4. Bereket Habte Selassie, *Review* of Haggai Erlich, *The Struggle Over Eritrea: 1962-178, Eritrea Information*, 5, 9, (1983) p. 10.
5. *Indian Ocean Newsletter* 124 (1984).
6. Carl von Clausewitz, *On War*, ed. Anatol Rapoport (Harmondsworth, Penguin Books, 1968) p. 313.

I

Retrieving the Past

1

IS ERITREA A NATION?

Nations, created over longer or shorter periods of time, with their own speech and culture and beliefs and institutions, are virtually indestructible; persecution and massacre more often intensify than eliminate their national feeling; and continuous repression serves to keep them in an explosive condition.

—SETON-WATSON, *Nations and States: An Enquiry Into the Origins of Nations and the Politics of Nationalism[1]*

The concept of self determination has exercised the minds of political theorists since the Middle Ages; it is almost universally agreed that to be legitimate, government must be based upon the consent of the governed. Most liberal observers argue that the potential of individuals can be realized fully only within a nation. Liberal theorists support secession if this is the wish of a cohesive group which is badly governed by the state to which it "belongs."[2] The fight for national self determination (mainly within colonial boundaries) became the priority of most African intellectuals and activists from the first World War onwards.

Once independence was eventually obtained, however, the new African governing elites took a very different approach. Since its foundation in 1963, the Organization of African Unity (OAU) has downplayed the concept of self-determination and has stood out firmly against the "balkanization" of Africa—even though the balkanization of Eastern Europe liberated many peoples from oppressive rule.[3] Not the least of the reasons for this stance is that the heads of state who attend the OAU summits are, in the main, military dictators, or men who have a tenuous power base, dependent upon the support of ethnic minorities. Consequently, the leaders are extremely wary of any change in the fragile boundaries imposed upon Africa by the European powers.

No country in Africa, with the exception of Somalia, has an homogenous population, where all speak the same language, practice the same religion and share a common history and culture. And as the Somali nation is distributed among five sovereign states, there is no country in Africa where state and nation overlap completely. Consequently, no country in Africa is immune from conflict over the nationalities question—and, to a lesser extent, religion. It is worth remarking that the "inviolability of colonial boundaries" is not (as is commonly stated) written into the OAU charter and that the 1964 resolution on this matter was intended to cover future disputes—not the Eritrean conflict which had been underway some three years by that date.[4]

Eritrea is a small, poor country in the Horn of Africa; it is bordered on the East by the Red Sea, on the North and West by the Sudan and on the South by Djibouti and Ethiopia. Since 1889, it has existed within the same external boundaries and internally divided into eight provinces, the dimensions of which have not been altered in any significant manner during a succession of administrations.

Eritrea's population is around 3.5 million. About eighty percent of the population are agriculturalists, agro-pastoralists and pastoralists. The other twenty percent of the population live in the towns and cities, the major ones being Asmara, the capital, Keren and the two major ports of Massawa and Assab. There are two main religions, Islam and Coptic Christianity, with sizable Catholic and Protestant congregations and adherents to animistic faiths.

The population contains nine nationalities, each with their own language. The most widely used languages are Tigrinya and Tigré, spoken by some eighty percent of the population. The other nationalities are Afar, Baria, Bilein, Hedareb, Kunama, Rashaida and Saho; all have their own language, live in defined areas and are at different levels of socio-economic-political development.[5] Tigrinya speakers are the most numerous and live predominantly on the Kebessa plateau, in the three highland provinces of Hamasien (they form a majority of Asmara's population), Seraye and Akele-Guzai. Some ninety-three percent of Tigrinya speakers are Christians and seven percent Muslims (Jiberti), the latter being merchants and urban dwellers. Tigré is spoken in the northeastern coastal plains (Sahel and Senhit) and the western lowlands (Barka) and in the Dahlak Islands. Most of the Tigré nationality are Muslims; with the exception of two-thirds of the members of the Mensa clan who are Christians. The Saho live on the eastern edge of the highlands in Massawa and Semhar Province and in the foothills of the coastal plain in Akele-Guzai Province; only three percent are Christian (Irob). Bilein is spoken by Eritreans in Keren and other parts of Senhit Province; seventy percent are Muslim and thirty percent are Christian. The Afars are all Muslim; they form a majority of Assab's population and inhabit the Danakil Province and the Dahlak Islands. The Kunama inhabit the area between the Gash and Setit rivers in Barka Province; they are mostly Muslims and Animists but include some Christians. The Baria occupy eastern Gash in the western lowlands; all are Muslim. The Hedareb are a nomadic nationality living in the northeast and northwest. All speak Beja, are Muslim and some have tribal links with Sudan. The smallest and most recent nationality are the Rashaidas who settled on the Sahel coast in the 1860s; they speak Arabic and are Muslims.

Eritrea has an extremely complex history, a history which is dominated by a fight against invaders. Since the sixteenth century, it has been occupied in turn by Ottoman Turks, Egyptians, Italians (from 1886 until 1941), the British (who defeated Italian forces in

Eritrea during the second World War) until 1952, and the Ethiopians ever since. The Ethiopians persist in their occupation, even though in the treaties of Uccialli and Addis Ababa, signed in 1889 and in 1896 after they had defeated Italy in the battle of Adua, if they agreed unilaterally to the Italian claim to Eritrea. An indication of the peripheral importance of Eritrea to Ethiopia is the fact that until the Ethiopian occupation in 1952, Amharic, the official language of Ethiopia, was only spoken by a handful of Eritreans, mainly those who had been educated or worked in Ethiopia. In spite of over thirty years of Ethiopian occupation—and probably because of this alien presence—few Eritreans speak Amharic willingly. Linguistically, Tigrinya is significantly different from Amharic, whereas Tigré is by no means as distinct from Tigrinya.[6] Notwithstanding the cogent and energetic opposition of most Muslim Eritreans and a growing number of Christians, Britain and the United Nations determined in 1950 on a federation of two disparate bedfellows—Ethiopia and Eritrea. The British government's motives were fairly clear; it was under considerable pressure in India, Palestine and West Africa as well as Eritrea to relinquish the burdens and benefits of empire. Moreover, the United States, which was relishing its new position of political, economic and military hegemony, had decided that a union of Ethiopia with Eritrea would best serve its strategic interests. It seems, however, that a majority of Eritreans were opposed to this move. Ethiopia also accepted federation under protest—it wanted unconditional union with Eritrea.

The ten years after federation saw a creeping imposition of Ethiopian direct rule. Toward the end of 1952, *La Voce dell'Eritrea*, a newspaper critical of the federation, was closed down. In 1956, all political parties were banned, and in 1958, following the suppression of a general strike, the Eritrean General Union of Labour Syndicates was banned. In 1960, the Eritrean flag was lowered and separate courts abolished. In 1962 Eritrea was forcibly annexed by Ethiopia.

The armed struggle for national liberation began in 1961, with the formation of the Eritrean Liberation Front (ELF). By late 1977, it and the Eritrean People's Liberation Front (EPLF), which split from the ELF in 1970, controlled most of the countryside. The EPLF also occupied most of the port of Massawa, had the Ethiopian garrison in Asmara under siege, and was in total control of all other towns and provinces, with the exception of the northern province of Barka. Here, the ELF had expanded from a well established base.

Fierce fighting over sixteen years had driven many tens of thousands of refugees into the Sudan. Many of these refugees subsequently formed part of an even wider diaspora. Many more Eritreans became displaced from their homes and sought refuge in other parts of the country, which were under the control of the liberation forces.

Until 1980, the EPLF and ELF waged a bitter civil war, a war which reflected badly on both parties; such fighting also seriously affected the chances of success for the war of national liberation. In the view of some writers the impact was permanent. The major reason, however, for the inability of the revolutionary forces to achieve independence in the late 1970s was the intervention of the Soviet Union on the Ethiopian side. The United States had also remained a backer of Ethiopia; in 1953, the two countries signed a twenty-five-year defense treaty, a major feature of which allowed the United States to lease the Kagnew Communications Base in Asmara, a facility which at its height employed 3,000 United States personnel. After a group of army officers seized power from the semifeudal regime of Haile Selassie in 1974 and subsequently proclaimed themselves Marxists, the United States gradually scaled down its economic and military assistance. The USSR and Cuba filled the political vacuum left by the United States. Massive supplies of military equipment and personnel, together with substantial training assistance from the USSR and its allies, helped the Ethiopian forces inflict a decisive defeat upon the ELF. On the other hand, the EPLF was not broken in the fighting, but made a strategic withdrawal from the towns it had liberated to a secure rear base in the mountainous northern province of Sahel.

Since the strategic retreat of 1978, the EPLF has not only been able to mount a classic guerrilla campaign throughout occupied Eritrea, but has also used the highly coordinated and disciplined forces which form the Eritrean People's Liberation Army (EPLA) to wage a prolonged conventional war.

In spite of such bitter conflict which has cost the lives of so many men and women, the destruction of hundreds of villages and thousands of acres of crops, the decimation of livestock and the continual risks of MIG and sporadic ground and artillery attacks, the EPLF can be said to be in effective control of eighty-five percent of the country.

Although the EPLF could not have survived without a broad base of support among the mainly rural population or without a deep-seated resentment against Ethiopian domination, many writers have been content to repeat well-worn cliches about the essential unity of Ethiopia and Eritrea, a unity broken by the Turks in the sixteenth century, to be remedied by the United Nations in 1950. For a brief period in its long history, Abyssinia did hold some of Eritrea. But such talk of "unity" is illusory; Ethiopia is a colonial occupying power—an empire, akin to the British, French, German and Italian empires, all of which have crumbled. Indeed, Abyssinia was an observer at the Berlin Conference of Emperors, held during 1884-1885, which resulted in the imperial carve up of Africa; Ethiopia arose from a division of the spoils of imperialism.[7] During a fifty-year period from 1883 until 1935, the ancient Solomonic Kingdom of Abyssinia, assisted and abetted by a number of the European powers, expanded over three-fold to become the Ethiopian empire.

A sense of Eritrean identity was formed during the Italian colonization of Eritrea. As mentioned earlier, there are nine nationalities in Eritrea; many other African nations face problems caused through an even greater ethnic diversity than Eritrea. Ethiopia has over fifty ethnic groups, Zaire seventy-seven, and Tanzania no less than 120.[8] Italian colonialism broke down the semifeudal and semicommunal administrations of the various Eritrean nationalities and brought them together in a centralized state. However, not all nationalities were affected to the same degree. The Tigrinya nationality is cohesive, with common administrative laws, tradition and mostly Christian; it also inhabited the area which felt the greatest impact of colonialism. The members of the Tigré nationality extend through four provinces, but are all Muslim and share common spiritual and cultural traditions, while their administrative laws differ only slightly. The Bilein nationality's population share strong economic, ethnic and cultural ties and was greatly influenced by Italian conquest. The Afars share a pastoral life style and inhabit a defined geographical area. Some of the Afars and Saho were affected by Italy, some hardly at all. The Baria (Nara) speakers are settled Muslim farmers with a strong sense of nationality and little affected by the Italian conquest. The Kunama are also a cohesive nationality, little affected by the main religions of Eritrea; they have been influenced by Italian colonization. The Beja-speaking Hedareb are thinly spread over the lowlands with little sense of nationality. The Rashaida speak Arabic and have not mixed with their neighbors at all. Neither of the two latter nationalities had much to do with the Italian colonizers.[9]

Tekeste has argued that if colonialism is such a major influence on national consciousness, it should have affected the Tigrinya to a greater degree than the other nationalities.[10] At the end of Italian colonial rule, a substantial section of Tigrinya opinion did not espouse a specific Eritrean nationalism. The EPLF would argue that Ethiopian rule is a continuation of colonialism and this has accelerated the formation of national consciousness.[11] One of the consequences of Italian colonization was the development of a substantial Eritrean petit bourgeoisie. Its influence was also felt outside the colony. Eritreans made a substantial contribution to Ethiopian central government service during the Italian and British occupation of Eritrea; their involvement increased during the period of federation with Ethiopia and the imperial annexation. During the 1941-1966 period, nineteen out of a total 138 senior officials (ministers, ministers of state and vice ministers) in Ethiopia were Eritrean.[12] Incidentally, conclusive evidence of Amhara dominance in the federation is that ninety-six were Amhara—eighty-five from Showa alone—while only three were Muslims.[13]

Before the nineteenth century, there did not exist a centralized Ethiopian state but merely a "number of kingdoms, principalities and feudal baronages."[14] It is of course also true to say that before Italian rule, no distinct and united area corresponding to present day Eritrea had a fully independent existence. The administrative boundaries of Eritrea, however, were fixed in 1889 by the treaty of Uccialli, signed by Italy and by the Emperor of Ethiopia, who thereby freely acknowledged Italy's rule over Eritrea. Therefore, Eritrea exists not only by virtue of Italian creation but also by an explicit Ethiopian renunciation.[15] It is also worth citing the International Council of Jurists' opinion on the Western Sahara; in their opinion, the right of the Saharawi people to decolonization takes precedence over any historical rights the Moroccans had in the area.[16] Eritrea was administered as a separate entity for as long as a period as most independent African states of the present day. There are many spurious historical claims of a "Greater Ethiopia"; it is sufficient here to reiterate the point that, even if Axumites, Abyssinians or Ethiopians had governed parts of Eritrea before the Italian colonization, this does not justify their forcible incorporation into modern day Ethiopia.[17]

Self-determination has been a key concept in the decolonization of Africa; however, it is the colonial entity rather than nationality that has usually been the framework for any liberation movement's operation. As Africans were "prepared to die as tribes and be born as nations," independence inevitably reopened ethnic grievances.[18] The United Nations General Assembly Resolution No. 2625 XXV deals with the right of peoples for self-determination and says in part that the United Nations "affirms the legitimacy of the struggle of peoples under colonial and alien domination recognized as being entitled to the right of self-determination to restore to themselves that right by any means at their disposal."[19]

There has been a great deal of discussion over whether the Eritrean people are entitled to the right of self-determination and whether they constitute a colony. The United Nations has come to accept the position that a colony has to be geographically and/or ethnically and culturally separate from the territory administering it.[20] It has rejected the rival thesis which recognizes the possibility of internal colonialism. But no matter what the UN, OAU or any other international body or state government says, the issue of self-determination will be a dominant force in world politics, perhaps for centuries to come.[21] There are numerous examples of countries where nationalism has lain dormant for many years and then becomes the dominant issue around which people organize.

Seton-Watson compares the Ethiopians to the Hapsburgs and the Eritreans to Balkan nationalists—an apt, but uncomfortable, comparison. Another liberal writer has also reflected that he cannot imagine two large, politically viable, independence-worthy, cultures cohabiting under a single political roof without distinct cultural political units being formed.[22]

Although some African leaders, such as the late President Samora Machel of Mozambique and President Siad Barre of Somalia have supported the right of Eritreans to choose independence, such leaders did not raise the matter in the United Nations, the OAU, nor in any other of the many forums where they debated at great length. Kamanu has argued that the leaders are shortsighted in this respect. "Secession" may, conceivably, facilitate the process of pan-African unity by lessening the fear that smaller states have of domination by the huge multinational states. This process would enable them to consider participation in supra-national arrangements, which arguably could bring about an era of peace and economic prosperity.[23] It is also instructive to consider the effect of Nyerere's support of the right to Biafra to secede from Nigeria during their civil war of 1967-1970. There is no evidence that this stance caused Nyerere to lose any of the immense prestige he had earned in Africa and the rest of the world; nor did it lead to calls for secession from nationalities on the mainland of Tanzania or demands from the island of Zanzibar for the right to secede from Tanzania.

It must be deemed unlikely, however, that many African leaders would be able to tolerate the development of a sense of ethnic (national) solidarity by any of the multitude of ethnic groups which comprise their nations—based upon shared culture, language and history—as this would pose a possibly mortal danger to the existence of a central state and their own power.[24] But, in spite of these constraints, all Islamic African states, as well as Benin, Côte d'Ivoire, Malagasy Republic, Mozambique, Niger and Togo have all announced their support for Eritrean self-determination.[25]

In 1950, the United Nations, after intense United States lobby-
ing on Ethiopia's behalf, resolved that Eritrea should be federated
with Ethiopia.[26] The United States' position was clearly stated by
John Foster Dulles, later to become the secretary of state. This was
that the eastern part of Eritrea should be incorporated within Ethiopia to prevent it being used as a base to attack Ethiopia. A separate
solution should be sought for the western part.[27] Later on, the
United States changed its position, arguing that the strategic interests of the United States in the Red Sea basin and considerations of
security and world peace made it necessary for the two countries to
be joined together.[28]

There is nothing to prevent the United Nations from reopening
the Eritrea file; indeed, it has a duty to do so, as the 1950 resolution
on Eritrea was violated by the Ethiopians when they dissolved the
federation in 1962.[29]

In 1950, the Soviet Union favored independence for Eritrea
and said to the General Assembly that, "We base our argument on
the fact that all peoples have a right to self-determination and
national independence.[30] Since 1950, however, the Soviet Union
has never again pressed the Eritrean claim although its client states,
Bulgaria and Cuba, gave some material assistance to liberation
groups until 1977. Since 1977, material and intellectual support
has ceased and in a number of Marxist circles the argument is heard
that the Eritreans have yet to justify their case for self-determination. Writers closer to the Soviet point of view even claim that, as
a "socialist revolution" has been established in Ethiopia, all traces
of colonialism have withered away. They usually describe Eritrean
revolutionaries as "separatist bandit gangs," and dismiss any view
that Ethiopia is an imperial presence suppressing Eritrea.[31]

The view is also put forward that although Eritrea has the theoretical right to self-determination, this is an undesirable option
because an independent Eritrea would come under the control of
reactionary classes. Moreover, secession would be a threat to the
socialist Ethiopian regime which is threatened by United States
imperialism.[32] This view persists despite the fact that a reading of
Lenin indicates that the "correct" theoretical line is that annexed

and oppressed nations retain the right to secession, even after a socialist party has seized power.[33]

As Marx did not offer a systematic position on self-determination, and other Marxist writers have often changed their position, the issues of nationalism and self-determination have been a major source of contention in Marxist criticism. The "correct" attitude to any nationalist movement stems not from the progressiveness of the movement, but its relationship to the international proletarian movement.[34] Support is dependent upon matters such as the position and strategy of the class struggle, the character of the state and economic and other ties between the imperial core and other areas. One of the main problems in developing a Marxist approach toward self-determination lies in the fact that, when Marx wrote of nations, he took an essentially economic view and often seems to have had in mind multinational states rather than nations (national states).[35] On other occasions, he draws a distinction between state and nation.

Engels developed the concept of "non historic" nations when he referred to peoples such as the southern Slavs and Basques, who, as "ethnic trash" or "people without history," were destined to be people without a future. Rosa Luxemburg also saw no future for small independent nations; in her view they would inevitably be economically dependent upon larger neighbors—as Poland was upon Russia.[36]

However, V.I. Lenin's view was more positive. He argued that while socialists are not obliged to support the aims of nationalist movements, they have the right to support the right of seceding nations to determine the issue for themselves. He did not limit the right of separation to developed capitalist communities; even when there were no workers—only slave owners and slaves—the demand for self-determination is obligatory for every Marxist.[37] He also thought that the bourgeoisie of any colonial country could have a role, possibly a leading one, in liberation. Admittedly, Lenin hoped that, as "nationalism is a fundamentally bourgeois ideology," nations will not exercise this right to secede once the transition to socialism has begun. It seems clear that he never intended to allow nations the right to secession once a communist party has achieved complete power. He seems then to hope that nationalism will be discouraged by keeping the party free from all nationalist proclivities and by the assimilation of nations.[38] Indeed, he argues that social democrats from small nations must also insist on the freedom to integrate with a neighbor state.[39]

In the present world when we can more realistically talk of post-Marxist societies rather than states in the transition to socialism, discussion of the Marxist approach to nationalism may seem peripheral. Prior to the 1974 revolution, however, the Ethiopian left ceaselessly debated the national question. Its members were aware that the decisive factor in determining the victory of the Bolsheviks in the civil war in Russia was the promise to give self-determination to nationalities. For the Ethiopians, three issues were involved: the nature of Ethiopian feudalism; the extent to which Ethiopia acted as a *de facto* colonial state; and the quality of Amhara domination over other nationalities.[40] John Markakis and Nega Ayele make the most informative analysis of these questions; they point out that there is a vast difference in modes of production between the north and the south of Ethiopia. The north comprises the heart of the old Axumite Empire and includes Tigray, Showa, Gondar, Gojjam and Wollo. The south comprises the more recently colonized, and mostly Muslim, areas inhabited by the Oromo and Somali peoples.[41]

After the military coup of 1974, the arguments over the national question became ever more tortuous. In *Combat*, the journal of the Ethiopian Students Body, it was argued that as colonialism can only be a product of capitalism "it is a self-evident truth that a colonial relationship does not (and cannot) possibly exist between oppressor and oppressed nationalities in Ethiopia."[42]

The twists and turns of the Ethiopian left were paralleled by Eritrea's erstwhile supporters, the Cubans. As late as March 1975, they were arguing that as Eritrea had a separate cultural, ethnic, linguistic and religious identity it constitutes a nation. After Mengistu had seized power in February 1977, Eritrea was abandoned.

The military rulers of Ethiopia chose to quote Joseph Stalin's *Marxism and the National Question* rather than Lenin. Stalin defines a nation as one having common territory, common language, common psychological make-up manifested in a common culture, and a historically constituted stable community of people formed on the basis of a common, advanced economic life.[43] The Dergue claims that as Eritrea does not qualify as a nation, the Eritrean struggle is a counter-revolutionary movement, serving the interests of imperialism. That under Stalin's definition, Ethiopia does not qualify as a nation seems not to have concerned the Dergue. Neither does the Dergue give rigorous attention to the undisputed fact that Eritrea had a higher state of capitalist development than Ethiopia, and is therefore closer to Stalin's definition of a nation.

There has been a great deal of discussion over the nature of the Eritrean and Ethiopian revolutions, and which class has been the beneficiary. One view is that as the Ethiopian revolution broke out spontaneously—at a time when there was no working class party—the army, which was the only institution which remained intact, had the mandate to rule.[44] The first years of the Ethiopian revolution can be characterized as being the dictatorship of the army whose major civilian support came from the lumpen proletariat, and the southern peasants.[45] It has also been argued that the main beneficiaries of the revolution have been the Amhara and Amharized petit bourgeoisie, which has emerged unscathed from the overthrow of the emperor, the Red Terror, land nationalization and the other traumas of the revolution.[46]

The Dergue soon adopted the mantle of socialism and found Marxist-Leninist texts to justify its determination to crush the Eritrean, leftist and nationalist movements. The Chinese communist Chang Chih-i argued in the 1950s that once national liberation has been achieved, the oppression of nationalities no longer exists. Moreover, Ho Chi Minh, the inspiration of so many liberation fighters, said that once an oppressor has been overthrown, formerly oppressed nations no longer have the obligation to secede.[47]

The history of Eritrea over the past 100 years is one of a people subjected to colonial, alien domination, slowly developing national consciousness and, in the process, developing a common culture, a *lingua franca*, and a relatively advanced economic life. The Italians claimed to be protecting the "ethnic individuality" of

Eritreans by giving instruction in Christian areas in Tigrinya and in Muslim areas in Arabic.[48] Italian strategy was to separate Eritrean Christians from Ethiopia. They tried to take Eritrean members of the Ethiopian Orthodox Church away from Addis Ababa's jurisdiction. They also tried to convert them to Roman Catholicism— with dismal lack of success; by 1928, after fifty years of proselytism, there were still only 8,473 Roman Catholics in Eritrea.[49] For a time, Italian policies led to separate development of Muslims and Christians, leading to divisions within the liberation ranks which are only now beginning to heal. During the latter part of Italian rule, Eritrea became the industrial heart of Mussolini's fascist, East African empire. Manufacturing industries, roads, railways and service industries were established in the highlands and along the Red Sea coast around the growing ports of Massawa and Assab. This development was particularly rapid in the years before the Italian conquest of Ethiopia in 1936, and during the Second World War. Substantial numbers of Eritreans entered the industrial work force to form the basis of a politicized proletariat, some of whom later assumed leadership roles under British rule. Bhardwaj has argued that the dominance of foreign capital held back the growth of indigenous Eritrean capital.[50] That may be, but what cannot be disputed is the exploitation of peasant and worker that took place; the resentment this caused found its outlet in the resistance described in chapter three.

The Eritrean middle class was small in number, as virtually all public servants, shopkeepers, large farmers and business managers were Italian settlers. By 1940, Italians numbered 60,000 out of a total population of less than one million; they alienated most of the best arable and grazing land, taking some away from the clergy and other large landholders, but also dispossessing many small farmers who tried to find work in the towns. All sections of society suffered under fascist, racist legislation, so the British occupation of 1941 was initially popular. The British allowed political organization, removed most of the worst, racist aspects of society and improved education and health services to some extent. But as the British allowed the former departments of the fascist, Italian administration to function much as before, with the same personnel, and raised taxes in a largely fruitless attempt to balance increased expenditure, it cannot be said that the Eritreans were much better off than they had been under the Italians.

The most vocal political group in Eritrea was based in the Ethiopian Orthodox Christian community but, as the British administration wore on, fewer and fewer Eritrean Christians supported union with the Amhara-dominated Ethiopia. The Muslims, who possibly formed at least half the population, were almost unanimous in their opposition to Ethiopian rule, while a sizable minority of Christians—particularly among workers in Asmara—also wanted independence, not subservience to such a ruler as Haile Selassie.

During the 1945-1951 period, however, Britain was faced with almost overwhelming problems of social and economic reconstruction and determined to divest itself of its more troublesome colonies and mandates—India, Palestine and Eritrea—as soon as possible. Eritrea was supposed to retain legislative, executive and juridical autonomy over domestic affairs under the sovereignty of the emperor, but Ethiopia totally disregarded the crucial autonomy clause. Tigrinya and Arabic were abolished as the official languages of Eritrea and replaced by Amharic.

The socialist Dergue continued this policy of cultural imperialism, following a pattern set in other communist states. Socialist language policy often follows this path. First, a policy of linguistic pluralism is proclaimed; with great publicity, literacy campaigns are carried out in most languages. Then bilingualism becomes the official policy, to be followed fairly rapidly by an emphasis on monolingualism. Finally, an attempt is made to eradicate all languages other than "the language of success."[51] This policy has been tried in Eritrea and has been accompanied by other acts of cultural imperialism. The emperor abolished the separate courts; many industries were dismantled, with the buildings, plant and workers being transferred *en bloc* to Ethiopia. Many Ethiopians were sent to the major Eritrean cities to take up key administrative posts. Some Ethiopian settlers arrived in the Eritrean towns. This follows a pattern set in other communist states; it is an attempt to dilute minority nationalities with the dominant group, which has a monopoly of top security, party, police and military posts. The preferred outcome of Leninist national policy is the merging of the nations and nationalities into a single whole; however, this could take a very long time.[52]

Because of the discontent of minorities, the national question often becomes the main priority in socialist societies. For example, in China of 1956-1957 during the "Let a Hundred Flowers Bloom" period, the unity of nationalities was recognized by Mao to be the main priority.[53] Although most communist states claim to have solved the nationalities question, they also acknowledge that nationalism, "the chief political and ideological weapon of international reactionaries," remains the principal obstacle to the building of communism.[54] One of the dilemmas facing any communist government is how to deal with Lenin's argument (put forward shortly before his death) that the best way to deal with the national question might be decentralization to the point that all matters other than military and foreign policy would be the responsibility of the national republics.[55] The Ethiopian communist government faced this dilemma. There is a precedent in recent Marxist history for the formation of a new nation. This happened in the case of the German Democratic Republic; it was argued that although all Germans shared a common nationality, the GDR was a separate nation.[56]

In 1962, Eritrea was incorporated fully into Ethiopia. Rather than wait for the final act of colonization, the Eritrean Liberation Front (ELF) began the long, and still incomplete, struggle for independence. It began the armed struggle from a fairly narrow base among the nomadic, Muslim, Tigré-speaking Beni Amir people of Barka Province. Chapter two shows that they have never been under firm central control. Barka remained a base for the ELF for almost twenty years; the ELF did not concern itself unduly with radical social change. It was the creation of the EPLF which transformed a purely national struggle into one which "is an integral part of the international socialist revolution."[57]

The Dergue reacted to the success of the Eritrean nationalist and revolutionary movements by announcing a national Democratic Revolution Program in April 1976 designed to solve the

"national question" once and for all. It was following a pattern set
by all besieged communist states. Paragraph 5 of the program
states:

> The right to self-determination of all nationalities will be
> recognized and fully respected. No nationality will domi-
> nate another.... This means that each nationality will have
> regional autonomy.... The right to determine the contents
> of its political, economic and social life, use its own lan-
> guage and elect its own leaders and administrators to
> head its internal organs.[58]

This proposal was dismissed by most Eritreans; however,
some Afar leaders (mainly from the Wollo, Hararghe and Tigray
provinces of Ethiopia) saw more merit in it and began to work with
the Dergue toward the establishment of an autonomous Afar state.
Afars differed on this subject, however. In 1965, the emperor
announced plans to merge the Danakil Province of Eritrea with
Wollo; after protests the plan was changed and a separate Assab
region proclaimed.[59] In April 1977, the Dergue convened an Afar
congress and in May 1978, Assab became a separate administrative
region. The Dergue also installed Afars in such administrative
posts as governor of Assab.[60] It seemed for a time that the Dergue
would use its seemingly successful approach to the Afar question
as a model for the settlement of the entire national question through
the creation of a series of autonomous regions.[61] There are now few
signs that the Dergue is serious about regional autonomy.[62]

The Dergue has continued to agonize over autonomy. An
uncritical supporter strongly promulgated the view that nationalism is a variant of false consciousness diverting people away from
the true class-based nature of the Ethiopian revolution.[63] In March
1983, the Dergue established an Institute for the Study of Ethiopian
Nationalities headed by Ashagre Yigletu, an Amhara. The nationalities issue, however, is as far from being solved as ever. The Dergue would have just as much difficulty in controlling an Ethiopia
restructured on ethnic lines, as it does with a socialist-oriented state
within the old imperial framework of fourteen provinces, in all of

which there is armed struggle. Restructuring into six or seven large national regions would still leave a number of them very ethnically diverse. The Institute has paid a great deal of attention to Soviet writing on nationalities, and, if the Dergue were able to carry out a redistribution—as distinct from announcing policies—they would presumably have to adopt the model of two-nation autonomous regions such as the Northern Caucasus of the USSR. The Soviets have also advised Mengistu that "one cannot resolve the national question by purely administrative measures."[64]

In 1987, the Dergue's new assembly (Shengo) had another go. It announced that five regions—Tigray, Diredawa, Ogaden, Eritrea and Assab—would have internal autonomy; but what this means in theory, let alone in practice, is far from clear. One year after this announcement, none of these "autonomous" regions—nor the twenty-four administrative regions announced—had been formed.[65]

The Dergue's pronouncements on the national question, together with the developing position of the other liberation fronts, has caused the EPLF some problems. All national liberation fronts agree that all nationalities in Ethiopia, apart from the Amharas, are exploited. The EPLF position was stated in 1985: apart from the case of Western Somalia, there was no case for secession among any of the oppressed nationalities. The main reason for the EPLF's position is a belief that secession of Oromia, Tigray, etc., would damage their economic development.[66] The EPLF, therefore, shares a number of theoretical assumptions with the Dergue, the most important being that the correct solution to the problems of the oppressed nationalities of Ethiopia is unity based on equality and unity based upon diversity.[67] It is perhaps inevitable that the EPLF would adopt this position. If it accepted the right of the Afars of Tigray and Wollo to press for a nation state, there can be no reason why Afars living in Eritrea and Djibouti should not join them.[68] There would be no justification for all of Djibouti to be part of an Afar state. The bulk of the population of Djibouti are Somalis—they are descendants of very recent migrants, but would certainly resist absorption into an Afar state.[69] It is difficult to escape the conclusion that the Afar have fared worse from the carve-up of

Africa than their neighbors, the Somalis, some of whom do have their own state. Some Eritrean Afar also have yet to be convinced that their future is best served in an Eritrean, rather than an Ethiopian, state.

The Eritreans have addressed themselves to the national question. One of the eleven objectives of their democratic program adopted in 1977 reads "Ensure the Equality and Consolidate the Unity of Nationalities." Attempts are made to train cadres from all nationalities and to preserve and develop their spoken and written languages. There is at least one representative from each national minority on the Central Committee of the EPLF.[70] The program safeguards "progressive culture and traditions," but vows to combat "narrow nationalism."[71] The 1987 program added a clause to the effect that each nationality could establish its own democratic administration.[72] A number of writers have stressed that there is an element of opposition within Eritrea towards the dominant nationalities—Tigrinya and Tigré. Gilkes has claimed, for instance, that the Kunama (Baza) "are the only one....which have largely and consistently supported the Ethiopian Administration."[73] It is noticeable that when Ethiopian troops have gone through the Gash area they destroy Baria villages but leave the Kunama alone.[74] Kunama support for whoever was in effective control of their center of population, Barentu, dates back to Italian times.[75] In recent years, however, there have been signs that the Kunama are giving increasing support to both the EPLF and the Tigray People's Liberation Front (TPLF).[76] Kunama intelligence and logistical support were vital in the EPLF capture of Barentu in July 1985, whilst large numbers of Kunama militia also defected from the Ethiopian side. Fayotingun Longhi, once the leader of a *shifta* Kunama band, a member of the Eritrean parliament and imprisoned by the Ethiopians, became a supporter of the EPLF.[77] The EPLF are also careful not to impose the Tingrinya language on the minorities.[78]

In a memorandum of August 1978, the EPLF used traditional Marxist arguments to push its case. It started with the premise that the ultimate aim of all progressive forces is to do away with national boundaries. However, it saw that the priority was to build socialism within the historically developed nation of Eritrea.[79] The national struggle is subordinate to the class struggle, but, in theoretical and strategic terms, when one nation is colonized by another, the national struggle must be waged simultaneously with the class struggle. The EPLF still states quite unequivocably that the question of nationality is the foremost question of democracy.[80] The EPLF also recognizes, in principle, the right of Eritrean nationalities to secede, once there is a genuine revolutionary organization in power in Eritrea.[81] However, the fact will remain that the new state will be within colonially determined boundaries and will contain nine nationalities—who may have differing priorities.

The EPLF and the Dergue have very different views on the domination of the Amhara nationality. The EPLF shares a view held by the majority of Horn of Africa scholars, that, as the majority of the members of the Dergue and the Central Committee of the Workers Party of Ethiopia (WPE) are of Amhara nationality—in addition to being serving or ex-military officers—the other nationalities of Ethiopia suffer from Amhara oppression. A minority of scholars speculate over the degree to which some members of the two bodies have more Oromo in their makeup than Amhara.[82] the EPLF also argues that the bulk of Amharas suffer from oppression and supports "democratic" opposition to the military dictatorship.

In early 1986, the Dergue distributed a draft constitution. The text was prepared by the Institute of Nationalities. As it is a generally faithful duplication of the Soviet Constitution of 1977, it is not surprising that the national question plays its part.[83] There are conventional expressions about the "equality of nationalities," but at the same time, an emphasis that all state activities will be conducted in Amharic.[84] It is envisaged that the Shengo will, at some unspecified time in the future, decide on the setting up of administrative and autonomous regions—presumably to accommodate some of the nationalities.[85] The Shengo is a very unrepresentative body—in the first election to the body, all candidates in Eritrea were Army officers and mostly Amharas.[86]

The endless talk about nationalities has inevitably raised the expectation of the various subject peoples. But it is still true to say that "the derg proposes to weld the rural and urban masses of Ethiopia into a unified political movement that will subsume legitimized ethnic differences without revealing a strategy by which this result can be achieved."[87] When the nationalities try to obtain some recognition of their national rights, the Dergue represses them. One cannot see the Dergue doing anything to extend human rights in this regard.[88]

It is clear that there is no significant body of opinion within Eritrea supporting the concept of a Greater Ethiopia. It is also clear that as there is no national consensus within Ethiopia, the possibilities of plural democracy are extremely remote unless the EPLF gains total control of Eritrea, and Eritrea then forms the model for a restructuring of the Ethiopian state. This is the WPE's nightmare: it has even been suggested that the party is so fearful of the explosive potential of the nationalities that it emasculates its only other rival—the armed forces—by forcing it to engage in endless unwinnable positional warfare in Eritrea.[89] The Ethiopian constitution guarantees freedom of the press, meeting and association, freedom of correspondence and the right to criticize the public sector.[90] It is obvious that these rights cannot be enjoyed unless there is a multiparty system and a clear division between state and party.[91]

The EPLF has observed that a rigid application of Marxist-Leninist tenets has caused tremendous problems in all transitional socialist states. It is trying to fuse together all of the various intellectual traditions about nationalism. It is succeeding largely in this task and in the process learning a great deal about nation-building. In the chapters that follow, it will be shown that the development of the Eritrean nation was accelerated by the imposition of Italian colonization, Ethiopian occupation and prolonged armed and political resistance to external intervention in Eritrean affairs. A nation has been formed which is a far cry from its ancient roots as a battleground for invaders and migrants.

Notes

1.   Hugh Seton-Watson, *Nations and States: an Enquiry into the Origins of Nations and the Politics of Nationalism* (London, Methuen, 1977) p. 482.

2.   Benjamin Neuberger, *National Self-determination in Post-colonial Africa* (Boulder CO, Lynne Reiner, 1986), pp. 3, 69.

3.   Neuberger, 'National Self-determination,' p. 95.

24 • ERITREA: EVEN THE STONES ARE BURNING

4.   A.M. Babu, 'The Eritrean Question in the Context of African conflicts and Superpower Rivalries,' *The Long Struggle of Eritrea for Independence and Constructive Peace*, eds. Lionel Cliffe and Basil Davidson (Nottingham, Spokesman, 1988), pp. 47-63; Alain Fenet, 'The Right of the Eritrean People to Self-determination,' *The Long Struggle of Eritrea for Independence and Constructive Peace*, eds. Lionel Cliffe and Basil Davidson (Nottingham, Spokesman, 1988), pp. 33-45.

5.   Eritrean People's Liberation Front, *Memorandum* (1978) p. 5.

6.   Edward Ullendorff, *The Ethiopians: an Introduction to Country and People* (London, Oxford University Press, 1965) p. 129.

7.   Bereket Habte Selassie, 'The American Dilemma in the Horn,' *Journal of Modern African Studies*, 22, 2 (1984) p. 254.

8.   Tesfatsion Medhanie, *Eritrea: Dynamics of a National Question*, (Amsterdam, B.R. Grüner, 1986) pp. 270-1.

9.   Eritrean People's Liberation Front, *Political Report and National Democratic Programme* (1987) pp 56-61.

10. Tekeste Negash, *Italian Colonialism in Eritrea, 1882-1941: Policies, Praxis and Impact* (Uppsala, Uppsala University Press, 1987) p. 148.

11. Eritrean People's Liberation Front, 'Political Report' p. 2.

12. Donald L. Horowitz, *Ethnic Groups in Conflict* (Berkeley, University of California Press, 1985) pp. 253-4.

13. Paul B. Henze, *Rebels and Separatists in Ethiopia: Regional Resistance to a Marxist Regime* (Santa Monica, Rand Corporation, 1985).

14. Addis Hiwet, *Ethiopia: From Autocracy to Revolution* (London, Review of African Political Economy, 1975) p. 1.

15. Crawford Young, 'Comparative Claims to Political Sovereignty: Biafra, Katanga, Eritrea,' eds. D. Rothchild and V.A. Olorunsola, *Managing Competing State and Ethnic Claims* (Boulder CO, Westview, 1983) p. 221.

16. Fenet, 'The Right of the Eritrean People,' p. 39.

17. Tesfatsion Medhanie, 'Eritrea: Dynamics,' p. 275.

18. Edmond J. Keller, 'Revolution, Class and the National Question: the Case of Ethiopia,' *Northeast African Studies*, 2, 3/3, 11 (1980/81) p. 44.

19. United Nations General Assembly, *Resolution 2625*, November 20 (1970).

20. Hakan Wiberg, 'Self-Determination as an International Issue,' *Nationalism & Self Determination in the Horn of Africa*, ed. I.M. Lewis (London, Ithaca, 1983) p. 48.

21. David B. Knight, 'Territory and People or People and Territory?,' *International Political Science Review*, 6, 2 (1985) p. 272.

22. Hugh Seton-Watson, 'Nations,' p. 482; Ernest Gellner, *Nations and Nationalism* (Ithaca, Cornell University Press, 1983) p. 119.

23. Onyeonoro S. Kamanu, 'Secession and the Right of Self-Determination: an OAU Dilemma,' *Journal of Modern African Studies*, 12, 3, (1974) p. 364.

24. S.K. Panter-Brick, 'The Right to Self-Determination,' *International Affairs* (London) 44, 2, (1968) p. 261.

25. Neuberger, 'National Self-determination,' p. 80.

26. United Nations General Assembly, *Official Records* 315th Plenary Meeting (1950).

27. United Nations First Committee, *Official Records*, 3rd Session (1949) p. 7.

28. Bereket Habte Selassie, *Conflict and Intervention in the Horn of Africa* (New York, Monthly Review Press, 1980) p. 58.

29. Gebre Hiwet Tesfagiorgis, 'Self-Determination: Its Evolution and Practice by the United Nations and Its Application to the Case of Eritrea,' *Wisconsin International Law Journal*, 6, 1 (1987) pp. 75-127.

30. United Nations General Assembly, *Official Records*, Supplement 8, (1950).

31. Georgi Galperin and V. Platov, 'Revolutionary Transformation in Ethiopia,' *International Affairs* (Moscow) (1982) pp. 58-66; K. Strzhizhousky, 'Ancient Ethiopia Builds a New Life,' *International Affairs* (Moscow) 2, February (1982) pp. 117-22.

32. Tesfatsion Medhanie, 'Eritrea: Dynamics,' p. 288.

33. V.I. Lenin, 'Discussion on Self-Determination Summed Up,' *Collected Works*, 22 (Moscow, Progress Publishers, 1964) p. 329.

34. Walker Connor, *The National Question in Marxist-Leninist Theory and Strategy* (Princeton, Princeton University Press, 1984) p. 14.

35. Connor, 'The National Question,' p. 9.

36. Michael Löwy, 'Marxism and the National Question,' *Revolution and Class Struggle: a Reader in Marxist Politics*, ed. Robin Blackburn (Glasgow, Fontana, 1977) p. 143.

37. Tesfatsion Medhanie, 'Eritrea: Dynamics,' pp. 268-9.

38. Connor, 'The National Question,' p. 38.

39. Lenin, 'Discussion,' p. 347.

40. Alessandro Triulzi, 'Comparing Views of National Identity in Ethiopia,' *Nationalism and Self Determination in the Horn of Africa*, ed. I.M. Lewis (London, Ithaca, 1983) p. 114.

41. John Markakis and Nega Ayele, *Class and Revolution in Ethiopia* (Trenton NJ, Red Sea Press, 1986) p. 23.

42. Triulzi, 'Comparing Views,' p. 117.

43. Joseph Stalin, 'Marxism and the National Question,' *Collected Works*, 2 (Moscow, Foreign Languages Publishing House, 1953) p. 307.

44. Raúl Vivó Valdés, *Ethiopia: the Unknown Revolution* (Havana, Social Sciences Publishers, 1977) p. 29.
45. Rene Lefort, *Ethiopia: An Heretical Revolution?* (London, Zed Press, 1981) p. 170.
46. Michael Chege, 'The Revolution Betrayed: Ethiopia, 1974-9,' *Journal of Modern African Studies,* 17, 3, (1979) p. 375.
47. Connor, 'The National Question,' pp. 119-20.
48. Corrado Zoli, 'The Organization of Italy's East African Empire,' *Foreign Affairs,* 16, Oct. (1937) p. 84.
49. Tekeste Negash, 'Italian Colonialism,' p. 127.
50. Raman G. Bhardwaj, *The Dilemma of the Horn of Africa* (New Dehli, Sterling Press, 1979) p. 89.
51. Connor, 'The National Question,' p. 269.
52. Connor, 'The National Question,' p. 388.
53. Anne Fremantle ed., *Mao Tse-Tung, an Anthology of His Writings* (New York, Mentor, 1962) p. 289.
54. Connor, 'The National Question,' p. 477.
55. Connor, 'The National Question,' p. 481.
56. Connor, 'The National Question,' p. 453.
57. Timothy Oberst, 'Eritrea and the Era of National Liberation,' *Northeast African Studies,* 2, 3/3, 1 (1980-81) p. 135.
58. Government of Socialist Ethiopia, *The National Democratic Revolution Program* (Addis Ababa, 1976).
59. *Adulis* IV, 5 (1987).
60. Kassim Shehim, 'Ethiopia, Revolution and the Question of Nationalities: the Case of the Afar,' *Journal of Modern African Studies* 23, 2 (1985) pp. 345-6.
61. Kassim Shehim and James Searing, 'Djibouti and the Question of Afar Nationalism,' *African Affairs,* 79, April (1980) p. 210.
62. Kassim Shehim, 'Ethiopia,' p. 347. There were no Afars on the 136-man Central Committee of the Worker's Party of Ethiopia.
63. Tarekgn Adebo, 'Ethnicity vs. Class: Concepts in the Analysis of the Ethiopian Revolution,' *Proceedings of the Seventh International Conference of Ethiopian Studies,* ed. Sven Rubenson (Addis Ababa, Institute of Ethiopian Studies, 1984) p. 546.
64. Georgi Galperin, *Ethiopia: Population, Resources, Economy,* trans. J. Shapiro (Moscow, Progress Publishers, 1981) pp. 73, 75.
65. *Adulis* V, 9 (1988).
66. *Adulis* II, 11 (1985).
67. *Adulis* IV, 1 (1987).
68. *Adulis* II, 11 (1985).

69. Neuberger, 'National Self-determination,' p. 57.

70. Peter With, *Politics and Liberation: the Eritrea Struggle, 1951-1985* (Denmark, University of Aarhus, 1987) p. 65.

71. James Firebrace (with Stuart Holland), *Never Kneel Down: Drought, Development and Liberation in Eritrea* (Trenton NJ, Red Sea Press, 1985) p. 158.

72. Eritrean People's Liberation Front, 'Political Report,' p. 177.

73. Patrick Gilkes, 'Centralism and the Ethiopian PMAC,' *Nationalism and Self-Determination in the Horn of Arica,* ed. I.M. Lewis (London, Ithaca Press, 1983) p. 203.

74. Gaim Kibreab, *Refugees and Development in Africa: the Case of Eritrea* (Trenton NJ, Red Sea Press, 1987) p. 51.

75. The Duke of Pirajno, *A Cure for Serpents: An Italian Doctor in North Africa* (London, Eland Books, 1985) p. 171.

76. Frits N. Eisenloeffel and Inge Rönnbäck, *The Eritrean Durrah Odyssey* (Utrecht, Dutch Interchurch Aid, 1983) p. 13.

77. Jordan Gebre-Medhin, *Peasants and Nationalism in Eritrea: A Critique of Ethiopian Studies* (Trenton NJ, Red Sea Press, 1989) p. 160.

78. Eritrean People's Liberation Front, 'Political Report,' p. 90.

79. Eritrean People's Liberation Front, 'Memorandum,' p. 18.

80. Eritrean People's Liberation Front, 'Political Report,' p. 106.

81. Eritrean People's Liberation Front, 'Memorandum,' p. 27.

82. Henze, 'Rebels and Separatists,' pp. 65-66.

83. *Eritrean Information,* 8, 10 (1986).

84. Government of Socialist Ethiopia, *Constitution,* Articles 2, 117 (1986).

85. Government of Socialist Ethiopia, *Constitution,* Article 60.

86. Christopher Clapham, *Transformation and Continuity in Revolutionary Ethiopia* (Cambridge, Cambridge University Press, 1988) p. 96.

87. Teferra-Worq Besah and John W. Harbeson, "Afar Pastoralists in Transition and the Ethiopian Revolution.' *Journal of African Studies,* 5, 3, Fall (1978) p. 267.

88. Patrick Gilkes, 'Centralism,' p. 209.

89. Eritrean People's Liberation Front, 'Political Report,' p. 109.

90. Government of Socialist Ethiopia, *Constitution,* Articles, 48, 50, 52.

91. *Eritrea Information* 9, 1 (1987).

2

Eritrea, Ethiopia and the Red Sea

The claim [that Eritrea is a lost province of Ethiopia] is based, in the official document, upon some rather indefinite references to early history and migrations, almost every sentence of which cries out for comment or correction.

—MARGERY PERHAM, *The Government of Ethiopia*[1]

I n ancient times, Eritrea was called *Medri Geez*, the land of the free, *Medri Bahri*, the land of the sea and *Mareb Mellash*, the land beyond the river. Although these names indicate that Eritrea and Ethiopia have divergent histories, and although many writers have given clues to some of the reasons for the divergent cultures, Ethiopian centralists claim that Abyssinian control extended to the Red Sea throughout most of history.[2] A recent article even claims that the whole of the Horn of Africa was under the control of the emperors of Ethiopia from about the beginning of the Christian era until the sixteenth century.[3] Such writers are giving a version of the past which "is not an objective, historically factual portrayal of the past, rather it constitutes an imaginative reconstruction of the past."[4] In times of change and stress Ethiopian and Abyssinian rulers invariably manipulated inherited ideologies, often with considerable skill.[5] Statesmen (and historians) are not the only ones proselytizing the Ethiopian cause. "To the missionaries in particular, championing Ethiopian claims to Massawa, meant gaining greater favour in the various courts of local Ethiopian rulers."[6]

A more plausible thesis, however, is that Massawa, the major Eritrean port, captured by the Turks in 1517, was part of the Red Sea world, and looked eastward, rather than inland to the African continent. While the Ethiopians were effectively cut off from the outside world for over three centuries, the Eritreans enjoyed continuous contact with the Middle East, a contact which resulted in a distinctive economic and political development.[7]

Ethiopia's claim to Eritrea is based upon dubious arguments that there has been continuity of rule from the Axumite period through Menelik and Haile Selassie to Mengistu. Axum was at its height in the fourth century A.D. having expanded as far as Meroe (Sudan) and across the Red Sea into Yemen.[8] It has been argued forcefully, however, that it is the Eritreans, rather than the Ethiopians, who have a better claim to be the legitimate descendants of the Axumite civilization.[9] It has been suggested that the Tigré and Tigrinya languages are older than Amharic—further grounds for this claim.[10] Also, there is no doubt that although the people of Tigray and Eritrea were considered by different Ethiopian rulers as their subjects, "an Ethiopian might not have been seen within these areas for decades."[11]

There is plenty of room for dispute in historical research; one of the greatest historians has said, "there is not anywhere upon the globe a large tract of country which we have discovered destitute of inhabitants, or where first populations can be fixed with any degree of historical certainty."[12] Eritrea is no exception; its history is one of waves of migrations and invasions. "Migrants" are people who move into a territory, and over generations, peacefully adapt to or perceptibly change the prevailing civilization. "Invaders" usually try to force the inhabitants to adopt different religions, languages and ways of life. They are often successful, but are sometimes resisted with strong and sustained courage.

The first inhabitants of Eritrea migrated there from the Southern Nile Valley, one of the cradles of civilization. They settled in the Gash-Setit lowlands and expanded into the interior of the country; they were pushed back into the lowlands by the second wave of migration from the northwest.[13]

Around 2,000 B.C. pastoral people from the deserts of southern Egypt and northern Sudan entered the Barka Valley and northern highlands, pushing the first wave southwards. These people were forerunners of the Beja tribes, who for many hundreds of years seem to have been the only independent pastoralists in Africa. They were later converted to Islam.[14] Indeed, the Beja may have been the founders of Axum. They later conquered parts of the Eritrean (Hamasien) central plateau and the coastal plains between Massawa and Aqiq; remains as early as 750 A.D. have excavated.[15] The Beja founded states in the ninth century and were still inhabiting the same areas in the twelfth century.[16]

Many of Eritrea's inhabitants are descended from Sabean migrants who came from the Arabian peninsula from 1,000 B.C. and established trading posts, and later city states, on the plateau and on the Eritrean coast.[17] By the end of the fifth century B.C. there is evidence of social and political organization in south Akele-Guzai.[18] Egyptians may well have used the port of Adulis some 1,400 years before the birth of Christ.[19] By the time the Greek text, *The Periplus of the Erythraean Sea*, was written around the turn of the first century A.D., Adulis' importance had declined; it is described as a village of but moderate size with no harbor.[20]

This wave of migrants brought with them an advanced culture, commerce, agricultural technology and a written language. They founded the Axumite empire in the second century A.D. and settled much of the highlands of Eritrea.[21] By the third century

A.D., Axum regarded itself as the third among the great world powers and the King of Axum regarded Ethiopia as a foreign country.[22] In 640 A.D., however, Adulis, which had become part of Axum, was destroyed by Arab invaders—the Ummayad Caliphates, who had occupied the Dahlak Archipelago and much of the Eritrean coast.[23] In the following year, the Moslem conquest of Egypt closed the Mediterranean trade routes to the Axumite kingdom, leading to a further decline in its importance and ultimately to the fall of the empire.[24] The Axumite kings stopped using coins in the middle of the eighth century.[25] By the end of the ninth century, the Axumite rulers had been overrun by the next wave of migrants, the Agaw, who were first subjects and then masters. The Beja also moved into their territory from the north and established five independent kingdoms—Nagic, Baklin, Giarin, Bazen and Kata'a—covering much of Eritrea and northeastern Sudan.[26]

The Agaw migrated from the Lasta region of Abyssinia to Eritrea. To this day, they maintain a shrinking linguistic identity around the city of Keren.[27] During the time of the Agaw, Zagwe dynasty (1130-1270) Christians controlled only a small part of the three highland provinces of Eritrea.[28] The last king of Zagwe was killed in 1270, by Yikuno Amlak, an Amhara who claimed descent from Solomon.[29]

The Eritrean Dahlak islanders were the first East Africans to be converted to Islam in the eighth century; they founded a semi-independent kingdom of considerable importance, possessing its own navy and ruling part of the Yemen coast.[30] In 935 A.D., the Red Sea coast town of Massawa was reported as being inhabited by Muslims. The town passed into the hands of the rulers of the Dahlak Islands from the late fourteenth-early fifteenth century.[31] With the advent of Islam, the center of Abyssinian government power moved away from Tigray to the south, while links between Eritrea and the Middle East grew stronger.[32] Dynamic Muslim mercantilism was the factor that led to the conversion of coastal communities and people living along the trade routes to Islam.[33]

No Abyssinian king ruled the Eritrean plateau in this period and powerful Ifat and Adal sultanates also prevented the Abyssinians from controlling the coast.[34] The Adal kingdom included Dankalia (now in Eritrea); in the sixteenth century it even overran the Abyssinian highlands.[35] Even such an energetic emperor as Galawdewos (1540-1559) did not attempt to capture any part of the coast.[36] The Eritrean Afar kingdoms which had been converted to Islam in the eighth century maintained a practical independence until the Italian conquest.[37]

In 1329—at the time of the "glorious victories of Amda Seyon" (1314-44)—it was clear that Muslims controlled the area from the coast of Eritrea, across the Mareb and all of Tigray south of Axum.[38] The Abyssinians gained a tenuous foothold in the highlands of Eritrea during the fourteenth to sixteenth century.[39] Even in those distant times, however, it is clear that the land and people of highland Eritrea were distinct from the people of Tigray, even though they spoke the same language—just as the Austrians, Swiss Germans and the Germans of today are very different people.

The culture of the Abyssinian settlers in the highlands gradually became diluted with that of the Beja. Their descendants retained nothing of their Abyssinian past but names and genealogies.[40] Examination of historical or contemporary records, which are invariably written from an Ethiopian centralist perspective, show, nevertheless, continuing resistance to Abyssinian or Amhara rule. For example, in the early part of the fourteenth century, in the reign of Amda Seyon I, the king had no authority to nominate the *Bahr Negash* (the Lord of the Sea).[41] Moreover, the *Bahr Negash* was not a vassal of the Lord of Tigray. The *Bahr Negash* often rebelled and his writ ran at most to the highlands.[42] As far as the rest of the Eritrea is concerned, "an occasional raid-frankly for slaves and cattle, or alleged as tribute collection-was the limit of State activity."[43] The Portuguese expedition of 1539 to 1540 discovered that "Moors" near the sea "paid the Bahr Negash nothing."[44]

Zara Yaqob (1434-68) established Shoan military colonies in the Eritrean plateau during 1448-1449, but their "reception by the local people was clearly hostile."[45] The most distinguished settler in the highlands was Meroni, descendant of Menab, the captain of the army of Menelik I. It is said that from Meroni's three sons are descended many of the major families of Hamasien and Akele-Guzai. Such traditional myths have played a great part in building the Eritrean highlanders' consciousness of their differences from their neighbors in Tigray.[46] During times of Ethiopian control, governors on both sides of the Mareb were appointed from traditional ruling families; they held "complete administrative and judicial authority." It is impossible to consider this nucleus of "Christian" Abyssinia as one unit.[47]

By the beginning of the sixteenth century, Eritrea was divided into four distinct parts. The Barka lowlands and the northern highlands were ruled by the Funj. The central plateau ruled by the Beja was in constant battle with the Abyssinian kings. The Danakil was under the Adal Sultan. Massawa and the surrounding coast was governed by the Turks and the Naib of Hirgigo.[48] In 1523, Brother Thomas observed that although the *Bahr Negash* claimed to control the whole Red Sea coast from Suakin to the Gulf of Aden, the area between Massawa and Suakin was wild and "unpacified."

In 1557, Issak, was appointed *Bahr Negash* by Galawdewos, the Abyssinian negus (emperor); however, Issak was a virtually independent ruler of the plateau for some twenty years. He first fought the Turkish invaders who had seized Debarua and later the Ethiopians, after he had ceded all the country between Debarua to the coast to the Muslims. He was beheaded by the negus after the defeat of his armies.[49]

At this point, it is worth reiterating that throughout recorded history, all of Eritrea, except the highlands, was either independent or subject to the payment of tribute to non-Abyssinian rulers. The highlands were subject to tribute to an Abyssinian emperor for limited periods only.[50] Even the Christian strongholds of

Hamasien and Bogos were only nominally under the Ras of Tigray.[51] A respected centralist writes that Abyssinian rule, coming from distant Showa from the fifteenth to early seventeenth century, and from Gondar after the mid-seventeenth century, was "tenuous."[52] One should also mention that throughout the seventeenth century and the first half of the eighteenth century, much of northern Ethiopia also enjoyed almost complete independence from the negus and his imperial court.[53] In the nineteenth century, the rulers of *Mareb Mellash* were the clan leaders of Hazzega and Tsazzega who were appointed by the rulers of Tigray. The role of the central state in the highlands, however, was limited to the fixing of a certain amount of tribute at the *medri* (district) level.[54]

This is not to deny that Abyssinia tried very hard to expand and defend an empire. The list of Abyssinian rulers who lost their lives in fifteenth to sixteenth century empire-building is not only an indication of the tenacity with which the largely Amharan-Showan core of the empire tried to hold onto power, but also a tribute to the fighting effectiveness of the peripheral peoples. The list includes: Dawit (1413); Tewodros (1414); Yeshaq (1429); Eskender (1494); Naod (1508) and Galawdewos (1559).

The memoirs of eighteenth century European travelers such as James Bruce show that although the rulers of Tigray could at times extract tribute from coastal dwellers, in no sense did Abyssinia control the coast.[55] Debarua belonged to the Naib of Hirgigo, leader of the Beni Amir of the Semhar plain. The Naib was appointed by the Pasha of Jeddah and became the most important ruler on the coast; his authority being recognized in parts of the Hamasien highlands.[56] His authority was also recognized by the Saho and Habab and he succeeded in restricting Abyssinian contact with the coast to regulated commerce through Massawa.[57] Regardless of the Ethiopians, the Naib's agents ranged far inland collecting tribute and spreading the word of Allah.[58] Indeed, the Beni Amir kingdom had been important before the Turkish occupation, flourishing in the country between the Sudan and Massawa since the late fourteenth century.[59] The town of Digsa, fifty miles from Massawa, also belonged to the Naib. Digsa, the second customs post on the Massawa-Adua road, formerly belonged to the *Bahr Negash*.[60]

There was, of course, much internal migration within Eritrea. For example, in the early sixteenth century, the Beit Asgade—ancestors of present-day inhabitants of the Keren area of Eritrea—descended from the plateaus of Akele-Guzai and succeeded in subjugating the land between the Anseba and the sea.[61]

The Ottoman Turks occupied Massawa in 1517, to be displaced as rulers by Egypt in 1848. After considerable fighting, the Seraye was conquered by the Muslims in 1534; Abbas Afra was appointed *Bahr Negash* and ruled from the Gash to Massawa on their behalf.[62] In 1589, the Abyssinians under Sarsa Dengel (1563-97) reoccupied some of the plateau; their rule took the form of pitiless looting of highland villages. Their troops were attempting to crush the rebellion of Walda Ezum, who had also made terms with the Turks.[63] The negus was unsuccessful in his attempts to capture Hirgigo.[64] He bestowed titles and levied taxation on the highland people, on a regular basis; but as far as the rest of Eritrea is concerned, he "looted the country from Halhal to Kassala."[65] The office of *Bahr Negash* was abolished in 1580.[66] It has been suggested that the negus did this because the *Bahr Negash* had become too powerful.[67] A more likely explanation might be that as the Abyssinians had resigned themselves to the fact they would not be able to capture the coast, the position had become irrelevant. There was still frequent trouble between the rulers of Massawa and the Abyssinians, however. The Abyssinians were clearly too weak to seize Hirgigo and Massawa, but they feared that were Eritrean noblemen to overthrow the Turks without their assistance, they would then deny allegiance to Abyssinia. A Portuguese map of 1660 shows *Medri Bahri* as covering most of the three highland provinces of Eritrea and distinct from Ethiopia.[68]

Idris Uthman, Naib of Hirgigo in 1805 indicated the erosion of Abyssinian influence, writing, "but my friend understand that I am the gate of Abyssinia and that no person either goes there or returns except through me."[69] By the 1830s, the Naib received the income from Halay and eight other villages on the edge of the plateau.[70] Some indication of the penetration of Eritrea by Muslim culture is shown by the fact that in 1842, a European traveler coming from the coast did not encounter a Christian village, Halhal, until thirty miles from the coast and a height of 6,000 feet. The Regent of Tigray sent 20,000 men against Hirgigo in 1848; local resistance was so fierce that they were compelled to retreat.[71]

Mansfield Parkyns traveled from Massawa to Adua on a route somewhat different from that taken by other European travelers and found that the first Christian village, Kiaquor, under the control of the Abyssinian Dejazmatch Wube, was well inside Hamasien.[72] By the 1860s, the Naib's authority extended from the bay of Aqiq in the north to Zula in the south.[73] Around 1871, his area of influence was expanded even further to some forty Hamasien villages.[74] The nomadic Saho, although virtually independent, also paid occasional tribute to the Naib..[75] It was not until the 1860s that the Dahlak islands were captured by the Turks.[76] The island of Dissei and the bay of Adulis were captured on December 14, 1861 and the bay of Amphylla on March 25, 1862.

At the beginning of the sixteenth century, the Funj kingdom which ruled Sinhar, now part of Sudan, began to push into the Gash and Barka lowlands, home of the Beni Amir.[77] They were followed by the Abyssinians. In 1692, the negus, for the first time in recorded history, led a raid on the Barka valley and the Kunama. Many hundreds of slaves and cattle were taken but the Baria and Beni Amir fought back fiercely and massacred many of the retreating Ethiopians.[78] The Funj also attempted, without much success, to levy tribute on the Beni Amir. Like other nationalities in Eritrea, the Beni Amir exercised a considerable degree of autonomy.[79] At the end of the eighteenth century, the power of the Funj kingdom began to decline; in 1819, Mohamed Ali Pasha, with little difficulty, took the area for the next invaders, the Egyptians, who for twelve years controlled three-quarters of present-day Eritrea and began the long process of unifying the disparate parts of Eritrea.[80]

After Sudan became a province of Egypt in 1820, raiding parties from Kassala probed into Eritrea. By 1832, many sheiks and rulers on the slopes of the plateau began to pay tribute to Egypt.[81] In 1848, Massawa was leased by the Turks to the Egyptians. The first major raid into the Bilein area occurred in 1853, and in 1854, the Egyptians built a fortress at Kufit in Beni Amir country. The rulers of the Bilein and Beit Asgede were converted to Islam.[82] By 1872, Egypt had expanded its control to much of Eritrea—a control which lasted until the Italian conquest of 1886. A nineteenth century visitor wrote, "were it not for the protection given to Abyssinia by the English, the Egyptians would have eaten it up long ago."[83] The Muhafazate of Massawa alone extended some 8,700 square miles.[84]

A crucial role in the Egyptian conquest was played by Pasha Münzinger who became governor of Massawa in 1871 and annexed the area around Keren in 1872. The decision of this Swiss adventurer to enter the service of the Egyptians has been seen as the first determining factor in the creation of modern Eritrea.[85] Moreover, it has been argued that the Egyptians began the unification of the *Medri Bahri*, a process completed by the Italians.[86] For example, in 1873, the Egyptians built a stone road lining Kassala, Keren and Massawa for the first time.[87] Telegraph lines were also laid between Massawa and Kassala, whilst the Ailet area between Massawa and Hamasien was placed under Egyptian protection.[88] A number of Hamasien chiefs and tribal Danakil leaders begged Münzinger to occupy their land. Although the Egyptians were defeated by Abyssinian troops at Gundet on November 14, 1875, and at Gura in the following month, they remained rulers of most of Eritrea.[89]

During the eighteenth century the law of the Abyssinian negus was inoperative in Eritrea; the highlands paid tribute to Tigray, although the Ras had often only a single representative in the country. The tyrant. Ras Mikael Suhul. was unwilling or unable to punish the Naib of Hirgigo in 1745; indeed, he gave him more grants of lands.[90] In 1800, the Naib did not pay tribute to the emperor.[91] Eritrea was far from passive after the death of Mikael; in 1839, Hailu, the ruler of Hamasien, rebelled. In 1843, the British traveler Plowden reported that, "the people of Hamazien and Serowee... are a fierce and turbulent race." and are "still scarcely considered by the people of Teegray as a portion of that country." Five years later he reported that the Abyssinian army of Dejazmatch Wube had plundered the whole country as close to the coast as Domona.[92] Plowden's companion, Parkyns, also observed that the war had resulted in whole villages being burned to the ground and their lands laid waste.[93] Wube pillaged Hirgigo and Monkulo and 15,000 inhabitants of Semhar sought refuge in Massawa.[94] However, like many Abyssinians before him, he could not take Massawa and in 1844, was forced to retreat inland; by 1846, he had also left Tigray.[95]

A renewed European interest in Abyssinia saw the arrival in the country of many explorers, adventurers and missionaries. In 1837, Father Guiseppe Sapeto started his Lazarist missionary work in the highlands. Around 1852, the center of his activity was a number of villages in Akele-Guzai. A Catholic Church developed which was largely beyond the control of Dejazmatch Wube.[96] The most important convert from the Ethiopian Orthodox faith was Negusie, Ras of Tigray. Swedish missionaries opened a school in Massawa in 1872 and in the following year in Tsazzega in the Hamasien.[97]

With the restoration of imperial power in Abyssinia in 1855—after the eighty-nine year "era of the princes," a period when Emperors were more shadowy and weaker figures than usual—the troops of Emperor Tedros (1855-1868) continued the Abyssinian tradition of oppressing the peripheral peoples. They destroyed many Eritrean villages during the 1858 campaign, in the course of which Tedros succeeded in ending the six-year rule of Negusie.[98] But the highland provinces were never cowed for long; it was said of the situation around Halay that, "some parts of the country were merely in nominal subjection to Theodore," and more generally, that the "Habesh [Abyssinians] could never be united."[99] During the Napier campaign of 1868, Eritreans, in particular Hailu, the governor of Hamasien, were of great assistance to the British. Hailu was arrested later by the Abyssinians and imprisoned for alleged relations with the Egyptians.[100] Abyssinian control stopped at the Mareb River; Senafé, forty-five miles from Annesley Bay, was a Muslim village and did not pay tribute to Tigray.[101]

In 1873, Emperor John (1872-1889) sent troops to occupy Hamasien and Seraye; they so terrified the population—held to Ethiopia by "the slenderest of threads"—that delegations appealed to the Egyptians to come to their assistance.[102] In December 1875, the emperor appointed a new governor of Asmara; he attempted to prevent trade with Massawa by penalizing offenders with the confiscation of their goods for the first offense and amputation of their hands for the second. By all accounts, the inhabitants were unwilling to pay taxes and were in a rebellious mood.[103] In 1875, Wolde Michael, the Koraj of Hamasien, destroyed Asmara in the course of his campaign against the emperor.[104] In turn, John ordered the destruction of entire villages known to support the Koraj.[105] And Ras Alula, during his brief period of rule as lord of the lands of *Mareb Mellash* (1885-1889), excluded all local leaders from political life and attempted to confiscate ten percent of the land. He was "fiercely and successfully" opposed by the local inhabitants.[106] Moreover, it was reported in 1893 that the men of Akele-Guzai were not obliged to serve in the Abyssinian army—nor did they pay any taxes.[107] Of course, Abyssinian armies were remarkably effective in subjugating other neighboring states and bringing them into the Ethiopian empire. The Mensa ruling clans of the western lowlands became Muslim as a reaction to the merciless raids of the Christian overlords of Tigray. The Abyssinian governor of Adiabo in Tigray exacted tribute from some of the Kunama. If tribute was not paid the Christians would raid, kill, emasculate or enslave Kunama and Baria. Both groups fought Abyssinian and Turk alike.[108]

Italian rule brought all of the inhabitants of Eritrea under the rule of a single power for the first time in the territory's history. Eritreans, already distinctive from their Ethiopian neighbors, developed in a radically different manner. Some indication of the hostility felt by Eritreans for Ethiopia is shown in the casualty figures for Eritreans fighting alongside the Italian forces at the battle of Adua, which took place in 1896; 2,000 were killed and 300 prisoners taken. These unfortunate men were victims of Ethiopian atrocities. They all had at least one of their limbs amputated.[109] many were castrated, a favorite punishment; among many reports, one, in 1930, is of an armed band from Ethiopia emasculating four children of a Kunama village who refused to help them.[110]

From the onset of Italian rule, Muslims obtained religious liberties that were unknown in Abyssinia, a measure of self-government and subsidies for the construction of mosques etc.[111] Such treatment led to an independent development which set them further apart from their co-religionists in Ethiopia. Moreover, the impact of foreign missions and customs on Ethiopian Orthodox Christians led Eritrean Christians down a path of development very different to that taken by Ethiopians.

The experience of being colonized by a European power for sixty years is one of the most important factors in the distinctive development of Eritrean nationalism. The next chapter will show that all Eritreans were by no means reconciled to the rule of the Italian invaders and that there was significant resistance. Such resistance is just one of the many features that have contributed toward the building of the Eritrean nation.

Notes

1.   Margery Perham, *The Government of Ethiopia* (London, Faber and Faber, 1969) p. 481.

2. Sylvia E. Pankhurst & Richard K.P. Pankhurst, *Ethiopia and Eritrea: the Last Phase of the Reunion 1941-1952* (Essex, Lalibela House, 1952) p. 13.

3. Getachew Haile, 'The Unity and Territorial Integrity of Ethiopia,' *Journal of Modern African Studies*, 24, 3, (1986) p. 465.

4. Frank Hearn, 'Remembrance and Critique: the Uses of the Past for Discrediting the Present and Anticipating the Future,' *Politics and Society*, 5, 2, (1975) p. 201.

5. Donald Crummey, 'Imperial Legitimacy and the Creation of Neo-Solomonic Ideology in 19th-Century Ethiopia,' *Cahiers D'Etudes Africaines*, XXVIII (1), 109 (1988) pp. 13-4.

6. Ghada H. Talhami, *Suakin and Massawa Under Egyptian Rule 1865-1885* (Washington D.C., University Press, 1979) p. xi.

7. Dan Connell, 'The Birth of the Eritrean Nation,' *Horn of Africa*, III, 1 (1980) p. 14.

8. David Pool, 'Ethiopia and Eritrea: the Precolonial Period,' *The Eritrean Case*, (Rome, Research and Information Centre on Eritrea, 1980) p. 35.

9. Araia Tseggai, 'The Case for Eritrean National Independence,' *The Black Scholar*, June (1976) p. 21.

10. Getachew Haile, 'Some Notes on the History of Ethiopia: a Reexamination of the Documents,' *Quo Vadis Ethiopia*, ed. P. Adwoa Dunn (Washington D.C., Howard University Press, 1983) p. 19.

11. Mordechai Abir, *Ethiopia—the Era of the Princes: the Challenge of Islam and the Re-unification of the Christian Empire 1769-1855* (New York, Praeger, 1968) p. 117.

12. Edward Gibbon, *The History of the Decline and Fall of the Roman Empire*, Vol. I (London, Folio Books, 1983) (first published in 1776) pp. 203-4.

13. Eritrean Liberation Front, *The Eritrean Revolution* (Beirut, ELF Foreign Information Centre, 1977) p. 18.

14. Robert Machida, *Eritrea: the Struggle for Independence* (Trenton NJ, Red Sea Press, 1987) p. 6.

15. Andrew Paul, *A History of the Beja Tribes of the Sudan* (London, Cambridge University Press, 1954) pp. 37, 80.

16. Edward Ullendorff, *The Ethiopians: an Introduction to Country and People* (London, Oxford University Press, 1965) p. 65.

17. Czeslaw Jesman, *The Ethiopian Pradox* (London, Oxford University Press, 1963) p. 10.

18. Tadesse Tamrat, *Church and State in Ethiopia 1270-1527* (Oxford, Clarendon Press, 1972) p. 11.

19. Carlo Conti Rossini, *Storia D'Etiopia* (First Part) (Bergamo, Instituto Italiano d'Arti Grafiche, 1928) p. 48.
20. G.W.B. Huntingford, ed. *The Periplus of the Erythraean Sea* (London, Hakluyt Society, 1980) p. 20.
21. Yuri M. Kobishchanov, *Axum* trans. Lorraine T. Kapitanoff (University Park, Pennsylvania State University Press, 1979) p. 35.
22. A.H.M. Jones and Elizabeth Monroe, *A History of Abyssinia* (London, Oxford University Press, 1935) pp. 23-4; Semere Haile, 'Historical Background to the Ethiopia-Eritrea Conflict,' eds. Lionel Cliffe and Basil Davidson *The Long Struggle of Eritrea for Independence and Constructive Peace* (Nottingham, Spokesman, 1988) p. 12.
23. Eritrean Liberation Front, *Political Programme* (Second Edition) (The Field, 1977) p. 19.
24. *Eritrea Information*, 1, June (1979) p. 9.
25. Tadesse Tamrat, 'Church and State,' p. 32.
26. Franz Amadeus Dombrowski, *Ethiopia's Access to the Sea* (Leiden, E. J. Brill, 1985) p. 6; Machida, 'Eritrea,' p. 8.
27. Eritrean Liberation Front, 'The Eritrean Revolution,' p. 18; Tadesse Tamrat, 'Processes of Ethnic Interaction and Integration in Ethiopian History: the Case of the Agaw,' *Journal of African History*, 29, 1 (1988) p. 6.
28. Taddesse Tamrat, 'Church and State,' p. 65
29. Semere Haile, 'Historical Background,' p. 13.
30. J. Spencer Trimingham, *Islam in Ethiopia* (London, Oxford University Press, 1952) p. 170.
31. Richard K.P. Pankhurst, *History of Ethiopian Towns: from the Middle Ages to the Early Nineteenth Century* (Wiesbaden, Franz Steiner, 1982) p. 83.
32. Stephen H. Longrigg, *A Short History of Eritrea* (Oxford, Clarendon Press, 1945) p. 14.
33. Mordechai Abir, *Ethiopia and the Red Sea: the Rise and Decline of the Solomonic Dynasty and the Muslim-European Rivalry in the Region* (London, Frank Cass, 1980) p. xviii.
34. Abir, 'Ethiopia and the Red Sea,' p. 36.
35. Pool, 'Ethiopia and Eritrea,' p. 42.
36. Abir, 'Ethiopia and the Red Sea,' p. 105.
37. I.M. Lewis, *Peoples of the Horn of Africa: Somali, Afar and Saho* (London, International African Institute, 1955) p. 157.
38. G.W.B. Huntingford ed., *The Glorious Victories of Amda Seyon: King of Ethiopia* (Oxford, Clarendon Press, 1965) p. 2.
39. Longrigg, 'A Short History,' p. 25.

40. G.K.N. Trevaskis. *Eritrea-A Colony in Transition: 1941-52* (London. Oxford University Press, 1960) p. 6.

41. G.W.B. Huntingford, *The Land Charters of Northern Ethiopia* (Addis Ababa, Institute of Ethiopian Studies, 1965) p. 10.

42. Dombrowski, 'Ethiopia's Access,' p. 14.

43. Longrigg, 'A Short History,' p. 43.

44. Castanhoso, *The Portuguese Expedition to Abyssinia in 1541-43,* ed. R.S. Whiteway (London, Hakluyt Society, 1967) p. 268.

45. Taddesse Tamrat, 'Church and State,' p. 260.

46. Longrigg, 'A Short History,' p. 29.

47. Abir, 'Ethiopia and the Red Sea,' pp. 52-3.

48. Amdemichael Kahsai, 'The Eritrean Struggle in Historical Perspective,' *Islamic Defense Review,* 5,3, (1980) p. 11.

49. Richard Leonard, 'European Colonization and the Socio-Economic Integration of Eritrea,' *The Eritrean Case* (Rome, Research and Information Centre on Eritrea, 1980) p. 84.

50. David Pool, 'Ethiopia and Eritrea: the Precolonial Period,' *Eritrea Information,* II, 10 (1980) p. 9.

51. Talhami, 'Suakin and Massawa,' p. 64.

52. Tekeste Negash, 'Review Article,' *Northeast African Studies,* 5,1 (1983) p. 71.

53. James C. McCann, *From Poverty to Famine in Northeast Ethiopia: A Rural History 1900-1935* (Philadelphia, University of Pennsylvania Press, 1987) p. 102.

54. Tekeste Negash, *Italian Colonialism in Eritrea, 1882-1941: Policies, Praxis and Impact* (Uppsala, University Press, 1987) pp. 31, 34.

55. James Bruce, *Travels to Discover the Source of the Nile,* Book V (Dublin, Porter, 1791) pp. 328-30.

56. Abir, 'Ethiopia,' p. 5.

57. Lewis J. Krapf, *Travels, Researches and Missionary Labours* (London, Frank Cass, 1968) (first published 1860) p. xxxvii.

58. Longrigg, 'A Short History,' p. 63.

59. Paul, 'A History of the Beja,' p. 65.

60. Bruce, 'Travels,' pp. 391, 413.

61. Paul, 'A History of the Beja,' p. 81.

62. Longrigg, 'A Short History,' p. 48.

63. Longrigg, 'A Short History,' p. 54.

64. E. van Donzel, *Foreign Relations of Ethiopia 1642-1700: Documents Relating to the Journeys of Khodja Muråd* (Leiden, Netherlands Historisch-Archaelogisch Institut Te Istanbul, 1979) p. 218.

65. Richard K.P. Pankhurst. 'The History of Taxation in Northern Ethiopia (later Eritrea),' *Horn of Africa*. IV, 2 (1980) p. 28.
66. Huntingford. 'The Land Charters.' p. 9.
67. Dombrowski. 'Ethiopia's Access.' p. 24.
68. Raman G. Bhardwaj. *The Dilemma of the Horn of Africa* (New Delhi. Sterlin. 1979), p. 39.
69. Sven Rubenson ed., *Correspondence and Treaties 1800-1854 Acta Æthiopica* Vol. 1 (Evanston, Northwestern University Press, 1987) p. 3.
70. Pankhurst, 'History of Ethiopian Towns.' p. 244.
71. Krapf. 'Travels.' pp. xxxviii. 18.
72. Mansfield Parkyns. *Life in Abyssinia*. Vol. 1 (London. John Murray. 1853) p. 127.
73. Talhami. 'Suakin and Massawa.' p. 58.
74. Richard K.P. Pankhurst. 'Tribute. Taxation & Government Revenues in Nineteenth and Early Twentieth Century Ethiopia (Part III). *Journal of Ethiopian Studies*. VI, 2 (1967) p. 102.
75. Lewis, 'Peoples of the Horn.' p. 176.
76. Talhami. 'Suakin and Massawa,' p. 15.
77. Richard Sherman. *Eritrea: the Unfinished Revolution* (New York. Praeger, 1980) p. 7; Talhami. 'Saukin and Massawa.' p. 101.
78. Longrigg. 'A Short History,' p. 71.
79. Pool, 'The Eritrean Case.' p. 41.
80. D.C. Cumming. 'The History of Kassala and the Province of Taka.' *Sudan Notes and Records*, XX. Part 1 (1937) p. 6.
81. Abir. 'Ethiopia The Era of the Princes.' p. 99.
82. Longrigg. 'A Short History,' pp. 85-6.
83. Sir S.W. Baker. *Exploration of the Nile Tributaries of Abyssinia* (Hartford, O.D. Case & Co.. 1868) p. 576.
84. Talhami. 'Suakin and Massawa.' p. 101.
85. Sven Rubenson. *The Survival of Ethiopian Independence* (London. Heinemann. 1976) p. 292.
86. Richard Greenfield. 'Pre-Colonial and Colonial History.' *Behind the War in Eritrea*. ed. Basil Davidson et. al. (Nottingham. Spokesman. 1980) p. 23.
87. Talhami. 'Suakin and Massawa.' p. 85.
88. Talhami. 'Suakin and Massawa,' p. 145.
89. Longrigg. 'A Short History,' pp. 106, 108-9.
90. Longrigg. 'A Short History,' pp. 76-8.
91. Richard K.P. Pankhurst. 'Ethiopia and the Red Sea and Gulf of Aden Ports in the Nineteenth and Twentieth Centuries,' *Ethiopia Observer*. VIII, 2 (1964) p. 39.

92. Walter Chichele Plowden, *Travels in Abyssinia and the Galla Country With an Account of a Mission to Ras Ali in 1845* (Farnborough Hants., Gregg, 1972 (first published in 1868) pp. 39, 373.

93. Parkyns, 'Life in Abyssinia,' p. 130.

94. Pankhurst, 'Ethiopia and the Red Sea,' p. 48.

95. Abir, 'Ethiopia-The Era of the Princes,' p. 121.

96. Donald Crummey, *Priests and Politicians: Protestant and Catholic Missions in Orthodox Ethiopia 1830-1868* (Oxford, Clarendon, 1972) p. 71.

97. Gustav Aren, *Evangelical Pioneers in Ethiopia: Origins of the Evangelical Church Mekane Yesus* (Stockholm, EFS Förlaget, 1978) p. 164.

98. Longrigg, 'A Short History,' p. 93.

99. Henry Dufton, *Narrative of a Journey Through Abyssinia in 1862-3* (Westport CT, Negro Universities Press, 1970) pp. 208, 335.

100. Longrigg, "A Short History,' p. 101.

101. Clements R. Markham, *A History of the Abyssinian Expedition: With a Chapter Containing an Account of the Mission and Captivity of Mr. Rassam and His Companions* (London, MacMillan, 1869) p. 193.

102. Talhami, 'Suakin and Massawa.' p. 147.

103. Pankhurst, 'Ethiopia and the Red Sea.' p. 67.

104. Augustus B. Wylde, *'83 to '87 in the Soudan: With an Account of Sir William Hewett's Mission to King John of Abyssinia* (London, Remington, 1888) p. 216.

105. Talhami, 'Saukin and Massawa,' p. 147.

106. Haggai Erlich, *Ethiopia and Eritrea During the Scramble for Africa: A Political Biography of Ras Alula, 1875-1897* (Michigan State University, African Studies Centre, 1982) p. 80.

107. James T. Bent, *The Sacred City of the Abyssinians: being a Record of Travel and Research in Abyssinia in 1893* (London, Longmans Green, 1896) pp. 206-7.

108. Aren, 'Evangelical Pioneers,' pp. 204, 132.

109. Addis Hiwet, *Ethiopia: From Autocracy to Revolution* (London, Review of African Political Economy, 1975) p. 12.

110. Duke of Pirajno, *A Cure for Serpents: An Italian Doctor in North Africa* (London, Eland Books, 1985), p. 171.

111. Jonas Iwarson, 'Islam in Eritrea and Abyssinia,' *Muslim World*, 18 (1928) p. 357.

3

Resistance to the Italian Occupation

Throughout the Italian regime the Eritrean remained content, docile and obedient to his rulers.

—G. K. N. TREVASKIS, *Eritrea: A Colony in Transition*[1]

Trevaskis' assertion is a fair example of the usual interpretation of the history of Eritrea during the more than seventy years of Italian occupation. A closer examination of the evidence, however, shows that a persistent tradition of Eritrean resistance and opposition runs throughout the Italian period. It should not be surprising that recorded cases of sustained peasant resistance, not to mention peasant revolutions in the Italian colony, should be few and far between.[2] Everyday forms of resistance rarely find their way into historical accounts. However, a pattern of behavior can be discerned which has had significant influence on the development of a specific Eritrean consciousness. The Italian invasion had particularly profound effects on this development. Of course, ethnic and national linkages, which cross international boundaries, remained. For example, Eritrean nomads would sometimes sojourn in Ethiopia as well as the Sudan. And in the Tigray province of Ethiopia, Tigrinya speakers felt that they had a common, if tenuous kinship with other "Tigray" regardless of their place of residence.[3]

The long period of Italian rule has received little attention by writers in English; the most influential work being that of Tekeste Negash. He argues that the Italian aim to settle Eritrea with poor southern Italian peasants in the late nineteenth century was thwarted by a fear of Eritrean resistance and that "the sparse and scattered acts of resistance, however, appeared to have limited the full implementation of many colonial policies."[4] Even so, Tekeste underestimates the extent of Eritrean resistance and the role it played in developing a distinct Eritrean nationalism. The Italian invaders did not always find conquest to be an easy matter. During the early years after the occupation of Assab, Italian troops began to occupy the fishing village of Beilul; the son of the local leader, Akiato, overpowered the Italian garrison.[5] In 1881, thirteen Italian explorers led by Giulietti and Biglieri were killed by Danakils and, in 1884, Bianchi, Diana and Monari met a similar fate. These and other such attacks, provided Italy with the *causus belli* for the seizure of much of the Red Sea coast.[6]

Italian missionary work began in Abyssinia and the Red Sea area in 1837 when Guiseppe Sapeto, a young Lazzarine monk, escorted by the d'Abbadie brothers, first came to Eritrea. Antoine d'Abbadie was French envoy to the negus and an influential intermediary; by the 1850s, missionary work was well under way in an area centered around Keren.[7] Italian commercial relations with Abyssinia began in 1859, with a treaty between the Kings of Sardinia and Ethiopia.[8] The opening of the Suez Canal in 1869 increased the commercial and strategic importance of the Red Sea and its ports, and led to a more substantial Italian presence in Eritrea. The presence lasted over seventy years, from November 15, 1869 until April 2, 1941; i.e. from the acquisition of land at the northern end of Assab bay by Father Sapeto, on behalf of the Italian government, until the day the British military took over the administration of Asmara, following the Italian withdrawal.[9] The Rubattino Shipping Company ultimately purchased the territory around Assab for 8,100 Maria Teresa dollars from sultans Hassan and Ibrahim Ahmad, Abdullah Sciahim and Burhan Dini, but it was run in Italy's national interest. Assab was chosen for its strategic location near the straits of Bab el Mandeb, and the possibility that it could become an important trading station between Ethiopia and Arabia.[10]

As the Italians expanded their control into the highlands, they proceeded to coopt or eliminate local chieftains. Debbeb Araya became an outlaw in 1882 and entered the service of the Egyptians at Massawa in 1883 and the Italians in 1887. In the middle of February 1888, he deserted the Italians and justified himself by asserting, "I submitted to them thinking that all other Abyssinians dependent on them will be under my orders. I wished to be the only Chief without having other Chiefs on my side: they made other Chiefs, that made me angry."[11] Between August 1889 and December 1890, the Italians killed about a dozen chiefs together, with some 800 followers, who would not submit; they thereby reduced the elite by half.[12] Some highland Eritrean peasants accepted the rule of the new Italian rulers with a degree of enthusiasm, possibly as it was a change from the Abyssinian rulers foisted upon them periodically. The Habab, Mensa, Marya, Baria, Kunama, Bogos and Saho people of the lowlands also collaborated. To them, Italian rule meant an end to the generations-old practices of periodic Abyssinian invasion, pillage, rape and slavery.[13] The Asawerta of the Sahel south of Massawa were alienated from Abyssinia as a result of repeated punitive expeditions mounted against them.[14]

There was also some notable resistance to encroaching Italian government. The Italians became so doubtful of the loyalty of Kefle Iyesus, who occupied Keren on their behalf, that they arrested him in May 1889; he died in prison in Assab.[15] In 1891, Hadgham Basah, chief of Adi Tekelezan (although originally from Gondar), joined other rebels in action against the Italians.

He hit Captain Bettini in the face and was imprisoned for his pains.[16] Dejazmatch Aberra from Hamasien killed Captain Bettini in February 1892; after the assassination, he hid in Asmara, evaded the Italians, fought at Adua and ended his life in exile in Showa.[17] In 1892, Ledj Beyené, another Eritrean rebel, raided Italian property in Seraye. Ras Alula, Tigrayan governor of the lands of *Mareb Mellash* for four years until 1889, in the hopes of enlisting Italian support for his campaigns against the Showan Lords, summoned Beyené to his headquarters in Adua and imprisoned him.[18] Beyené's village was then forfeited to the Italian state.[19] That Beyené was not an isolated malcontent is shown by the fact that, on March 20, 1895, the Italian government declared all lands belonging to rebels to be state land.[20]

In 1893, it was reported that "the revolt of the dervishes have kept the Italian government active [around Keren]."[21] Dervishes pushed to within seven miles of Massawa and the army was continually in action. Italian troops were stiffened with numerous Eritreans recruited since 1890; these soldiers known as *askaris* acquitted themselves magnificently at the battle of Agordat fought on December 21, 1893. A defeat here would have meant the end of the Italian colony.[22]

Many Italian officials held to the view that the highlands of Eritrea were ideally suited to European colonization and that "native" land rights should be curtailed in the interest of white settlers.[23] Moreover, they held the erroneous view that ownership of land in the highlands was traditionally vested in the sovereign of Ethiopia who could appropriate and distribute it at will. In fact, the greater part of the land on the Eritrean plateau was vested in the community and could not be alienated except in special circumstances.[24] Neither did the Ethiopian Orthodox Church own more than a few highland villages.[25] However, decrees establishing state land and reserving it for Italian colonists were first enacted on May 11, 1893.[26] Within a year, nearly a fifth of all arable land—over one million acres—had been expropriated.[27]

As direct consequence of this expropriation, rebellion became more common. The most significant acts took place in Akele-Guzai. On December 15, 1894, Dejamatch Bahta Hagos, who had been given 287 guns by the Italians and raised to the position of chief of Akele-Guzai and Seraye provinces in gratitude for his support, rebelled. It is said that he was discontented at the increasing alienation of land, particularly from the clergy.[28] His defection has also been attributed to the influence of the French Lazzarists, by whom he was converted to Catholicism. He could also have been fearful that he would be sent by his Italian masters to fight the dervishes in the northern reaches of Eritrea.[29]

Bahta Hagos, accompanied by his brother Sengal and his son Gebre Medhin, took Lieutenant Sanguinetti, the commander of the Italian garrison at Segeneiti, as a prisoner and cut communication links with the rest of Eritrea. Bahta, continuing the long tradition in Eritrea of opposition to invaders—whether from beyond the Mareb or from across the Red Sea—proclaimed himself "an avenger of their rights trampled on by the Italians."[30] He also claimed that, "the Italians curse us, seize our land; I want to free you...let us drive the Italians out and be our own masters."[31] The rebellion lasted only three days, and Bahta was killed, his body left unburied and his brother fled to join Ras Mengesha in Tigray. Bahta is reputed to have written repeatedly to the rulers of Tigray and to Menelik pleading for their support. No support was forthcoming and none of the letters have been traced.[32] The rapid collapse of the rebellion has been ascribed to the less than wholehearted devotion of Akele-Guzai villagers to a chief foisted upon them in the first place by the Abyssinians. There is a very democratic tradition in the highland villages of Eritrea, with male villagers accustomed to electing leaders by popular assembly.[33] Bahta was also a convert to Roman Catholicism, and like many such, implacable in his opposition to those still adhering to the old faith.[34]

The incident took its place in Eritrean folklore and signaled the start of extensive fighting and unrest; this culminated a year later with the defeat of the Italians by the Ethiopians at Adua.[35] Bahta Hagos' son escaped to Tigray and between 1896 and 1904 repeatedly and unsuccessfully tried to involve the rulers of Tigray in his fight against the Italians. He joined up with another famous "bandit," Mohammed Nuri, settled in Senafé and continued to harass the Italians.

Other Eritreans also found that the costs of supporting Italy were too high. Sheik Thala, a respected leader in the Danakil, had joined Major Toselli, the victor over Bahta, with some 300 of his followers. But after the battle of Amba Alagi on November 24, 1895, in which 1,300 Eritrean soldiers and virtually all their white officers, including Toselli, were killed by the Ethiopians, Thala and his men defected, spreading far and wide news of the Italian disaster. By 1896, Italy was seen to be vulnerable, and all doubting Ethiopians and Eritreans joined the negus before the battle of Adua.[36] Ras Sebhat and Hagos Tefri defected from the Italians with 500 men.[37] Before the battle, Tigrinya women, who had the free run of the Italian camp, often worked as Menelik's spies. The role of women in the Eritrean resistance must not be discounted; a visitor to the country in 1886 said "we will teach these people a lot of things that as yet they do not know exist. Women will hear of independence."[38] Only in 1897, was pacification of Eritrea considered to be complete and a civilian governor appointed. Even so, at the turn of the century, the new governor, Ferdinando Martini, still reported that desertion and small scale armed confrontations were *"il menu quotidiano"*—daily occurrences.[39]

By 1900, the population of Eritrea, ravaged by constant wars, disease and resultant famines, was estimated to be no more than one-fifth of that estimated by Münzinger some thirty years before.[40] The great famine of 1888-1892 killed many Eritreans as well as possibly one-third of the population of Ethiopia and is still remembered as *kifu qan* (evil days).[41] Augustus Wylde, the British traveler and later vice-consul in Massawa, saw villages in ruins around Dongola. The villagers had been punished for looting and killing Italians fleeing after their defeat at Adua in 1896.[42] In Adi Quala, he was informed of "terrible accounts of famine and cholera." Locusts destroyed the grain crops, then rinderpest killed seventy-five percent of the cattle; this disaster was followed by failures of the winter and spring rains. Although some Italian officers fed the Eritreans out of their own pockets, the government (like succeeding colonial governments) did nothing.[43]

Italian authorities persisted in their claim that land abandoned largely as a result of the great privations suffered by the Eritreans had reverted to the state and could be settled by Italians.[44] Martini, governor of Eritrea for nine years from 1898, reported that hasty appropriations of land by the state without taking account of local customary rights had serious consequences.[45] Armed rebellion was scattered through the country. Comments such as, "no Ethiopian fifth column" existed in Eritrea after the Italian defeat at Adua, are not accurate.[46]

A major cause for complaint was the question of expropriated land. Although the office of colonial settlement was abolished in 1895, and laws of 1903, 1909 and 1926 recognized the rights of indigenous inhabitants, resulting in the return of some of the expropriated land, a minimum of 16,250 acres of land was still in the hands of sixty-two Italian farmers. In 1905, people of Hamasien and Akele-Guzai demanded their land back. They were not successful[47]

A number of Eritreans were imprisoned for political offenses. Toward the end of 1899, some 109 of these, detainees on Naqura prison island near Assab, escaped to Tigray.[48] Ali Osman Bore, a Danakil patriot, organized the escape.[49] Among the escapees was the writer Gebre Igziabiher who was Sanguinetti's secretary but had fallen foul of the government. Although Gebre Igziabiher apparently regarded himself as an Ethiopian, he was at the same time a vigorous critic of the decadent Ethiopian political system.[50]

Although the first thirty-five years of this century were years of relative calm in the Italian colony of Eritrea—certainly compared to the thirty-eight year period that has elapsed since the British left Eritrea in 1952—there were tensions. In 1913, it was admitted that, "the attitude of the Arab population was such" that the Italians could not place any reliance on them as troops.[51] From 1907, Eritrean *askaris* played a vital role in the subjection of Somalia, and from 1912, they formed the bulk of the colonial army in Libya. They were joined by 100,000 men from Tigray, Wollo and Gojjam.[52] During the Libyan pacification, Eritreans were vital and they became aware of how much better they performed than Italian troops.[53] Much of Eritrea was left untouched by Italian colonization, and until the fascist era, Eritrea "stagnated." Apparently, Italian law did not reach very far and "in out of the way places," the Italian district governor concerned himself "only with offenses brought explicitly to his attention."[54]

The conventional view was that Eritrea was "a peaceful, loyal and contented colony."[55] At least this was the impression gathered by King Vittorio Emmanuele and General de Bono, minister of colonies, on their 1932 visit to Eritrea for celebrations marking the fiftieth anniversary of the Italian occupation.[56] The fascist regime began the development of modern Eritrea and sent increasing numbers of settlers to Eritrea. The Italian population was some 70,000 in 1941; in 1905, there had been only 1,617 adult male Europeans in the colony.[57] Eritrea provided a major stimulus for the development of a cash economy in the north of Ethiopia; it drew much of the region into its hegemony.[58]

It is clear, however, that Eritreans were not invariably loyal; there was opposition to the decree of February 7, 1923, which declared increased areas of Eritrean land to be the exclusive property of the state. Kentiba Tessema, ruler of Enda Gebre-Kristos district in Hamasien, resisted the policy of land alienation and was dismissed from office.[59] Of highland land assessed as cultivable, totaling 445,000 acres, sixteen percent, 70,000 acres, including much of the most fertile land was placed under Italian control.[60] Food production declined from 1921 through 1931.[61] One contributory factor may well have been the fact that many Eritrean peasants were forced off productive land and migrated into cities and into marginal farming areas. According to one writer, virtually none of the Italian owners farmed themselves. They did however, take profits from their sharecroppers.[62] Some 25,000 acres were given as a concession for palm cultivation, 7,500 acres for cotton and 12,500 acres reserved for coffee plantations. Of the latter, 1,250 acres were taken up immediately by twelve Italians. By 1947, however, only six Italians were involved on a total of 750 acres; there was resentment at the extent of unutilized land.[63] Many areas still remained out of the reach of the Italian government. In the Afar areas, it was the practice of the Danakil to kill any stranger on sight.[64] They did this because "the natives understand perfectly that it is better no one should know their country—that this is the only safeguard to their independence."[65] A revolt against government authority beginning in northern Wollo, which spread to include most of eastern Tigray and southern Eritrea in 1929-1930, is just one indication of underlying discontent.[66]

Prior to 1935, many hundreds of dissident Eritreans left the colony and found exile wherever anyone would welcome them. Many ended up in Addis Ababa and made a considerable contribution to their new country. One of these, Ato Lorenzo Taezaz, frustrated at the lack of opportunity in Eritrea, eventually became private secretary to the emperor and head of the secret police.[67] He accompanied the emperor into exile in London.[68] He was one of the three Ethiopian delegates at the September 1936 session of the League of Nations, which recognized the credentials of Ethiopia in spite of strenuous Italian objections.[69] Lorenzo also visited Ethiopian guerilla forces in Gojjam during 1939-1940 and established that the emperor would receive support on his return to Ethiopia.[70] Among other notable Eritrean exiles, Efrem Tewolde became a minister in Haile Selassie's government in exile in London and Issayas Gebre Selassie was placed in charge of Oromo affairs in the resistance Committee of Union and Collaboration, formed after the occupation—and later became a lieutenant general in the Ethiopian army.[71] Tekeste has argued that the emperor's "slow but steady progress" to a modern state was largely as a result of the influence of Eritrean migrants to Ethiopia. Italy feared it would lose its influence on the most dynamic section of the colony—the Tigrinya-speaking areas and invaded Ethiopia.[72] This seems to be over stretching the point; what cannot be denied is that Eritreans were granted a number of privileges in the East African empire and this "further strengthened the growth of a separate Eritrean identity."[73]

During the feverish build up to the invasion of Ethiopia in 1935, the Italians introduced conscription in Eritrea; this raised more than 65,000 *askari*—some forty percent of the active labor force.[74] There was increased Ethiopian espionage in the markets of Asmara and among the clergy of the Ethiopian Orthodox Church; a few defections occurred from the Italian Army.[75] The defections were particularly worrying as the Eritrean *askari* had been the backbone of the Italian colonial army since 1895. Men would enlist for five years and extend their service for two years at a time; they became skilled fighters and disciplined men, trustworthy and of marked endurance. During the 1935-36 war, there were many Eritrean heroes. Eritreans also fought in the specialized corps, for example, the Third Field Artillery was all *askari*.[76]

In spite of a superficial impression that during the invasion, "the Eritreans followed their white officers with ferocious devotion," there were numerous Eritrean defections from the army.[77] By December 1935, there was already a steady stream who were "indignant at being given the hardest and most dangerous tasks."[78] An eyewitness reported that the "Blackshirts were mere spectators of the gallantry of the askari."[79] Indeed, the initial slowness of the Italian advance has been attributed to the discontent felt by the Eritrean *askaris*. They were perturbed at the bombing of villages and field hospitals and over their continued deployment in dangerous operations. They were also aware of the successes (albeit only temporary) achieved by the Ethiopian armies on the Takkaaz front and concerned over civil grievances such as the curfew, racial discrimination and the shortage of supplies.[80]

After the opening phases of the war, with the exception of the battle of Mai Chew, Eritrean *askaris* were held in reserve and played from then on only an extremely small part in the great battles.[81] That the Italians had good cause to be concerned over the loyalty of the Eritreans was soon confirmed. Before the battle of Ganale Doria in January 1936, twelve men under Gerazmatch Gebrai deserted; during the night, several hundred more, under the command of Fitaurari Tegai Negussie, joined them. Eritrean troops mutinied after the attack, during which the Italians used mustard gas on the Ethiopians. Some 904 *askaris* of the Fourth Eritrean *Gruppo* attached to the Agostini column led by Colonel Maramarcio deserted. Some of these *askaris* had been fighting in Libya for over 20 years.[82] An additional 600 men marched along the Omo River to Kenya where they were interned in Isiolo at the No. 1 Eritrean Deserters Camp.[83] Fitaurari Haile Beyené was another leader of the mutineers.[84] The Fourth *Gruppo* was disbanded and the Eritrean *askaris* dispersed. In 1940, the Eritrean troops interned in Kenya were released to fight alongside other troops in the British-led liberation of Eritrea and Ethiopia.[85]

There were also desertions on the northern front. Shumbash Andom Tesfazien led 100 *askaris* into the Ethiopian camp after being ordered to leave Eritrean dead unburied. In March 1936, on the eve of the battle of Mai Chew, the emperor's last battle, Andom had over 1,000 Eritrean deserters under his command. He fought a guerilla war against the Italians for four years but was killed in the battle of Armchako. He was promoted to the rank of Dejazmatch on the eve of his death.[86] Other troops under Kegnazmatch Selebe also deserted.[87] Many Eritreans led by Fitaurari Tessema, also joined Ras Desta Domtu, son-in-law of the emperor, who maintained stout resistance in Sidamo until February 1937.[88]

During the years that Italy occupied Ethiopia, Eritreans carried out a number of spectacular acts of resistance, though within Eritrea itself, it is said, reports of overt opposition were rare.[89] There was bandit activity such as that of Hagos Temnewo, imprisoned for the first time in 1924, which could be said to have political overtones.[90] There is one report of a strike in Decamare on September 25, 1935 when forty men, led by an Italian married to an Eritrean woman, protested against racist laws.[91] A possible reason for the relatively low level of resistance recorded at this time, is that Italy began to favor Muslims and Christian elites in Eritrea (as well as in Ethiopia); this purchased the loyalty of over half of the population.[92] The first government school in Eritrea (Keren, 1911) was for the sons of Muslim chiefs and notables. Moreover, Eritrean Muslims took advantage of the boom years in Eritrea and joined the paid workforce for the first time. This not only muted their political activity, but also broke down the dependency of the Tigré-speaking serfs upon their Shumagelle lords; it also lessened sectarian divisions and helped to pave the way for the united opposition to Ethiopian colonialism that developed in the 1970s.[93]

Another reason for the relatively low level of overt opposition in Eritrea at this time, lies in the growing influence of Eritreans of mixed race. Until 1937, children who had an Italian father and Eritrean mother were considered to be Italians, providing the father acknowledged the child as his, and, unlike Eritreans, were given an education; they were placed in the care of the Catholic Church's St. Joseph Institute.[94] By 1937, there were some 35,000 Eritreans of mixed race. They began to play a leading role in Eritrean society. Other foreign missionaries also played a role in Eritrea; the Swedish Evangelical Church entered Eritrea in 1868 and, by 1935, were operating twelve schools and two hospitals. Seventh Day Adventists had worked in Eritrea since 1906. From as early as 1870, significant numbers of Eritrean elites were converted from adherents of the Ethiopian Orthodox faith to Evangelical Christianity—a conversion which clearly has its political significance.[95] General Graziani, Mussolini's overlord in Eritrea, expelled all foreign missionaries on December 20, 1935, angering many Eritreans.[96]

Italy pronounced the "Organic Law for Eritrea and Italian Somaliland" on July 6, 1933. This allowed for discrimination based on physical characteristics.[97] Italy began to enforce racist segregation laws in January 1937; these prohibited mixed marriages and assigned the mother's nationality to any child. The children were taken out of their privileged schools and assigned to menial occupations—agricultural labor for boys and domestic service for girls. This change caused resentment.[98] In 1940, all Eritreans of mixed race were declared to be natives.[99] The fascist racial laws were bitterly resented by all Eritreans.[100] Two Eritreans, Abraham Deboch, an interpreter in the Italian consulate in Addis Ababa, and Moghes Asegedom, a clerk living in the German legation, were (at least according to popular belief) discriminated against when they attended a cinema. The official Ethiopian version of the succeeding events is that, smarting under this racist insult, they attempted a "spontaneous" assassination of Viceroy Graziani on February 19, 1937.[101] It seems, however, that the assassination was not as "spontaneous" as it appears because Grazmatch Letibellu Gebre, who had retired to his estates after fighting bravely against the Italians, supplied the grenades.[102] Abraham and Moghes escaped capture by the Italians and attempted to join the Ethiopian forces of Abebe Aregai and Mesfin Silleshi; they were rejected because they were Eritreans.[103] They then disappeared—killed it seems by hostile Showan tribesmen when they were close to safety in Sudan.[104]

The attempted assassination of Graziani led to horrifying reprisals from the Italians, and stimulated further acts of resistance from Ethiopians and Eritreans. On May 21, 1937, on the first anniversary of the Italian occupation of Addis Ababa, Zerai Deres, an Eritrean youth, killed five fascist guards in Rome. Zerai used a ceremonial sword to carry out the killings in front of the gold lion of Judah statue which had been transported to Rome from Addis Ababa.[105]

For three years, Ethiopian patriotic forces maintained guerrilla opposition to the Italian invaders of their homeland. Eritrea was quiet until Italy declared war on Britain on June 10, 1940. The British liberation offensive began in July 1940, with the Emperor of Ethiopia being brought back from Europe and installed in Khartoum. The British sought all allies in the fight, including those Eritreans, politicized by the activities of the 1930s into supporting Ethiopia. An imperial proclamation was dropped by plane over Eritrea and occupied Ethiopia, encouraging *askaris* to desert; many did so.[106] Leaflets and loudspeaker propaganda were also directed at the Eritrean troops facing General Wavell, the commander of the Allied troops in the Burye area; they were equally effective.[107] The British produced a newspaper, *Banderachin Negusachin* (Our Flag and Our King) for clandestine and general distribution; the chief compositor of the newspaper, Konstantinos Trage, was partly Eritrean.[108]

The British invaded Eritrea in January 1941 and in a rapid, effective campaign, captured Keren on March 27. According to G.L. Steer, chief of the British propaganda unit, 6,000 Eritreans deserted from their units at Keren; afterward the Italian command dispersed forty Eritrean battalions.[109] The success of the propaganda campaign was partly due to the very clever wording of the leaflets. Different versions were printed for Italian, Amhara and Eritrean troops. Those aimed at Eritreans read: "Eritreans! You deserve to have a flag!... This is the honorable life for the Eritrean: to have the guts to call his people a Nation."[110]

Resistance to Italian settlement continued during the British administration. The seven urban communities created by the Italians in Asmara, Massawa, Keren, Decamere, Adi Ugri, Adi Quala and Assab became the centers of protest and confrontation against continued European rule.[111] From 1941-1944, the British appropriated a further 10,000 acres of land and gave it to Italian settlers.[112] The number of Eritrean farm workers, which in 1937 had been 1,915, most being former peasant farmers, continued to grow.[113] There was consequently much friction between Eritreans and Italians; property was destroyed and crops burned in an attempt to drive the Italians from Eritrea.[114] Many groups of bandits, known as *shifta*, often composed of disbanded soldiers, roamed the countryside. The famous Mossazghi brothers had all been with the Italian forces; the eldest, Wolde Gabriel, served in Libya and Gondar, while Beyené, the second oldest, had seen action in Gondar.[115] The youngest brother was killed by an Italian *carabinieri* in December 1948; in revenge, at least eleven Italians were killed in the highlands. The Mossazghi brothers were revered as anti-Italian resistance fighters far beyond their immediate locality.[116] Much of the folk culture of the Eritrean peasant amounted to a legitimation of celebration of bandit activity.[117] All too often though, bandits, such as the brothers, were given arms, money and refuge by Ethiopian officials in Tigray in exchange for terrorizing Eritrea into a federation with Ethiopia.[118] It is probable, however, that the techniques that the Eritrean peasants devised to deal with their Italian masters were extremely useful in their later armed resistance to the Ethiopian state.

The Italian influence on Eritrea extended well into the period of federation. In 1970, Italians still held the most important civic positions in Asmara, including those of chief secretary, chief engineer, sanitary officer, medical officer, road maintenance technician, sanitary inspector and surveyor.[119] Many of the other important positions were held by Ethiopians. The new generation of Eritreans, educated under British rule, deeply resented their continued inferior status. They came to see the British as just one more set of invaders. Just as many of the deserting *askari* in the 1930s and 1940s fled to join their brothers across the Mareb, who were fighting a European invader, a number of educated, mainly middle-class, Christian highlanders believed that their true loyalties lay with Ethiopia. The views of these articulate men received great prominence during the post-war debates over the future of Eritrea and will be discussed briefly in the next chapter. The views of the mass of men and women are less familiar; it is unlikely they will ever be fully known. The long history of resistance to Italian occupation, however, is largely their monument.

Notes

1.   G.K.N. Trevaskis, *Eritrea—A Colony in Transition: 1941-52* (London. Oxford University Press, 1960) p. 29.
2.   Jim Scott, 'Everyday Forms of Peasant Resistance in South-east Asia,' *Journal of Peasant Studies*, XII, 3 (1985) p. 5.
3.   Dan F. Bauer, *Household and Society in Ethiopia: an Economic and Social Analysis of Tigray Social Principles and Household Organization* (East Lansing, Michigan State University Press, 1977) p. 116.
4.   Tekeste Negash, *Italian Colonialism in Eritrea, 1882-1941: Policies, Praxis and Impact* (Uppsala, University Press, 1987) p. 122.
5.   Araia Tseggai, 'The History of the Eritrean Struggle' eds. Lionel Cliffe and Basil Davidson, *The Long Struggle of Eritrea for Independence and Constructive Peace* (Nottingham, Spokesman, 1988) p. 70.
6.   Ghada H. Talhami, *Suakin and Massawa under Egyptian Rule 1865-1885* (Washington D.C., University Press, 1979) pp. 212-3.
7.   Agatha Ramm, 'Great Britain and the Planting of Italian Power in the Red Sea, 1868-1885,' *English Historical Review*, 59 (1944) p. 214.
8.   Norman Bentwich, *Ethiopia, Eritrea and Somaliland* (London, Gollanca, 1945) p. 6.
9.   Ramm, 'Great Britain and the Planting of Italian Power,' p. 214; Talhami, 'Suakin and Massawa,' p. 199.
10. Richard K.P. Pankhurst, 'Eritrea and the Red Sea and Gulf of Aden Ports in the Nineteenth and Twentieth Centuries,' *Ethiopia Observer*, VIII, 2 (1964) p. 64.
11. Richard Caulk, 'Bad Men of the Borders: Shum and Shefta in Northern Ethiopia in the 19th Century,' *International Journal of African Historical Studies*, 17, 2 (1984) p. 212.
12. Tekeste Negash, 'Resistance and Collaboration in Eritrea: 1882-1914,' *Proceedings of the Sixth International Conference of Ethiopian Studies*, ed. Sven Rubenson (Addis Ababa, Institute of Ethiopian Studies, 1984) pp. 317-8.
13. Tekeste Negash, 'Resistance and Collaboration,' p. 322.
14. Caulk, 'Bad Men of the Borders,' p. 225.
15. Chris Prouty, *Empress Taytu and Menelik II: Ethiopia 1883-1910* (Trenton NJ, Red Sea Press, 1886) p. 59.
16. James T. Bent, *The Sacred City of the Abyssinians: being a Record of Travel and Research in Abyssinia in 1893* (London, Longmans Green, 1896) pp. 79-80.
17. Tekeste Negash, 'Resistance and Collaboration,' p. 318.
18. Haggai Erlich, *Ethiopia and Eritrea During the Scramble for Africa: A Political Biography of Ras Alula, 1875-1897* (East Lansing, Michigan State University Press, 1982) pp. 173-4.

19. Bent, 'The Sacred City,' p. 90.
20. Richard K.P. Pankhurst, 'Italian Settlement Policy in Eritrea and its Reper-cussions 1889-1896,' *Boston University Papers in African History Volume I* (Boston, Boston University, 1964) p. 144.
21. Bent, 'The Sacred City,' pp. 79-80.
22. E. Arimondi, 'The Italian Operations at Agordat in the Eastern Sudan,' trans. A. Paget, *Journal of the Royal United Service Institution,* XXXVIII (1894) p. 846.
23. Pankhurst, 'Italian Settlement Policy,' p. 123.
24. Pankhurst, 'Italian Settlement Policy,' p. 131-2.
25. Tekeste Negash, 'Italian Colonialism,' p. 6.
26. Pankhurst, 'Italian Settlement Policy,' p. 143.
27. Tekeste Negash, 'Resistance and Collaboration,' p. 319.
28. Harold G. Marcus, *The Life and Times of Menelik II, Ethiopia 1844-1913* (Oxford, Clarendon Press, 1975) pp. 153-5.
29. Roberto Battaglia, *La Prima Guerra d'Africa* (Turin, 1958) p. 595.
30. Sylvia E. Pankhurst, *Eritrea on the Eve: the Past and Future of Italy's "first-born" colony, Ethiopia's Ancient Sea Province* (Woodford Green Essex, New Times and Ethiopia News, 1952) p. 45.
31. Richard Caulk, '"Black Snake, White Snake": Bahta Hagos and his Revolt against Italian Overrule in Eritrea, 1894,' ed. Donald Crummey, *Banditry, Rebellion and Social Protest in Africa* (London, James Currey, 1986) p. 301.
32. Tekeste Negash, 'Italian Colonialism,' p. 124.
33. O. Baratieri, *Memoires d'Afrique: 1892-1896* (Paris, Charles De la Grave, 1899) p. 110.
34. Caulk, 'Black Snake, White Snake,' p. 305.
35. Pankhurst, 'Italian Settlement Policy,' p. 148.
36. Battaglia, 'La Prima Guerra,' p. 675.
37. Prouty, 'Empress Taytu,' p. 152.
38. Prouty, 'Empress Taytu,' pp. 359, 233.
39. Tekeste Negash, 'Resistance and Collaboration,' p. 318.
40. G. F-H Berkeley, *The Campaign of Adowa and the Rise of Menelik* (London, Constable, 1935) p. 386.
41. Amartya Sen, *Poverty and Famines: An Essay on Entitlement and Deprivation* (Oxford, Clarendon, 1982) p. 86.
42. Augustus B. Wylde, *Modern Abyssinia* (London, Methuen, 1901) p. 107.
43. Wylde, 'Modern Abyssinia,' p. 105.
44. Pankhurst, 'Italian Settlement Policy,' p. 132.
45. Trevaskis, 'Eritrea,' p. 54.
46. Trevaskis, 'Eritrea,' p. 29.
47. Tekeste Negash, 'Resistance and Collaboration,' p. 320.
48. Tekeste Negash, 'Resistance and collaboration,' pp. 318-9.
49. *Adulis,* IV, 5 (1987).
50. Tekeste Negash, *No Medicine for the Bite of a White Snake: Notes on Nationalism and Resistance in Eritrea 1890-1940* (Uppsala, University Press, 1987) p. 7.
51. Emilio de Bono, *ANNO XIIII: the Conquest of an Empire,* trans. B. Miall (London, Cresset Press, 1937) p. 31.
52. McCann, 'From Poverty to Famine,' pp. 189-90.

53. Tekeste Negash. 'Italian Colonialism.' p. 116.
54. Harald P. Lechenberg, 'With the Italians in Eritrea.' *The National Geographic Magazine*, LXVIII, 3 (1935) p. 293.
55. Anthony, Mockler, *Haile Selassie's War: the Italian-Ethiopian Campaign, 1935-1941* (New York, Random House, 1984) p. 27.
56. Angelo Piccioli, *La Nuova Italia D'Oltre Mare: l'Opera Del Fascimo Nelle Colonie Italiane* (Verona, A. Mondadori. 1933) pp. 264-76.
57. Pankhurst, 'Italian Settlement Policy.' p. 155.
58. McCann, 'From Poverty to Famine.' p. 129.
59. Jordan Gebre-Medhin. *Peasants and Nationalism in Eritrea: A Critique of Ethiopian Studies* (Trenton NJ, Red Sea Press, 1989) p. 108.
60. John Markakis. *National and Class Conflict in the Horn of Africa* (Cambridge, Cambridge University Press, 1987) p. 58.
61. James C. McCann, *A Great Agrarian Cycle? A History of Agricultural Change in Highland Ethiopia, 1900-1987* (Boston, Boston University Press, 1988) p. 3.
62. Tekeste Negash. 'Italian Colonialism.' p. 61.
63. Tekeste Negash, 'Italian Colonialism.' pp. 71, 43: Tekeste Negash 'No Medicine for the Bite of a White Snake.' p. 89.
64. L.M. Nesbitt, *Hell-Hole of Creation: the Exploration of Abyssinian Danakil* (New York, Knopf, 1935) p. 56.
65. Werner Münzinger, 'Narrative of Journey Through the Afar Country.' *The Journal of the Royal Geographical Society*, 39 (1869) p. 195.
66. McCann, 'From Poverty to Famine.' p. 155.
67. Evelyn Waugh, *Waugh in Abyssinia* (London, Methuen, 1984) p. 75.
68. Haile Selassie I, trans. E. Ullendorff, *My Life and Ethiopia's Progress. 1892-1937* (London, Oxford University Press, 1976) p. 299.
69. Stephen U. Chukumba, *The Big Powers against Ethiopia: Anglo-Franco-American Diplomatic Maneuvers During the Italo-Ethiopian Dispute 1934-1938* (Lanham MD, University Press of America, 1979) p. 446.
70. George L. Steer, *Sealed and Delivered: A Book on the Abyssinian Campaign* (London, Hodder and Stoughton, 1942) pp. 8-9.
71. Richard Greenfield, *Ethiopia, a New Political History* (London, Pall Mall, 1965) p. 243.
72. Tekeste Negash. 'Italian Colonialism.' p. 129.
73. Tekeste Negash. 'Italian Colonialism.' p. 156.
74. Timothy Fernyhough, 'Social Mobility and Dissident Elites in Northern Ethiopia: the Role of Banditry, 1900-69.' ed. Donald Crummey, *Banditry, Rebellion and Social Protest in Africa* (London, James Currey, 1986) p. 159: Tekeste Negash, 'Italian Colonialism.' p. 43.
75. De Bono. 'ANNO XIIII.' pp. 168-170.
76. J.F.C. Fuller. *The First of the League Wars: Its Lessons and Omens* (London, Eyre and Spottiswode, 1936) pp. 59, 67.
77. Waugh. 'Waugh in Abyssinia.' p. 157.
78. Mockler. 'Haile Selassie's War.' p. 85.
79. Fuller, 'The First of the League Wars.' p. 59.
80. Fuller, 'The First of the League Wars.' pp. 29-31.
81. Marshal Badoglio. *The War in Abyssinia* (London, Methuen, 1937) p. 175.
82. Angelo del Boca, trans P.D. Cummins, *The Ethiopian War 1935-1941* (Chicago, Chicago University Press, 1969) p. 122.

83. Mockler, 'Haile Selassie's War,' p. 94.
84. Mockler, 'Haile Selassie's War,' p. 433.
85. Harold Marcus, 'Ethiopia (1937-1941),' eds. D.M. Condit et. al., *Challenges and Response in Internal Conflict*, III (Washington D.C., American University, 1968) p. 15.
86. del Boca, 'The Ethiopian War,' p. 122.
87. Haile Selassie, 'My Life.' p. 241.
88. Alberto Sbacchi, 'Ethiopian Opposition to Italian Rule, 1936-1940,' ed. R.L. Hess, *Proceedings of the Fifth International Conference of Ethiopian Studies*, Session B. (Chicago, University of Illinois Press, 1979) p. 588; Alberto Sbacchi, *Ethiopia under Mussolini: Fascism and the Colonial Experience* (London, Zed Books, 1985) p. 188; Salome Gebre Egziabher, 'The Ethiopian Patriots 1935-1941,' *Ethiopia Observer*, XII, 2 (1968) p. 79.
89. Sbacchi, 'Ethiopian Opposition,' p. 591.
90. Jordan Gebre-Medhin, 'Peasants and Nationalism,' pp. 124-5.
91. Thomas Charles Killion, *Workers, Capital and the State in the Ethiopian Region 1919-1974*, (Stanford, Unpublished Ph.D. Thesis, 1985) p. 276.
92. Sbacchi, 'Ethiopia Under Mussolini,' pp. 164-5.
93. Roland Marchal, 'Birth, Development and Crises of the Muslim League in Eritrea,' Paper presented to the Conference of Northeast African Studies, Michigan State University, (1989) p. 12; Killion, 'Workers, Capital and the State,' p. 282.
94. Sbacchi, 'Ethiopia Under Mussolini,' p. 172.
95. Gustav Aren, *Evangelical Pioneers in Ethiopia: Origins of the Evangelical Church Mekane Jesus* (Stockholm, EPS Förlaget, 1978) p. 204.
96. Ingeborg Lass-Westphal, 'Protestant Missions During and After the Italian Ethiopian War 1935-1937,' *Journal of Ethiopian Studies*, X, 1 (1972) p. 95.
97. Richard K.P. Pankhurst, 'The Development of Racism in Fascist Italy's Colonial Empire (1935-1941),' *Ethiopian Journal of African Studies*, 4,2, September (1987) p. 31.
98. The Italian Foreign Minister, Galleazzo Ciano, commented in January 1939 that "Amhara was still in a state of complete revolt." Galleazzo Ciano, *Diario: Volume Primo, 1939-1940* (Milano, 1946) p. 1. Note that one translation into English misread *Amhara* for *Asmara*, and this error has been perpetuated by some writers relying upon secondary sources.
99. Tekeste Negash, 'Italian Colonialism,' p. 109.
100. Sbacchi, 'Ethiopia Under Mussolini,' pp. 172-3.
101. Mockler, 'Haile Selassie's War,' p. 415.
102. Greenfield, 'Ethiopia,' p. 240.
103. Sbacchi, 'Ethiopia Under Mussolini,' p. 193.
104. Mockler, 'Haile Selassie's War,' p. 415.
105. Greenfield, 'Ethiopia,' p. 232.
106. Mockler, 'Haile Selassie's War,' p. 232.
107. W.E.D. Allen, *Guerilla War in Abyssinia* (Harmondsworth, Penguin, 1943) pp. 73-4.
108. Steer, 'Sealed and Delivered,' pp. 96-7.
109. Steer, 'Sealed and Delivered,' p. 175.
110. Steer, 'Sealed and Delivered,' p. 174.

111. Getahn Dilebo, 'Historical Origins and Development of the Eritrean Problem 1889-1962,' *A Current Bibliography on African Affairs*, 7, 3 (1974) p. 237.
112. David Pool, *Eritrea: Africa's Longest War* (London, Anti-Slavery Society, 1982) p. 18.
113. Irma Taddia, *L'Eritrea—Colonia 1890-1952* (Milano, Franco Angeli, 1986) p. 252.
114. Trevaskis, 'Eritrea,' p. 55.
115. Fernyhough, 'Social Mobility,' p. 159.
116. Fernyhough, 'Social Mobility,' p. 163.
117. Scott, 'Everyday Forms of Peasant Resistance,' p. 29.
118. Fernyhough, 'Social Mobility,' p. 165.
119. John M. Cohen and Peter H. Koehn, *Ethiopian Provincial and Municipal Government: Imperial Patterns and Post Revolutionary Changes* (Ann Arbor, Michigan State University Press, 1980) p. 109.

4

Elections Under Britain and Ethiopia

The secretary-general of the Unionist Party, Mr. Tedla Bairu, admitted that the figures which he had supplied relating to the supporters of this party were inaccurate and that the Muslim population of the western lowlands had ceased to support union with Ethiopia. With regard to the eastern lowlands, he preferred not to give a categorical reply until the question had been studied by his party.[1]

—United Nations General Assembly

Over the fifty years that Italians ruled Eritrea, some of the linguistic, religious and ethnic divisions had broken down. Many people saw themselves primarily as Eritreans and not as Christians and Muslims, Tigrinya or Saho, farmer or merchant. Differences still remained, differences subsequently exploited very cleverly by Ethiopia and unionists within Eritrea. Ethiopia's strong arm tactics, however, alienated a majority of Eritreans, who came to see that the Ethiopians were merely the latest (and most oppressive) of a long line of invaders of their country.

As soon as Haile Selassie returned from exile in Europe in 1941, he began to annex Eritrea. He established The Society for the Love of the Land of Eritrea, an organization which aimed at the eradication of all vestiges of Italian colonialism. It was led by local notables, Ethiopian Orthodox churchmen and the petit bourgeoisie. In 1945, it became the Unionist party which stood for the unconditional union of Eritrea and Ethiopia; its most active member was Secretary General Tedla Bairu. Most Eritreans, however, were against unconditional union with Ethiopia.[2] In 1942, the British administration suggested that what little irredentism existed in Asmara stemmed from the head of the Ethiopian Church in Eritrea, Abuna Marcos.[3] Moreover, this "irredentism" could be seen rather as a protest at the British policy of retaining the fascist administrative system, than as a wish for union with Ethiopia.

Although most scholars would now agree that the United Nations observation quoted in the epigraph fairly represents the feeling in lowland Eritrea in the years before federation, they would probably still argue that, until as late as 1975 a majority of Christian Eritreans wanted union with Ethiopia. Tekeste has said that Tigrinyas "maintained, albeit unarticulated, sentiments of Ethiopianism."[4] And Okbazghi stated "[Eritrean] nationalism had failed to carry conviction in the 1940s."[5] A careful examination of the evidence, however, leads one to question this view. Not the least important fact is that the Ethiopians forced Tedla Bairu, one of the chief architects of union, to resign his position of Chief Executive in 1955, after he had expressed his disquiet over Ethiopia's policy of depriving Eritreans of the human rights promised them in the Constitution. In 1967, completely disillusioned with Ethiopia, he completed his political pilgrimage by defecting to the Eritrean Liberation Front (ELF).

A significant independence movement developed in the 1940s; a major contribution to which was made by the Muslim League. The Muslim League, formed in 1946 in Keren, called for an independent, unpartitioned Eritrea; it brought together almost all of the lowland Muslim communities under the leadership of the late Ibrahim Sultan.[6] The Eritrean Liberal Progressive Party— another precursor of the Eritrean liberation movement—was founded in February 1947. Its most active member was journalist Wolde-ab Woldemariam. The party linked up with the Muslim League in 1949 to form the Independence Bloc. This ferment of political activity took place in the context of a revolt in the western lowlands which lasted from 1942 to 1949. Serfs refused to pay taxes and tribute to their landlords.[7]

In 1947, indirect elections were held in Eritrea under the aegis of the United Nations Four Power Commission. Each village, family or clan was approached by the commission and asked to choose a representative; each representative was asked by the commission to declare which party he favored and how many people he represented.[8] Some 3,336 representatives voted in this curiously haphazard fashion and a minority of forty-eight percent declared for the Unionist party; forty-three percent voted for pro-independence parties and nine percent for a return to Italian rule or trusteeship. Some 675,000 Eritreans opposed union and 547,000 supported it.[9]

There was considerable intimidation of representatives and it is clear that, in many areas, supporters of the Liberal Progressive Party and the Muslim League were prevented from speaking to the commissioners. It has been claimed that the British Foreign Office sent Frank S. Stafford to Eritrea in order to disrupt the pro-independence campaign.[10] It is almost impossible to believe that in seventy-seven villages in south Hamasien and in another forty-six north Hamasien villages, there were no members and supporters of the Liberal Progressive Party.[11] Moreover, in western Seraye—with an estimated population of 80,818—there were reportedly no representatives who favored independence. A major role in the anti-independence campaign was played by the clergy of the Ethiopian Orthodox faith, who threatened excommunication, and refused baptism, marriage and funeral services to all Eritreans in favor of independence.[12] This message was conveyed by 5,000 Ethiopian Orthodox priests and 870 monks in 550 churches and fourteen monasteries.[13] Another powerful figure was Haile Selassie's liaison officer in Asmara, Colonel Negga Haile Selassie, who supplied large sums of money directly to the Unionist Party.[14] Many Eritreans were doubtful of the economic viability of an independent Eritrea; from 1945 until 1950 there was a decline in the economy as a result of British economic measures such as the dismantling of industrial capital investment set up during the war.[15]

The commission did not have a very high opinion of the "representatives" it met: "an impression was gained that the population will accept the decision of the Big Four even if it does not coincide with the opinions expressed by the representatives."[16] Two weeks after the commission left Eritrea, gangs of *shifta*—armed and supplied by Ethiopia—started a series of attacks against the lives and property of Italian, Muslim and, particularly, pro-independence supporters. After the Four Power Commission had presented its report later in 1948—a report which showed the Unionists to be in a minority—further acts of outright terrorism were perpetrated against the anti-unionists.

At the time of formation of the Independence Bloc in 1949, there were many defections from the Unionist party. Some, it must be said, defected because the terms that Ethiopia was offering to Eritrea in the mooted federation were not attractive enough. The United States ambassador reported that, "Keren branch...has defected en bloc....British administrator estimates privately...that independence bloc commands 75 percent of Eritrea."[17]

The United Nations addressed the question of Eritrea at its fourth session commencing on September 20, 1949. Four Eritrean political leaders were invited to appear before the subcommittee on Eritrea. Ibrahim Sultan, in particular, made such a favorable impression on the delegates with a well argued and eloquent appeal for Eritrean independence, that the subcommittee saw the need for further information.[18] The United Nations Commission arrived in Eritrea in February 1950 "to ascertain more fully the wishes and best means of promoting the welfare of the inhabitants of Eritrea."[19] A continuous violent campaign of intimidation, carried out by Ethiopia and the Unionist party, began to pay off within a few weeks of the commission's arrival. The Independence Bloc split into three factions. The Muslim League of the Western Province began to campaign for independence for western Eritrea and not for the whole country. The pro-Italy party began to lose support, while the Liberal Progressives changed their name to Liberal Unionist and their policy—in the last resort—to settle for federation with Ethiopia. The United Nations Commission performed its investigatory role in a most perfunctory manner; spending only seven weeks in the country and visiting few areas outside of Asmara. The commission reported that, "it is impossible to gauge accurately the permanence and exact strength of the political persuasions of the people of Eritrea."[20] However, three members of the five-nation commission, Burma, Norway and South Africa, seem to have had their minds made up before they entered the country and were eager to accept Ethiopia's case. The delegates of Guatemala and Pakistan were more cautious. They commented that many of the representatives who came forward to the commission supporting the Unionist cause were bogus.[21]

After prolonged debate, the General Assembly agreed to a compromise solution and voted on December 2, 1950, to federate Eritrea with Ethiopia. As with many compromises, this solution found few fervent supporters. An election to choose representatives to an Eritrean Assembly was held in Eritrea in March 1952. The election was supervised by the British using war powers gazetted in Proclamation 121. The electoral procedure adopted was essentially the same as in 1947 (i.e. representatives' views were solicited) with the exception of Asmara and Massawa, where a secret ballot was allowed. During February, potential electors in these two towns were asked to register; only half of them did so—a strong indication that they were not interested in voting for an assembly whose prime purpose would be to vote on a constitution which did not allow Eritreans the option of independence. As in 1947, women were excluded from the ballot.[22] Some sixty-eight constituencies were drawn up—supposedly based upon social, geographical and political considerations, but in reality gerrymandered so that Unionist areas were over represented.[23] Even so, the Independence Bloc (including Liberal Unionists) won eighteen seats, and the Muslim League (which had split away from the Bloc but still stood for independence) fifteen; the Unionists won thirty-two and there were three others. Some 51.5 percent of the seats went to pro-independence parties. The sixty-eight member assembly was evenly divided on religious lines and included thirty-four Christians and thirty-four Muslims.[24] Support for pro-independence parties would no doubt have been higher had there not been considerable intimidation of non-Unionists.

In January 1951, the British administration offered an amnesty to Unionist *shifta* who laid down their arms; some 296 did so—less than ten percent of those in the field. On June 19, another amnesty was announced and most of the rest (having achieved their objective of intimidating non-unionists) surrendered.[25] Estimates of grassroots support for the independence majority range from sixty to seventy-five percent.[26] Eritrean interest in politics was spread throughout the country. Even supporters of union with Ethiopia wanted autonomy for Eritrea in domestic affairs as a way of safeguarding some of the amenities that Italian and British rule had brought.[27] The British representative in Asmara during the first year of federation, commented that, "all sections of the people... would not at present welcome a complete merger with Ethiopia."[28]

On May 25, 1954, the Eritrean Parliament asked the prime minister to warn the Ethiopian government to provide the necessary safeguards to protect the sovereignty of the Eritrean Constitution within twenty days. In the event of Ethiopian noncompliance the prime minister was to ask the United Nations to intervene.[29] The United Nations informed the Eritreans that any complaint against alleged violations of the Constitution must be addressed to the United Nations via the federal government. This ruling has ensured that for the past thirty-five years the issue of Eritrea has never been heard in the United Nations.[30] It soon became transparently clear to Eritreans that a complete merger with Eritrea was the aim of Ethiopia. It remained the hope of a dwindling band of Eritrean Unionists.

After the 1952 election, the Unionists were able to command a majority in the assembly by dint of striking a deal with the Muslim League, convincing them that Unionists were determined that Eritrea's interests in the federation would not be subordinated to Ethiopia's.[31] As part of the deal, Ali Mohammed Mussa Radai of the Muslim League became the first president of the assembly after the establishment of the Federation on September 15, 1952.

The last session of the First Eritrean Assembly was held in March 1956 and elections for a new assembly were held on Sep-

tember 5, 1956. Article 45 of the Constitution stipulated the establishment of an independent commission to conduct the elections.[32]
This was never implemented. Instead, the elections were supervised by the emperor's right hand man, Asfaha Wolde Micael, who
combined the posts of chief executive and Ethiopian vice representative in Eritrea. By use of the same powers used by the British—
Proclamation 121—Asfaha was able to ban the participation of
organized parties and ensure a pro-Union majority. Women were
not permitted to vote or stand as candidates. The main role of the
new assembly was to vote its dying autonomy out of existence.[33] In
1957, Idris Mohammed Adam, the president of the assembly, was
forced by the chief executive to resign—further indication of the
waning influence of the assembly. Further examples of encroaching Ethiopia dictatorship were given in Chapter 1.

The end of federated Eritrea came with a "vote" in the Eritrean
Assembly in 1962, in favor of annexation by Ethiopia. Prior to the
vote, Ethiopia increased its campaign of bribery and intimidation.
Eritrean police surrounded the assembly; the police were surrounded by men of the Ethiopian Second Division under the command of General Abbiye Abebe, who controlled all urban areas and
most of the countryside. On November 13, a motion to dissolve the
federation was defeated four times.[34] No vote was taken on the next
day; Asfaha Wolde Micael merely read a statement prepared for
the emperor several weeks in advance by his advisor, John Spencer, requesting the assembly to dissolve the federation and unite
with "our motherland, Ethiopia."[35] Asfaha read the statement in
Amharic, a language understood by a only a handful of the Eritrean
representatives.[36] Several Muslim and a few Christian members
expressed their opposition. Indeed, Muhammed Omar Akito, an
Afar representative from Assab who made an eloquent speech on
Eritrean independence, refused to vote in favor, as did one other
member.[37] Tedla Ogbit, the Eritrean chief of police was active in
the assembly intimidating members; he repented later and
attempted to join the Eritrean resistance movement.[38]

On the following day, the emperor, without consulting the
United Nations, proclaimed Order No. 27, terminating Eritrea's
federal status. On December 4 and 11, demonstrations organized

by the Eritrean Liberation Movement's secret highland groups,
Mahber Shewate (the Association of Seven) were held in Asmara,
Massawa and Keren in support of Eritrean independence.[39]

With the end of the federation, Eritrean political life was
restricted to the participation of eleven Eritrean representatives in
the ineffectual Ethiopian parliament.[40] In the ten years after 1962,
the pro-Ethiopian lobby, which was ascendant in international,
diplomatic and scholarly circles, made a rigorous attempt to depict
the mood in the highlands as one of overwhelming support for
union with Ethiopia. The "Greater Ethiopia" thesis was strenuously propagated and became "a brilliant intervention at the ideological level for justifying the continued existence of the Ethiopian
Empire."[41] The reality was very different. For example, in 1964, a
returned Peace Corps volunteer reported from the village of Adi
Tekelezan (which later became an EPLF stronghold) that, "the
feeling of pride in the now dissolved institutions and the traditional
Tigrinya resentment of the ruling Amhara tribe [*sic*], are still real.
A few students...insist that they are Eritreans, not Ethiopians."[42]
The 1974 overthrow of the Emperor and his replacement by a provisional military government led to more oppression of Eritreans
by Ethiopians. By late 1974 and early 1975, oppression had
reached such a level that virtually no support remained within Eritrea for union or federation with Ethiopia. Christian recruits from
the Hamasien highlands were joining the EPLF in thousands.[43]
These young men and women were the heirs of a continuing highland resistance to alien domination. Chapter 7 deals with the
important role they have played in the military campaign that has
been waged against the Ethiopian regime since 1961. However, it
is useful to deal first with the Ethiopian perspective on the revolt in
Eritrea.

Notes

1. United Nations General Assembly, *Official Records Supplement 8* (1950) p. 31.
2. Lloyd Ellingson, 'The Emergence of Political Parties in Eritrea, 1941-1950,' *Journal of African History*, XVIII, 2 (1977) p. 261.
3. Sylvia E. Pankhurst and Richard K.P. Pankhurst, *Ethiopia and Eritrea: the Last Phase of the Reunion 1941-1952* (Essex, Lalibela House, 1953) p. 69.
4. Tekeste Negash, *Italian Colonialism in Eritrea, 1882-1941: Policies, Praxis and Impact* (Uppsala, University Press, 1987) p. 59.
5. Yohannes Okbazghi, 'The Creation and Termination of the Ethio-Eritrean Federation and the Rise of Eritrea to National Revolution' (University of Denver, Unpublished Ph.D. Thesis, 1986) p. 96.
6. Richard Leonard, 'European Colonization and the Socio-Economic Integration of Eritrea,' *The Eritrean Case* (Rome, Research and Information Centre on Eritrea, 1980) p. 92.
7. Araia Tseggai, 'The History of the Eritrean Struggle,' eds. Lionel Cliffe and Basil Davidson, *The Long Struggle of Eritrea for Independence and Constructive Peace* (Nottingham, Spokesman, 1988) p. 72.
8. G.K.N. Trevaskis, *Eritrea—A Colony in Transition: 1941-52* (London, Oxford University Press, 1960) p. 88.
9. Ellingson, 'The Emergence of Political Parties,' p. 270.
10. Peter With, *Politics and Liberation: the Eritrea Struggle, 1961-1986* (Denmark, University of Aarhus, 1987) p. 145.
11. Pankhurst and Pankhurst, 'Ethiopia and Eritrea,' pp. 317-8.
12. Bereket Habte Selassie, 'Eritrea and the United Nations,' *The Eritrean Case* (Rome, Research and Information Centre on Eritrea, 1980) p. 157.
13. Jordan Gebre-Medhin, *Peasants and Nationalism in Eritrea: A Critique of Ethiopian Studies* (Trenton NJ, Red Sea Press, 1989) p. 98.
14. Ellingson, 'The Emergence of Political Parties,' p. 269.
15. John Markakis, *National and Class Conflict in the Horn of Africa* (Cambridge, Cambridge University Press, 1987) p. 62.
16. Trevaskis, 'Eritrea,' p. 90.
17. Bereket Habte Selassie, 'Eritrea and the United Nations,' p. 126.
18. Tekie Fessehatzion, 'The International Dimensions of the Eritrea Question,' *Horn of Africa*, 6, 2 (1983) p. 12.
19. Trevaskis, 'Eritrea,' p. 95.
20. United Nations, 'Official Records,' p. 21.
21. United Nations, 'Official Records,' p. 31.
22. Pankhurst and Pankhurst, 'Ethiopia and Eritrea,' p. 279.
23. Tekie Fessehatzion, 'The International Dimensions,' p. 16.
24. Semere Haile, 'The Roots of the Ethiopia-Eritrea Conflict: the Erosion of the Federal Act,' *Journal of Eritrean Studies* 1, 1 (1986) p. 7.
25. Robert Machida, *Eritrea: the Struggle for Independence* (Trenton NJ, Red Sea Press, 1987) p. 26.
26. Leonard, 'European Colonization,' p. 96.
27. D.C. Cumming, 'The Dispersal of Eritrea,' *The Middle East Journal* 7, 1 (1953) p. 23.

28. E.R.J. Hussey. 'Eritrea Self-Governing.' *African Affairs*. 23. 213 (1954) p. 322.
29. *Adulis*, IV, 4 (1987).
30. With, 'Politics and Liberation,' p. 146.
31. Trevaskis, 'Eritrea,' p. 120.
32. *Journal of Eritrean Studies*. 1, 1 91986).
33. Haggai Erlich, *Ethiopia and the Challenge of Independence* (Boulder CO, Lynne Rienner. 1986) p. 219.
34. Tekie Fessehatzion, 'The International Dimensions.' p. 18.
35. Tesfatsion Medhanie, *Eritrea: Dynamics of a National Question* (Amsterdam. B.R. Grüner. 1986) p. 26.
36. Tekie Fessehatzion, 'The International Dimensions,' p. 18.
37. Kassim Shehim, 'Ethiopia, Revolution and the Question of Nationalities: the Case of the Afar,' *Journal of Modern African Studies*, 23, 2 (1985) p. 338.
38. Bereket Habte Selassie, *Conflict and Intervention in the Horn of Africa* (New York, Monthly Review Press, 1980) p. 62.
39. Tekie Fessehatzion, 'The International Dimensions,' p. 19.
40. Semere Haile, 'Historical Background to the Ethiopia-Eritrea Conflict,' eds. Lionel Cliffe and Basil Davidson, *The Long Struggle of Eritrea for Independence and Constructive Peace* (Nottingham, Spokesman, 1988) p. 23.
41. Jordan Gebre-Medhin, 'Peasants and Nationalism.' p. 8.
42. Anthony Vigo. 'Between Two Worlds,' *Africa Today*. October (1965) p. 6.
43. Bereket Habte Selassie, 'Conflict and Intervention.' p. 198.

5

Eritrea Under the Dergue

The right of the Ethiopian Nationalities to determine their own future will be translated into practice.

•

The oppressed people of the Eritrean region have no interests and aspirations different from those of the people of Ethiopia as a whole.

—*The Ethiopian Herald,* July 8, 1978[1]

I t cannot be denied that, during the past sixteen years, the Ethiopian military regime, or Dergue, has exercised control over much of urban Eritrea and established legitimacy in the eyes of some Eritreans, the most notable being Ammanuel Amde Michael, the first governor of post-revolutionary Eritrea, and—until his 1988 defection—vice-president of Ethiopia. It is extremely unlikely that the Ethiopian regime can ever exercise effective control over the bulk of Eritrea or command the allegiance of a majority of the population. The inherent contradictions in their Eritrean policy are nowhere more evident than in the above two slogans.

The inability of the semi-feudal regime of Haile Selassie to contain the Eritrean liberation movement was one of the most important factors leading to its downfall. Without the inspiration of the ELF, which commenced the armed struggle on September 1, 1961, the effective guerrilla actions of the Eritrean Liberation Front (ELF) and Eritrean People's Liberation Front (EPLF), and the vanguard role played by many Eritrean students, workers and intelligentsia residing in Addis Ababa, it is unlikely that the momentous revolution of February 1974 would have occurred.

The men of the Second Division of the Ethiopian Army who had borne the brunt of Ethiopia's war against the ELF and EPLF forces were exceedingly restive over pay and conditions; they mutinied in Asmara in February 1974. Most of their demands were met; this encouraged other units to rebel. The collapse of imperial authority in Ethiopia led to a creeping transfer of power to the military. This resulted in the formation of the Dergue—the Provisional Military Armed Council (PMAC)—in July 1974 and a Provisional Military Government (PMG) in September. A Workers Party of Ethiopia was formed in 1984, elections held in 1987 and a civilian socialist government proclaimed. In spite of numerous defections and executions, the core of the PMAC, centered on Chairman Mengistu, remained essentially unchanged from 1974 until 1989.

The first chairman of the PMAC was an Eritrean, General Aman Andom. In a September 1974 speech at Keren, he admitted that it was impossible to set up a stable administration in Eritrea through the sheer use of force. Accordingly, he appointed a new governor general. A draft constitution was proposed under which all fourteen provinces of Ethiopia would have regional assemblies and the power to issue laws (for Eritrea this would have been a return to the position that existed—at least on paper—in the 1952-1962 period). The Dergue's seriousness with regard to autonomy must be doubted. In spite of the relatively peaceful conditions that have existed in some other provinces over the past ten years, regional autonomy has never been enacted—as opposed to being proclaimed—in any part of Ethiopia, let alone in Eritrea. The Dergue and its supporters have continued to talk endlessly about the nationalities question; in March 1983, an Institute of Nationalities was established under the direction of Ashagre Vigletu, but few of the proposals of the Ethiopian National Democratic Revolutionary Program have been implemented.

After the Revolution, peace talks were held with some of the guerrillas; an attempt was made to persuade them that the Eritrean struggle was a residue of the feudal system; now that a socialist system was being introduced in Ethiopia their struggle was no longer necessary. This line of argument had some appeal and (discounting exaggerated reports) resulted in the return of some refugees and former fighters who took advantage of an amnesty. A number of Eritreans who acted as intermediaries for the Dergue took this opportunity to defect to the liberation forces; moreover, a steady stream of prominent Eritreans who had initially supported the Ethiopian revolution also went into exile.

Because of the authority possessed by Aman and the willingness of the liberation forces to test the Dergue's good will, the EPLF and ELF observed a virtual cease fire in Eritrea in the latter part of 1974. The Dergue took advantage of this respite to bring in 5,000 more troops. They then affirmed a clear policy that "the unity of Ethiopia and Eritrea is eternal and armed force will be used if Eritreans are not able to realize this."[2] Aman Andom and a number of prominent officials were clearly determined to work towards a negotiated settlement, but most Dergue members were not. In November 1974, Aman and a number of his supporters were killed by government forces. There were bomb explosions in Addis Ababa and many Eritreans were rounded up in late November 1974. ELF and EPLF urban guerrillas attacked many targets in Asmara and were only expelled from Asmara at great cost to the army and civilian population.

The military government was subject to a great deal of bitter infighting and consequently made a number of apparently contradictory statements. For example, General Teferi Bante—who replaced Aman Andom as head of state until he, in turn, was slain on Mengistu's orders—said in December 1974 that "peace and security prevails in all parts of country." But by February of the next year, a state of emergency was declared throughout Eritrea, "after fourteen years of continuous banditry."[3]

On May 18, 1976, the Dergue announced a nine-point plan on Eritrea; it promised to release some prisoners and lift the state of emergency, declared it would encourage exiles to return and promised that the entire Ethiopian people would discuss the nationalities question. The Dergue also expressed its willingness to exchange views with groups that were not in collusion with feudal, reactionary, imperialist forces—by this Dergue members implied that they would negotiate with the EPLF. After this pronouncement there were reports of huge rallies in support of the government. Indeed, as the Dergue's grip on Eritrea declined, the size of the crowds supporting the government's position increased—an unusual phenomenon to say the least. The Dergue hastened to inform the masses that its willingness to negotiate was not to be seen as a sign of weakness.

As Marxist-Leninist civilian influence on the leadership deepened, there were repeated statements that no contradiction existed between the peoples of Ethiopia and Eritrea. On the occasion of May Day 1977, a long unsigned article in *The Ethiopian Herald* attacked the EPLF position that it was fighting an anti-colonialist war. The author (presumably connected with the Yekatit 66 Ideological School) maintained that the struggle of the Eritreans could not be against colonialism, as Ethiopia was an underdeveloped neocolonial country and Eritrea was in a higher stage of capitalist development. (One might then wonder what advantage there would be for progressive Eritreans in a union with Ethiopia).

In August 1976, government spokesmen claimed that peace overtures were working. However, unity talks between the ELF and the EPLF were also held; the guerrilla leaders made it clear that no matter what the differences between them, neither front would do a separate deal with the Dergue. The Dergue was also faced with growing opposition in Addis Ababa as well as in the countryside, with the most formidable resistance to its dictatorship coming from the Ethiopian People's Revolutionary Party (EPRP). The EPRP was mainly composed of students and intellectuals; it had originally supported the military coup, but turned against the Army when it became clear that the military had no intention of relinquishing power to civilians. The EPRP, after much intellectual debate, eventually came out in support of the Eritrean struggle. The armed liberation fronts, in Ethiopia as well as Eritrea, received thousands of recruits as the government closed universities and schools in an effort to assert its will on the population.

On April 13, 1977, the Eritrean liberation forces attacked and later captured the towns of Om Hager and Afabet. Mengistu accused the Sudan of open armed intervention and blamed President Jaafer Nimeri for sabotaging peace talks and for preventing refugees from returning to Eritrea. Correspondents of Reuters, Agence France Press and *The Washington Post*, as well as all Western consuls resident in Eritrea, were expelled from Ethiopia. From that point, news about events in Eritrea came only from correspondents going into Eritrea under the auspices of the EPLF, or from the stories of reporters handpicked by Ethiopia, and escorted around a few carefully selected locations.

After a brief period during which it professed its willingness to talk with the guerrillas, the Dergue declared that all secessionists were reactionary. Mengistu used the crisis caused by the fall of the major towns of Keren, Tessenei, Nacfa and Karora to the EPLF and ELF to call for national mobilization. In consequence, thousands of untrained and poorly armed peasants were pressed into service. In a particularly badly planned operation they descended upon Tigray and Eritrea, where many met their death. This disaster was never admitted in the Ethiopian press. The only acknowledgment of the peasants' sacrifices was the construction of a heroes center and periodic medal-giving ceremonies.

The Dergue became steadily more Marxist and pro-Soviet in its pronouncements. A host of delegations from the socialist camp visited Ethiopia and began to send aid. On December 11, 1977, the

Cuban head of state, Fidel Castro, declared that while the Eritrean liberation movement had once been progressive it was now controlled by reactionary states such as Sudan and Saudi Arabia; this was why the Eritreans continued to fight against a socialist regime. In June 1980, Mengistu went even further when he said that the separatists were never progressive and cooperated with the feudal leaders of Ethiopia, even before the 1974 Revolution; no evidence was cited for this claim. The Dergue mounted a very skillful campaign in efforts to detach traditional supporters of the fronts and met with a major success in the case of the People's Democratic Republic of South Yemen (PDRY). It also continued its diplomatic assault on Sudan, which met with fluctuating successes and failures. The intricate bargaining is described in more detail in Chapter 6.

In spite of constant assertions that all sections of Eritrean society fully supported the Dergue and that Eritrea was an integral part of the motherland, the Dergue was forced to call for substantial outside assistance in order to enforce its claim to Eritrea. From early 1978, there was considerable Cuban, Soviet and Yemeni support in battles against the liberation forces. At the time, this vital military support was never officially admitted by the Dergue; but later on, much publicity was given to ceremonies decorating Cuban and Yemeni heroes of the campaign. The ELF lost a considerable number of men in the Soviet-led offensives. The EPLF also lost most of the urban areas it had captured during 1978; however, it executed a "strategic retreat" in an orderly fashion and retained most of its units and armor. After the fall of Keren in November 1978 the Dergue announced "the end of the 17-year-old separatist dream."[4] It even claimed (incorrectly) to have captured Nacfa, the capital of Sahel Province and an EPLF stronghold.[5]

The Dergue admitted that for a long time, in some cases almost four years, most Eritrean industries had ceased production. By late 1978, they claimed that these had begun to function again and were already operating at thirty percent capacity, although still suffering from shortages of power and materials. The extent of the devastating damage caused by the fighting was also admitted; damage for which the "bandits" were invariably held to blame—even when photographs showed that it was obviously caused by Ethiopian bombing, tanks and heavy artillery. The rebuilding of the economy was clearly moving at a very slow pace; in October 1980 it was admitted that there were few Eritrean peasant associations; this was due to the activities of *wenbede* "bandits."[6] The authorities were able to reopen Asmara University (with students drawn from all over Ethiopia) as well as an office for the Revolutionary Ethiopian Youth Association (REYA). There was some evidence that a number of guerrillas had defected from both fronts after interrogation, some were interviewed in public and claimed to be convinced that the Ethiopian revolution was genuine. They formally renounced their past as "bandits." The Dergue claimed without producing compelling evidence that thousands of former "so called ELF and EPLF fighters" had returned.

From 1981, arms were given to selected peasants (the EPLF maintains that these were usually the large landowners). The Dergue also used the *kebeles*—the Urban Dweller's Associations (UDA)—as an effective way to control localities in fourteen towns; the UDAs act as a security service for the Dergue, rooting out "anti people and anti unity elements;" members cannot change their residence without obtaining permission. There are Worker's Control Committees in offices and factories. Some of the *kebeles* in Asmara had non-Eritrean and Soviet members as many Ethiopians were brought in to work in sensitive areas and, at one time, close to 9,000 Soviet-block advisers lived in Eritrea.[7]

According to the official media, in late 1981 an atmosphere of peace, prosperity and optimism prevailed in Eritrea.[8] That this was hyperbole became evident on January 26, 1982, when Mengistu launched the multi-faceted Red Star Campaign on military, ideological, political, organizational, cultural and economic fronts "to end for once and for all the organized banditry."[9]

Large claims were soon made for the success of the Red Star military campaign; there were reports of hundreds of bandits being captured and demoralized by the superior fighting tactics of the Northern Command. "Bandits were trapped atop the summits of Sahel mountains lacking food, water and medicines."[10] This was all window dressing; the Dergue were even finding it difficult to control Asmara. In late 1981, the curfew was lifted from 7:00 p.m. to 11:00 p.m. but the result of this was that the EPLF cells which had remained in Asmara and other towns after the strategic withdrawal were able to maneuver more freely. On January 23, 1982, 2,500 EPLF fighters attacked the town, destroying two garrisons, the Thirty-fifth Brigade Headquarters, the Baratollo textile factory and much of Asmara airport. The town was bombarded four times in February and again in March. During this period, Mengistu visited Eritrea twice. There is some speculation that he was injured in an EPLF attack on Asmara airport; he did not appear in Addis Ababa for the victory parade commemorating the defeat of the Italian army at Adua in 1896. A BBC reporter claimed, however, that there was no sign of shelling at Asmara airport.[11]

The government claimed that production in 1981-1982 was forty percent greater than the year before. The Red Star Campaign, which absorbed ten percent of Ethiopia's non-military budget, was said to be a success. A British parliamentary delegation visited Asmara in the spring of 1982 and observed that, on entering or leaving Asmara, people had to pass through check points; also that there were no new buildings in the city.[12] One of the few Western reporters allowed in noticed "sandbags and machine guns at street intersections and on roof tops"; he also saw Soviet military personnel walking the streets.[13]

Government spokesmen continued to exhort Eritrean youth (or the few that remained under their control) to politicize, organize and enlighten the peasants; it appears that constant orientation, upgrading and reskilling seminars took place, all having a heavy ideological content and consuming a great deal of time that might have been more profitably employed on production. For example, in December 1982, there was a report that peasants in a seminar in Gash Setit district had "resolved to wipe out the bandits causing havoc to development," but acknowledged that this would take time. At the same seminar, the representative of the Organizing Committee for the Workers Party of Ethiopia (COPWE) claimed that the people had been totally liberated from the influence of the "bandits."[14]

One indication that the Red Star campaign had failed is that the first anniversary of the proclamation of the campaign passed unnoticed in the media; every other significant date in the revolutionary calendar receives maximum coverage. Indeed, at the Second COPWE Congress, held in January 1983, Mengistu announced that national military service was needed, a clear indication that the Red Star campaign had not met its objectives of weaning the civilian population away from the EPLF and "wiping out the bandits for once and for all." On May 5, 1983, conscription was introduced; all Ethiopians aged sixteen to thirty were required to undergo six months military training and then serve as a territorial reserve for a further twenty-four months. Those aged thirty to fifty were also registered for service in a commissariat and territorial militia.

In the 1980s, there were a number of visits by Western observers to Dergue held areas of Eritrea. For example, in July 1982 John Valner, the European Economic Community representative to Ethiopia, expressed satisfaction with soil and water conservation projects he examined in four provinces. Another visitor was the deputy director of the United Nations World Food Program who was impressed by the "enthusiastic involvement" of the peasants, and called for a vast international support to the Dergue.[15]

This vast support was not forthcoming. On March 6, 1983, a new crisis was announced; the Relief and Rehabilitation Commission (RRC) estimated that some 710,000 people in Eritrea were affected by drought and problems were compounded by the activities of bandits. In August 1983, the RRC claimed that Eritrea was in as critical a condition with regard to drought as in 1974, but that prompt action by the government had forestalled a potentially calamitous situation. This claim cannot be verified. Chapter 9, however, discusses the progress of the 1984-1985 famine and competing claims of the RRC and the Eritrean Relief Association (ERA) in greater depth.

In September 1983, the Amharic weekly *Ethiopia* published by the Second Army in Eritrea, reported on the success of the Red Star campaign. The Revolutionary Ethiopia Women's Association (REWA) claimed to have 300 groups in Eritrea with 83,600 members.[16] On the other hand, REYA was much less developed with only seventy-two associations with 6,031 members, none of whom were in Barka or Sahel. Only 200 former "separatists" had found employment, and 8,500 peasants had been supplied with arms. After training, many of the militias desert *en block* to the EPLF and few of the others attempt to engage EPLF forces; this is never directly admitted by the Dergue, but articles complaining of the lack of vigilance against "anti-people activities" show the true picture.[17]

Eritrea was said to be the hub of socio-economic activity, with fifteen major industrial complexes, producing at, or nearly at, projected levels. Eleven schools had been rebuilt and 141,000 students were said to be at school. Moreover, 231,000 people, half of them women, had become literate. The Dergue paid little attention to health services; the major hospitals in Keren, Massawa and Asmara had been rebuilt, but were full of military casualties. Moreover, the doctor/population ratio remained one of the poorest in the world.[18] In Asmara in 1988, there was one surgeon for a population of half a million, there was almost no running water and typhus was common.[19] In the rural areas, the lack of control by the military is clearly shown by Ethiopian complaints that a rinderpest and diphtheria vaccination campaign had been impossible because of "anti-people activities."

There was no direct reference in the Ethiopian press to the significant military setbacks suffered by the Dergue in 1984: events such as the Eritrean People's Liberation Army (EPLA) tank victories on the Northeastern Sahel front, the capture of the important town of Tessenei, and the attack on Asmara airport, when a fifth of the Ethiopian air force was put out of action, all went unrecorded. Neither were figures given of Eritrean registrations for military service under the Dergue. The conscription campaign led to the flight of many more Eritreans to the Sudan; some became recruits to the EPLF. The only (veiled) references to the military reversals were in the COPWE party organ, which said that "anti people elements" in certain areas were indulging in "vicious rumor mongering."[20] In July 1984, REYA members were urged to fight against the "cheap propaganda of the secessionist gangs." Many cadres said how much they appreciated the wise and dedicated leadership of Mengistu; indeed, one tangible result of Mengistu's triumph over the rest of the PMAC is that in Ethiopia's public places it was now his portraits which dwarfed those of Marx and Lenin.

From June 1984 until the tenth anniversary of the revolution in September, public activity in Ethiopia was dominated by endless meetings leading to the formation of the Workers Party of Ethiopia (WPE), and preparing for the OAU summit and the ten-year anniversary of the revolution, rather than on effective measures to combat drought. Not until September 18, 1984, did the government face up to the appalling crisis.

After the end of the costly anniversary celebrations, it became clear that the government was aware that the revolt in Eritrea was far from over; on September 25, a meeting of 1,700 government officials in Eritrea resolved to crush for once and for all the separatist "Mafia" and gave unqualified support for the ten-year development plan. The plan called for a 7.5 percent yearly increase in GDP (over twice the rate for 1977-1981) and was rightly dismissed by a World Bank economic mission as "overly ambitious in terms of both financial feasibility and implementing capacity."[21]

The Dergue received a timely shot in the arm during 1984-1985. According to a former head of the RRC, it used some of the vast sums of international aid forcibly to resettle peasants from the northern provinces in the southwest in a vain attempt to isolate the guerrillas who have always had wide support in the North. An indication of the inability of the government to control the situation in the North is shown in the report on the national census of May 9, 1984; the authorities were not able to cover Eritrea, Tigray, four provinces in Wollo and three in Gondar, or parts of southern Ethiopia.

The Ethiopian military government devoted the major part of its energy and the bulk of Ethiopia's scarce resources to constant, ineffectual attempts to defeat its opponents. Its most effective foe has been the Eritrean people. Today, the Dergue has even less hope than it did in 1975 of defeating the liberation movement. Even Asmara is "a tense and very heavily patrolled city that looks half empty of population."[22] In 1987, an aid worker encountered three checkpoints on the short ride from the airport to the city center. Asmara textile mills were functioning at only a quarter of 1974 production levels, and it was estimated that from sixty to seventy percent of the members of the Ethiopian National Trade Union were also clandestine members of the EPLF mass organization.[23] Even the Dergue's own statistics show a drop in Asmara's population; in 1975 it was 301,600 and in 1983, 275, 400.[24] In December 1979, there had been only 90,000 people in the capital.[25] In 1988, it was reported that "no one leaves the city, even for an hour, without written permission from city hall. Travel to the coast frequently is forbidden."[26] The Dergue has clearly failed to win the hearts and minds of the bulk of Eritreans who live under its military occupation. A careful reading of the government's own information and propaganda outlets bears out these assertions.

The Ethiopian government has devoted much of its energy to portraying the liberation movements as pliant tools of its Arab neighbors. At the same time it has waged a less public, but nevertheless effective, campaign to persuade or intimidate its neighbors to support its unification policies. It has also cultivated a surprising list of supporters. This area, to which the next chapter is devoted, is perhaps one of the most misunderstood features of the Eritrean struggle.

Notes

1. *Ethiopian Herald,* July 8 (1978).
2. *Ethiopian Herald,* October 11 (1974).
3. *Ethiopian Herald,* December 12 (1974): February 16 (1975).
4. *Ethiopian Herald,* January 7 (1979).
5. *Yekatit,* March (1979).
6. *Ethiopian Herald,* October 31 (1980).
7. Mary Dines, 'Ethiopian Violation of Human Rights in Eritrea,' eds. Lionel Cliffe and Basil Davidson, *The Long Struggle of Eritrea for Independence and Constructive Peace* (Nottingham, Spokesman, 1988) p. 141.
8. *Ethiopian Herald,* September 30 (1981).
9. *Ethiopian Herald,* January 26 (1982).
10. *Ethiopian Herald,* May 5 (1982).
11. *Africa News.* XVIII, 12 (1982).
12. Richard K. P. Pankhurst, 'Peace Returns to Asmara,' *Africa Today,* Second quarter (1982) p. 74.
13. Richard Caputo, *National Geographic,* 163, 5 (1983) p. 644.
14. *Ethiopian Herald,* December 3 (1982).
15. *Ethiopian Herald,* June 30 (1982).
16. Alemneh Dejene, *Peasants, Agrarian Socialism, and Rural Development in Ethiopia* (Boulder CO, Westview, 1987) p. 62
17. *Ethiopia,* September 7 (1983).
18. Peter Schwab, *Ethiopia: Politics, Economics and Society* (Boulder CO, Lynne Rienner, 1985) p. 90.
19. *The Age* (Melbourne), April 9 (1988).
20. *Serto Ader,* January 27 (1984).
21. World Bank, *Ethiopia: Recent Economic Developments and Future Prospects* Vol. 1 (Washington DC, 1984) p. 41.
22. David A. Korn, *Ethiopia, the United States and the Soviet Union* (London, Croom Helm, 1986) p. 160.
23. *New Africa News,* March-April (1988).
24. Mulatu Wubneh and Yohannis Abate, *Ethiopia: Transition and Development in the Horn of Africa* (Boulder CO, Westview, 1988) p. 139.
25. Dawit Wolde Giorgis, *Red Tears* (Trenton NJ, Red Sea Press, 1989) p. 96.
26. *The Age,* April 9 (1988).

II

The Struggle for Independence

The Struggle for Existence.

6

Eritrea, Ethiopia and the Middle Eastern Powers

Ethiopia, the oldest principality in Christendom is fighting a war against a dissident movement sponsored by the Arab world.

—*Christian Science Monitor*[1]

S ince the 1950s the Eritrean liberation fighters have been variously characterized as bandits, extremists, Muslim separatists, Marxists, ultra-leftists and a host of other epithets. A typical description of the EPLF is "a secessionist movement with a radical Marxist ideological position." In a large part of the literature—scholarly and ephemeral alike—it has become almost obligatory to analyze and speculate upon its reliance upon a changing cast of Middle Eastern powers for training, arms and support. The view is taken that without such assistance the Eritrean cause is doomed. This simplistic stereotype is impossible to reconcile with the many reports that a far-reaching, national democratic revolution is taking place in the areas of Eritrea controlled by the EPLF; a revolution which is self-reliant to an unusual degree. There is no need to adopt the thesis that Eritrean resistance is only possible because of Arab support. An independent, self-reliant spirit characterizes liberated Eritrea. This has been developed through centuries of exposure and adaptation to outside influences; some of the most important of these influences have emanated from the Middle East. As Chapter 2 argues, these predate the formal links with Ethiopia by several thousand years. This chapter begins in 1952—the year marking the end of British occupation of Eritrea and the beginning of the ten-year period of absorption by Ethiopia.

After the federation of Eritrea with Ethiopia in 1952, Sudan was a natural center for anti-unionist Eritrean exiles. Sudan was a British/Egyptian condominium with a tradition of allowing more political freedom to, and showing more tolerance of exiles than, anywhere else in the Middle East and North Africa. Khartoum was the political headquarters for the exiles, while Kassala became, to some extent, the nucleus of Eritrean armed opposition to the Ethiopian occupation forces. This resistance came initially from the Beni Amir people who live on both sides of the Eritrean/ Sudanese border. Some ninety percent of them live in Eritrea; most are adherents to the Mirghaniya sect of Islam, whose center is in Kassala.

As the Ethiopians tightened their grip on Eritrea, a steady stream of defectors entered the Sudan from Eritrea. Prominent Eritreans also went into exile in Cairo. Among them were: Idris Mohammed Adam, president of the Eritrean Parliament; Ibrahim Sultan Ali, secretary general of the Muslim League Party and Wolde-ab Woldemariam, president of the Eritrean Labour Unions and leader of the Independence Bloc. Wolde-ab's broadcasts from Cairo (until curtailed on Nasser's orders) did more than anything to make Eritreans aware of the brutality which accompanied Ethiopian occupation.[2] Gamel Abdul Nasser gave only verbal support for Eritrean independence because he valued good relations with the venerable Haile Selassie, and also because Ethiopia is the source of the waters of the River Nile, essential for Egypt's survival. Ethiopia mistrusted Nasser and was also anxious to remain on good terms with the western powers; this was highlighted during the Suez invasions of 1956, when the Egyptian military attache was ordered out of the country.[3] Egyptian logistical support was insignificant. There were also Eritrean exiles, mostly of the Afar nationality, in Somalia. In 1961, exiles in Saudi Arabia called upon Idris and Ibrahim, who were paying a visit to that country, to start an armed struggle against Ethiopian rule.[4]

Nasser's foe, Israel, has played an important role in Ethiopia's campaign against Eritrean rebels. Some links between the two countries predate Israel's independence. There is a long history of Jewish settlement in Ethiopia; at one time there was a village of the Beta Israel People (Falasha Jews) on the border between Eritrea and Tigray province. A number of Irgun and Stern Gang terrorists, including former Israeli Prime Minister Yitzak Shamir, were interned in Eritrea during the Second World War. They developed some contacts with local businessmen and politicians. Israeli and Italian Jewish business interests were involved in Eritrea; for example, they owned the Yonah Darom fish processing plant in Massawa. Ethiotextile, a large company employing about 2,000 workers, was also controlled by Israeli capital. Two meat-packing plants, INCODE and SOPRAL, were owned by Israelis and a third, the Red Sea Development Corporation, had substantial Israeli equity.[5] A synagogue established to serve the community in Asmara was reported—inaccurately—to have been destroyed during the 1975 fighting.[6]

Israel abstained from the United Nations vote which federated Eritrea with Ethiopia in 1950. There was, however, a secret security pact between Ethiopia and Israel; this was signed in 1954 at the instigation of the respective military establishments, with the particular blessing of General Moshe Dayan. The agreement was an integral part of Israel's peripheral strategy, which supposedly safeguarded her frontiers.[7] Diplomatic relations with Israel were not opened until 1961; Israel was eager for open relations but the emperor presumably wanted first to secure the support of

his Arab neighbors and then annex Eritrea, before recognizing a
state which was occupying Arab land and Christian shrines. A
break-through occurred largely as a consequence of the Ethiopian
Army's attempted coup in December 1960. Israel enabled the
emperor, who was on a state visit to Brazil, to communicate with
loyal troops under General Abbiye in Eritrea, and defeat the
rebels.[8]

Israel began to train Ethiopian police officers in counterinsurgency commando tactics designed to end the guerrilla (or *shifta*)
actions of the Eritrean Liberation Front, which had commenced
the armed struggle on September 1, 1961. Col. Ben Nathaw
headed the training school at Decamare and Col. Don was in
charge of the Ethiopian Marine Commando Forces training team.[9]
An Israeli served as military attache to Asrate Kassa, the governor
general of Eritrea from 1964-1970.[10]

The struggle was seen by Ethiopia, Israel and the United
States as Arab-backed, Muslim-extremist and separatist. If successful in winning independence for Eritrea, the liberation movement would be hostile to Israel and enforce a blockade of the Bab
el Mandab straits at the southern end of the Red Sea; Israel's position was partly based on the belief that Eritrea's population had a
Muslim majority. This belief is derived from approximate estimates made by Brigadier Drew in the early 1940s—presumably
based on the Italian census of 1931. The estimates cannot be substantiated.[11] There is no greater justification for accepting Longrigg's figures, which show Muslims to be in a minority, or
claims that Christians comprise more than two-thirds of the population.[12] A more recent estimate suggests that the Tigrinya-speaking (mainly Christian) proportion of the population is eighty
percent.[13] Since no comprehensive population census has ever
been carried out in Eritrea, it is difficult to place much confidence
in such guesswork.

The first major military actions of the Eritrean liberation
forces were reported in December 1962, after Ethiopia's annexation of Eritrea. General Abbiye, in charge of Ethiopian forces in

Eritrea, was attacked by guerrillas, reflecting the strong resentment felt in Eritrea against carpetbagging Amhara Christians who descended on Eritrea after its annexation to occupy the most profitable bureaucratic, business and administrative positions. Despite continued insistence that opposition to Ethiopian rule came in the main from extremist Muslims, it is clear that, "Eritreans did not and do not look on Ethiopia as the mother country."[14]

Israeli involvement in Ethiopia increased substantially. Ethiopia became a vital conduit for Israeli communication with the Anya Nya rebels in the Southern Sudan who had been fighting the Khartoum regime since 1964.[15] Starting in 1964, Ethiopian military officers in Asmara began to take charge of Anya Nya guerrilla rebels flown by Israel from a collection center in Uganda. They were driven to a camp close to Wukro in Tigray and trained in counterinsurgency operations by Ethiopian and Israeli advisers.[16] By 1966, Israel had a military mission numbering 100 men in Ethiopia; it was the second largest foreign military contingent in the country, although a distant second to the American mission. On average, the Israelis trained 1,000 men per year; by 1970, Israeli-trained forces reached battalion size.

Israeli intelligence services were also active in Ethiopia.[17] A communique in early 1975 claimed that guerrillas had destroyed the Israeli Intelligence Center in Asmara.[18] Intelligence operations were facilitated by the relatively large contingents of American troops training the Ethiopian Army and manning the Kagnew Communications Base in Asmara. Some 3,000 United States personnel were employed at the base. It is more than likely that some Israeli agents were among them. Troops trained by the Israelis and the United States began to take the initiative in Eritrea in late 1967. Borrowing tactics which had so alienated peasants in Vietnam, the army commenced the pacification and resettlement of villagers in an attempt to stop guerrilla activity. Attacks on civilians suspected of supporting the ELF led to an increasing exodus of refugees; by May 1967, there were 28,000 Eritreans in the Sudan.[19]

There was considerable cooperation between Israel, the United States and Ethiopia, which involved for example, the construction of an air base. There were also reports (denied by Ethiopia and the Israelis) that Israel had established bases on the Red Sea islands of Fatima, off Assab, and Hatmil in the Dahlak Archipelago.[20] It seems clear that there were complex radar stations on the islands in 1977.[21]

Such collusion between Israel and Ethiopia goes some way to explaining the liberation fronts' early uncompromising opposition to Israel. For example, the National Democratic Programme of the EPLF, published in 1977, had among its objectives to nationalize all industries in the hands of "Zionists;" to punish aliens who as "lackeys and followers of Zionism" spy on or become obstacles to the Eritrean people, and to support the struggle against "Zionism."[22]

Compared to the considerable support given to Ethiopia by the United States and Israel, the liberation forces received little foreign assistance. The ELF's most significant Middle Eastern backer was Syria. Three months after the Baath officers coup in March 1963, an ELF office was opened in Damascus and Osman Saleh Sabbe began to make radio broadcasts attacking Ethiopian policies in Eritrea. In 1964, twenty Kalashnikov rifles were supplied to the ELF, which had some 250 guerrillas.[23] According to one writer, year-long training of some of these Eritreans commenced in Syria's Aleppo Military Academy.[24] Another claims that Syrian support enabled the ELF to expand to a force of 2,000 men.[25] It seems unlikely that Syrian assistance could have been that significant, as by May 1966, it was estimated that the guerrilla forces numbered merely 500 men, and only 370 had modern weapons.[26] Syrian support remained consistent over the years, unlike that of many other Arab states, and an EPLF office in Damascus still exists.

Apparently, the Sudanese government authorized ELF activities in border areas for a short time in the mid-1960s, but this relaxation was short-lived;[27] in 1965, the Sudanese government reimposed restrictions after announcing with great indignation that it had seized eighteen tons of Czechoslovakian arms at Khartoum airport. The arms had presumably been shipped from Syria for use by the ELF.[28]

In July 1968, Baath Party army officers mounted a successful coup in Iraq; the new regime gave assistance to the ELF and trained officers. Iraq has continued to give minimum assistance to the Eritrean Liberation Front Revolutionary Command—a small body which split from the ELF and has no military presence in Eritrea.[29] An EPLF office remains open in Baghdad, but relations are strained.[30] In 1989, Ethiopia reopened diplomatic relations with Iraq for the first time since the days of the emperor.[31]

Nimeri's May 1969 military coup in the Sudan was of much more long-term significance to the fortunes of the liberation forces. Prior to 1969, "Sudanese aid was limited and inconsistent."[32] Even after Nimeri's coup, aid was spasmodic and unreliable. In agreements reached with Ethiopia over a two-period, the new ruler showed that good relations with his powerful, large neighbor were of paramount importance. The first was signed in 1971 after Nimeri had received a considerable shock from an attempted leftist coup. The other agreements made in February and June 1972 settled the southern problem for the rest of the decade. Police and army units from the two countries attempted to seal the border.

After Muammar Gadaffi came to power in September 1969, Libya began to funnel some supplies to the ELF. A Libyan delegation paid a visit to the liberated areas in 1973. One writer claims that Libya supplied the guerrillas with "considerable aid."[33] Somalia, after Siad Barre's military coup, also in 1969, was more sympathetic to Eritrean exiles in Mogadishu, while the radical regime of the PDRY—after independence in 1967—became a valuable friend of the Eritreans. Aden is only a short boat ride from the sparsely populated, 500-mile-long Red Sea coast and islands. During 1971-1972, arms given to the EPLF by friendly states were brought in this way.[34] Some ELF fighters were trained by Palestinian El-Fatah instructors in Aden, and in Somalia.[35] Osman Saleh Sabbe operated from Aden and the PDRY was the main conduit for finance and arms. But the most important source of supply was arms captured from Ethiopian troops and police or brought with them by Eritrean defectors from the occupying Ethiopian forces.

After the September 1969 Islamic Summit Conference held in Rabat, the ELF denied that it was a purely Muslim movement. At this stage, Arab support was of no more than token value; according to the testimony of Woldai Kahsai, a defector from the ELF, financial and military support from Arab states dried up after the June 1967 Arab-Israeli War.[36] Ethiopia was certainly concerned over the future, however. The first of many (largely ineffectual) agreements between Sudan and Ethiopia committed both countries to the control of dissidents residing in their respective capitals and provincial centers and the extradition of leaders and militants.

Israeli sources also emphasize Eritrean links with the Palestine Liberation Organization (PLO). The Israelis claim that Osman Saleh Sabbe was rejected by the Syrian and Iraqi Baath trained young commanders of the ELF, and while in a Jordan-based Palestinian camp in November 1969, gathered support for a splinter group of the liberation movement.[37] Once again this link is overplayed, the PLO has little influence on events in Eritrea; indeed the PLO's formal links with the Dergue are much closer than its liaisons with the Eritrean movement. A PLO office was opened in Addis Ababa in July 1978.

It is well to retain a sense of proportion when discussing the issue of how important foreign aid has been to the fluctuating fortunes of the liberation forces. Eritrean nationalists were always kept waiting by their Arab supporters, and according to Al-Amin Mohamed Said, EPLF Director of Information, not until 1971 did they receive any significant arms supplies from these sources.[38]

Most Arab regimes have tried to manipulate different factions of the Eritrean opposition. It has been claimed that the PDRY helped to build up the ELF and then attempted to take control of it during 1970-1971.[39] Isaias Afwerki, general secretary of the EPLF, said that "the Saudis' strategy is to use the Eritrean struggle as an external buffer area for balancing, creating pressures here and there to influence the situation in the Horn as a whole and Ethiopia in particular. For them Eritrea is an instrument."[40] By 1987, the Saudi Arabian authorities had closed the EPLF office in Jeddah and confiscated weapons that the EPLF had purchased.[41] The Saudis do not want to see an independent Eritrea under the leadership of the EPLF.[42]

By 1970, it is likely that the ELF and EPLF between them controlled two-thirds of Eritrea, and had 10,000 men under arms.[43] This impressive record of achievement was largely due to the fact that the fronts had been sympathetically received in most areas of operations in Eritrea. The ELF maintained that "the struggle is a national struggle with humanitarian aspects. Moslems and Christians alike were participating in the struggle." The Ethiopian authorities imposed martial law in 1970 and mounted a large-scale offensive in December of that year, using the sophisticated equipment and techniques taught them by Israel and the United States. It was such draconian techniques, involving whole scale bombing of villages, that curtailed the expansion of the Fronts and not the absence of Arab supplies. A major civil war which erupted between the ELF and EPLF, was also a reason for the decline in fortunes of the Eritrean liberation forces during 1971-1972. The Ethiopians again attempted to seal the border with the Sudan, and forced the temporary closure of ELF offices in Khartoum and Kassala. That the border was still open, in spite of Ethiopian efforts, is borne out by the increased flow of Eritrean refugees into the Sudan; by December 1972, there were 52,000.[44]

Many commentators, working on the commonly accepted hypothesis that foreign aid and the support of a bordering country is essential to the success of a liberation movement, have always been prepared to write off the Eritreans.[45] It is true that by the early 1970s the war showed significant internationalization which fueled the civil war.[46] But the long term significance of the split in the liberation forces can be over emphasized. However, vicious and sapping the internal war, the Eritreans were still able to inflict significant defeats on the Ethiopians during the winter of 1973-1974.[47] These defeats were one of the major reasons for the decline in morale of the army, its disillusionment with the emperor's command, and its determination to seize power. The emperor was also showing signs of eccentricity and senility too obvious to ignore.[48]

Although the emperor had broken off diplomatic relations with Israel on October 13, 1973, Israel's ostracism did not last long.[49] The "socialist" Dergue invited her back in 1975. The Israelis trained (at the Arba base) the *Nebelbal* (flame) Brigade—which was involved in the Anseba River battle of 1976, in an Ethiopian attempt to break the EPLF siege of Nacfa.[50] The Israelis directed the unsuccessful Ethiopian relief operations and continued to make little impact on the fighting; the last parachute instructors left in 1976.[51] However, the support of the Flame Brigade was vital to Mengistu in his power struggle with General Teferi Bante, the Ethiopian head of state.

Israeli technicians continued to service jets supplied by the United States. Arms, including anti-personnel cluster bombs, were sent to the Dergue at least until February 6, 1978.[52] Israel also trained Ethiopians to operate the tanks they had captured from the Somali army during the Ogaden Campaign of 1977-1978. The Dergue, however, was more than embarrassed by Israeli Foreign Minister Dayan's remarks that, as Israel was arming the Dergue, it ill became them to fulminate at "the racist, Zionist state of Israel."[53] The Ethiopian Ministry of Foreign Affairs dismissed the arms purchases as "a simple business deal made on a commercial basis."[54] It is claimed that all remaining Israeli military advisers were expelled; however, trade and development programs continued. Some forty percent of Ethiopia's export/import shipping trade was handled by the Israeli company Zima.[55]

Some observers subscribe to the thesis that when Ethiopia was weakened by revolution, the neighboring Arab states agreed to increase support to the guerrillas. For example, Saudi Arabia was reportedly generously aiding Osman Saleh Sabbe's group from June 1974 with small arms, anti-aircraft batteries and land mines.[56] Osman visited ten Arab countries in August-September 1974, and declared that, "all support our just cause in one way or another and some of them give full backing."[57] Such support, it is argued, accounted for the defeat of the Ethiopian forces in 1977-1978. Another writer claims, however, that since 1975, the EPLF has relied upon its own resources and merely receives nominal transport facilities for medicine and relief supplies from Sudan.[58] An EPLF commander stated that from 1980, no country gave the EPLF military aid; before that, Iraq, Kuwait and certain Palestinian organizations provided it with limited aid, especially shells and ammunition.[59] A judicious view would seem to be that Arab military support has been relatively modest; while financial assistance, although significant in early years, is by no means the primary reason for the success of the Eritrean liberation struggle.

In any case, any indication of support for Eritrea from Arab countries led to immediate diplomatic and media counteroffensives by the Dergue. When the Syrian Baath Party called for the liberation and independence of Eritrea, the PMAC made a statement accusing Idris Mohammed Adam and Osman Saleh Sabbe of selling the country to the highest bidder.[60] Such attacks in the media continued through March 1975. Another target of abuse was the Conference of Islamic States held in July 1975, which allocated $1.5 million to Eritrea. Ties were severed with Tunisia on July 16, 1975, when it supported the right of the ELF to have observer status at the Organization of African Unity summit meeting. Although Osman Saleh Sabbe claimed that the Arab world was behind the Eritrean cause, it seems that Libya, Egypt, Algeria, South Yemen and Sudan, after overtures from the Dergue, favored negotiations between the fronts and the Dergue.[61] Ethiopia, even an Ethiopia ripped apart by revolution and counter-revolution, was still a powerful international and regional actor and its views could not be ignored.

The ELF and the EPLF were also well aware that it was not only necessary to gain the support of all sections of the Eritrean population and win military victories over the Dergue, it was also essential to gain external diplomatic support in order to destroy the Empire's legitimacy. A 1975 tour of nine Arab states by a joint ELF-EPLF delegation was successful in eliciting verbal support.[62]

In April 1976, the PMAC announced that it was a genuine Marxist-Leninist body.[63] It was no nearer a political or military solution in Eritrea and was not yet able to garner support from the socialist camp; therefore, a renewed diplomatic offensive was mounted, aimed primarily at Arab supporters of the Eritreans. Major Berhanu Bayeh, chairman of the PMAC Legal Affairs Committee paid a three-day visit to Sudan. Nimeri, in a characteristic *volte face* on Eritrea, declared that Sudan supported Ethiopia's claim to Eritrea, citing as a precedent Ethiopia's recognition of the unity of Sudan.[64] Berhanu also toured most other states in the region and reported on his return that Algeria, Egypt, Kuwait, Libya, Saudi Arabia and North and South Yemen all supported the PMAC regime and would stop forthwith all aid to the liberation fronts.[65]

Whether or not Berhanu was speaking the truth, his visit coincided with the virtual cessation of Arab aid to Eritrea. But as the liberation movements gained strength in the field they also won some diplomatic battles. A delegation representing both wings of the liberation movement was granted observer status at the May 1976 meeting of the foreign ministers of Moslem states. In spite of Berhanu's efforts, the Dergue continued to be worried about Arab support for Eritrea. Accordingly, Lt. Col. Asrat Desta, chairman of the Information and Public Relations Committee of the PMAC, led another delegation to Sudan in August 1976.[66] As well as indulging in the conventional, flattering, diplomatic exchanges, the Dergue also vigorously condemned any pro-Eritrean sentiments. President Habib Bourguiba of Tunisia was abused again for allowing the opening of an ELF information office in Tunis. And, in November 1976, Ahmed Nasser of the ELF was reviled for visiting Iraq; the Baath Party's "expansionist aims" also came under attack.[67] At the end of 1976, there were some 90,000 Eritrean refugees in the Sudan; the Dergue declared that they were not refugees but people who were living in concentration camp conditions under the iron control of "so-called ELF and PLF." Dergue relations with Nimeri blew cold again when the Ethiopians put forward the ingenious—if provocative—argument that the Ethiopian government was protecting the refugees in the Sudan against attacks by the Sudanese government.[68]

Conservative Arab governments began to support the more traditional and conservative ELF to a greater extent from 1977 as the Dergue became increasingly aligned with the Soviet Union.[69] If one supports the thesis that Arab aid is indeed essential for success, one would have expected the EPLF offensive to falter. However, the EPLF—deserted by its erstwhile friends, the PDRY and Libya, and unsupported by the conservative Arab states—was still able to capture the towns of Karora, Elghena, Afabet, Nacfa, Keren, Decamere, most of Massawa and also have Asmara under siege for over a year. The ELF, supported by moderate and conservative Arab states, did not make such headway and controlled less territory. In any case, Al-Amin Mohammed Said, of the ELF-PLF splinter group, said that although aid was received from Arab states, there had been no material or military backing from either the Soviets or Saudi Arabia.[70] When "a prominent spokesman for the Eritrean liberation movement" appealed to the Arabs for $30 million in 1977-1978, there was only a "meager response."[71]

The battle for Arab diplomatic backing continued. Isaias Afwerki, then vice secretary of the EPLF, visited Saudi Arabia and in an interview with the paper *Al-Madina Al-Manawarrah* denied that either he or the EPLF were Marxist.[72] Although this remark would presumably have pleased the Saudis, the fact remains that the EPLF received no significant assistance from Saudi Arabia.

From early 1977, the PMAC came under increased opposition from many Arab and Muslim powers. This was not only because the country appeared to be on the verge of disintegration, but because the regime was discriminating against the sizable Muslim populations of Eritrea and Ethiopia. In January 1977, the ELF sent a message to the World Islamic League accusing the Dergue of waging war against the Islamic religion and the Arabic language. Later in the month, Nimeri and other OAU leaders called for the removal of the OAU offices from Addis Ababa. Teferi Bante denounced the ELF and accused Sudan and Somalia of plotting to attack Ethiopia.[73] Such is the uncertain world of politics under military dictatorship that on February 4, Teferi Bante was executed after being accused of the unlikely charges of plotting against the revolution and sympathizing with the ELF. The media made hysterical attacks on the increasing number of refugees in the Sudan, arguing that "the broad masses are better in the absence of such people."[74]

Mengistu, the new chairman of the PMAC, was eventually forced to admit that Ethiopia had lost control of significant areas of Eritrea. On April 13, 1977, he accused Sudan of open armed intervention; later in the same month, the government newspaper reported that ELF leaders had met with the Chiefs of Staff of the Egyptian and Sudanese Armies to plan a joint campaign.[75] The Sudanese consulate in Asmara was closed down; and in May, the Egyptian defense attache was ordered home.

The EPLF held its first congress in Eritrea in January 1977; it was attended by delegates from Iraq, Libya, Somalia, Sudan and Syria, as well as representatives from the radical Palestinian groups, the Democratic Front for the Liberation of Palestine (DFLP) and the Popular Front for the Liberation of Palestine (PFLP).[76] This Congress attracted some 311 delegates from all over Eritrea.[77] Representatives from Iraq, Egypt, Syria, Sudan, Somalia and the PLO attended the First Congress of the ELF-PLF held in Eritrea in March 1977. In August, the Arab Information Minister's Council issued a statement in support of Eritrea. Mengistu (after a speech at the OAU summit in Gabon, when he accused Nimeri of sabotaging the Dergue's peace initiative in Eritrea and hiring mercenaries who made daily incursions into Ethiopia) admitted that Keren, Tessenai, Nacfa and Karora were occupied by, "groups of secessionist bandits put together by foreign powers."[78] Keren fell to the EPLF after a four-day battle. In 1941, it took much larger and better armed British and French forces a month to take the city. Nevertheless, a staff writer on the government newspaper called the Eritrean rebels "traitors inspired by religious fanaticism, and intoxicated by hashish" and "brokers of Arab petro dollars ready to sell the country to the highest bidder."[79]

In December 1977, Fidel Castro unequivocally supported the Dergue; he said that although the liberation movement had initially been led by progressives it was now controlled by reactionary Saudi Arabia and Sudan. The Eritreans countered these charges immediately. Ahmed Nasser, chairman of the ELF Revolutionary Command said that "we have never accepted aid that had conditions attached," and, "are we therefore Baathists? No. Are we trying to be Arabs or Muslims? No."[80] In Freetown, Sierra Leone, Sudan and Ethiopia signed an agreement that they would observe a cease-fire along the border, stop all hostile acts and resume airlinks.[81] This did not halt the Eritrean advance.

During the Soviet-led offensive against the Eritrean liberation forces in 1978, the switching of PDRY support to the Dergue was crucial. The PDRY had been the most important foreign sympathizer of the EPLF; for a while, Aden was the conduit for arms, ammunition and supplies and a safe base to care for wounded fighters. It was also the site for abortive peace negotiations between the Dergue and the liberation movement in 1976. There were still signs as late as August 1979 that the PDRY was not completely hostile to the Eritreans. A delegation of General Union of Eritrean Workers—a part of the ELF—visited South

Yemen and were told that the workers of the PDRY offered full support to the Eritrean peoples' "right to self-determination."[82] By 1981, however, South Yemen, along with Libya, signed an agreement with Ethiopia which committed these two states to the Dergue. In spite of its own increasingly intimate links with the Arab world, the Dergue still emphasized Eritrea's "Arab influence." Whilst clearing "vast areas" of the coast and "annihilating secessionist pockets," the army found Saudi Rials—evidence, it was said, of substantial Arab support for the rebels. More likely it was the income of Eritrean and Saudi traders who do considerable business across the Red Sea.[83]

As the Ethiopian army drove the ELF out of its last strongholds in Barka Province, many more thousands of refugees fled into Sudan. There were talks "of extreme cordiality" between Ethiopian and top Sudanese officials—including the administrator of Kassala Province—which led to yet another commitment to control illegal activities along the border.[84] In May 1980, Mengistu visited the Sudan. A joint ELF/EPLF meeting, meanwhile, took pains to thank the government and people of the Sudan for their support.[85]

From July, there were monthly reports of refugees returning from the Sudan. The first group was met by Mengistu. By December, it was claimed that 2,500 people had returned but there were still 490,000 in Sudan and it was clear that, in spite of all Mengistu's overtures, few would return willingly to Ethiopia.[86] This reluctance is not surprising. Between September 1983 and December 1984, 32,000 refugees returned to Ethiopia from Djibouti; there were reports of forced repatriation and, in August 1984, at least twenty-five were shot by the Ethiopians. At least 10,000 of the returning refugees had once again moved back into Djibouti by the end of December.[87]

During 1981, Sudan's refugee population continued to grow—augmented by those fleeing from the fighting between ELF factions and EPLF and from renewed offensives by the Ethiopians. The Ethiopian attacks were now also directed at the

Tigrayans, who, under the leadership of the TPLF, were waging a determined resistance to Amhara domination. After July 1981, there were no more reports in the Ethiopian press of any refugees returning to Ethiopian-held areas, indicating that the liberation forces were once more in full control of the border regions.

A joint Algerian/Syrian communique of 1979 indicated that these two countries, in spite of strenuous wooing from the Dergue, still supported the right of the Eritreans to self-determination.[88] An Eritrean political office was opened in Algiers following a visit from a joint ELF/EPLF delegation.[89] The Thirteenth congress of the Baath Arab Socialist Party of Syria, meeting in August 1980, passed a resolution supporting the Eritrean struggle for self-determination—ironically at a time when Ethiopia's foreign minister, Col. Feleke Gedle Giorgis was in Damascus.[90] The Arab People's Congress, meeting in Beirut in June 1981, called upon the Dergue to enter into direct and democratic dialog with the Eritrean people. The Islamic Conference, held in Saudi Arabia in 1981, supported Eritrea for the first time. Following an official EPLF visit to Syria, Muhammad Haydar, chairman of the Syrian Foreign Relations Office gave, "firm and unwavering support" for the Eritrean struggle.[91] There was also a lot of sympathy in Kuwait and the United Arab Emirates (UAE) for the liberation movement. His Highness Sheik Zayed Ben Sultan Alnahyan, president of the UAE, pledged support for Eritrea.[92] The liberation forces were active and holding ground even though the Dergue had driven more refugees into the Sudan. There were 550,000 refugees by January 1982.[93]

In spite of the EPLF's ability to hold its own against Ethiopian attacks and evidence of continuing diplomatic support for the movement, writers continued to dismiss the EPLF. A new line of argument appeared on the left. As the Dergue's statement that it was instituting socialism was taken at face value, the Eritreans were advised to give up the fight and find their solution in a united revolutionary Ethiopia.[94] Not surprisingly, the Eritreans fought on.

Even though the ELF was by now no longer a significant military force, it maintained ties with some Arab states and organizations. And in 1979, it found a new friend, Ayatollah Ruhollah Khomeini in Teheran. After the overthrow of Haile Selassie, the ELF had refused to accept aid proffered by the Shah of Iran; they therefore built up credit with the new ruler, who also thought he was aiding a Muslim struggle. Tesfatsion Medhanie claims that Iraq continued to provide pharmaceutical and medical support to the EPLF, which included flying wounded fighters to Baghdad.[95]

The Dergue still worked hard at cultivating Nimeri; Berhanu Bayeh visited the Sudan again and yet another agreement was reached to close down all facilities used by "secessionist dissidents."[96] In July, the Sudanese vice president visited Ethiopia and promised measures to guarantee the safety of the common border. The visit was returned two months later by the Ethiopian minister of national defense, Tesfay Gebre Kidan.[97] In spite of all this diplomatic activity, the EPLF began to regain the military initiative; it was clear that the much vaunted Red Star campaign, launched with such enthusiasm in January 1982 had failed, exacting an enormous toll in money and men.

Following the severe military setbacks of 1984, Ethiopia once again called upon Israeli assistance. Arms sales were resumed through Amsterdam and a company known as Amiran based in Addis.[98] There were persistent reports of continuing discreet intelligence links and that secret agreements with the emperor have persisted under the Dergue.[99] One such intelligence area concerns the EPLF. When the Israelis occupied West Beirut in July 1982, they seized many documents belonging to the EPLF foreign mission and gave them to the Dergue. During 1985, Dawit Wolde Giorgis, who had acted as Ethiopia's foreign secretary on a number of occasions, met secretly with David Kimche, the head of Israel's foreign affairs department, and explored ways in which relations between the two countries could be improved.[100] In 1988, the negotiations bore fruit once again with the arrival in Ethiopia of Israeli military advisers.[101] Full diplomatic relations were restored in 1989, and transfer of anti-personnel cluster bombs followed shortly after.[102]

One of the key factors in the continuing success of the Eritrean struggle has undoubtedly been the ability of the Eritreans to remain in the Sudan where they have developed a very impressive series of garages, workshops and infrastructure to care for refugees and seriously injured fighters. Their ability to maintain relations with successive Sudanese administrations has been a major reason for this success. In part, these relations have been helped by a consistent commitment to having no armed EPLF fighters on Sudanese soil. Following the military coup of 1985, relations between the Sudanese government and the EPLF continued along the same lines although, with the disbanding of Nimeri's security service, which had closely monitored the activities of Eritreans, relations were more easy going. Elements of the Sudanese population have continued to express support for Eritrea; resolutions were passed at the Fourth Congress of the General Union of Sudanese Workers in May 1984 and the Fifth Congress of the General Union of Sudanese Women.[103] Moreover, the Sudanese know that should they try to eliminate ERA and EPLF from the Sudan and close down the "northern supply route," many more hundreds and thousands of Eritreans would flood into the Sudan in search of food presenting a totally unmanageable situation. Finally, the Sudanese simply do not have enough troops to close the border.

That the EPLF was a formidable force was shown in July 1985 when it captured Barentu, a stronghold of the Degree which had never fallen to the Eritreans in the previous twenty-four years of war. Today, there is only one unified liberation movement active in the field, even though some leaders of the splintered ELF still find some funds and support from some Arab states. The largest of the ELF splinter groups—ELF Central Command (Saghem) merged with the EPLF in March 1987. Two others appear likely to merge in time. ELF-RC (Teyar) was formed in 1982 and in

1987 was holding talks with the EPLF. The ELF-PLF United Organization will probably do so in the future.

The fate of the Eritreans will ultimately be decided by the success of the liberation struggles in the field. The Eritrean problem does have wide international dimensions and Eritreans are aware that diplomatic support is important. Representatives of the movement constantly seek support from Arab and African leaders and organizations. The remarks made by Wolde-ab Woldemariam, the grandfather of Eritrean liberation, a generation ago hold true today. He stated that "even if the government [of Sudan] has concluded a treaty of friendship [with Ethiopia] the people will continue to support us."[104] Isaias Afwerki left the field in 1988 for the first time in three years in order to hold talks with Sudanese leaders; the Sudanese President made an unequivocal statement of support for Eritrean independence. The EPLF also places as much emphasis on help from Western sources, especially churches, aid organizations and social democratic, liberal, conservative and labor parties. It is probable that, in the past, some Eritrean spokesmen may have exaggerated the extent of Arab support; this has misled many commentators. But, the fact is that the EPLF remains free from outside influence to a unique degree.

Notes

1. *Christian Science Monitor,* August 6 (1968)
2. Bereket Habte Selassie, 'Eritrea and the United Nations,' *The Eritrean Case* (Rome, Research and Information Centre on Eritrea, 1980) p. 147.
3. Czeslaw Jesman, *The Ethiopian Paradox* (London, Oxford University Press, 1963) p. 23.
4. Bereket Habte Selassie, 'Eritrea and the United Nations,' p. 151.
5. Andemichael Kahsai, 'Interview,' *MERIP Reports,* 62 (1977) p. 20.
6. *Vanguard,* (New York) 1, 13 (1976).
7. Michael Bar-Zohar, trans. L. Ortzen, *Ben-Gurion: the Armed Prophet* (Englewood Cliffs NJ, Prentice-Hall, 1968) p. 247.
8. Haggai Erlich, *The Struggle over Eritrea 1962-1978* (Stanford, Hoover Institution Press, 1983) p. 57.
9. Richard Lobban, *Eritrean Liberation Front: A Close-Up View,* Munger Africana Library Notes, 13 (1972) p. 16.

10. Richard Sherman, *Eritrea: the Unfinished Revolution* (New York, Praeger, 1980) p. 75.
11. Tekeste Negash, *Italian Colonialism in Eritrea, 1882-1941: Policies. Praxis and Impact* (Uppsala, Uppsala University Press, 1987) p. 150.
12. Sylvia E. Pankhurst and Richard K. P. Pankhurst, *Ethiopia and Eritrea: the Last Phase of the Reunion 1941-1952* (Essex, Lalibela House, 1953) p. 152; G.K.N. Trevaskis, *Eritrea—A Colony in Transition; 1941-52* (London, Oxford University Press, 1960) p. 46.
13. M.L. Bender et. al., eds., *Language in Ethiopia* (London, Oxford University Press, 1976) p. 17.
14. *Africa Confidential*, November 8 (1963).
15. Mohammed Omer Beshir, *The Southern Sudan: from Conflict to Peace* (New York, Barnes and Noble, 1975) p. 91.
16. Dawit Wolde Giorgis, *Personal Communication* (1986).
17. Abel Jacob, 'Israel's Military Aid to Africa,' *Journal of Modern African Studies*, 9, 2 (1971) p. 178.
18. *Eritrean Review*, 11, February (1975) p. 4.
19. Gaim Kilbreab, *African Refugees* (Trenton NJ, Africa World Press, 1985) p. 27.
20. *Ethiopian Herald*, October 17 (1974).
21. *Eritrean Revolution*, 2, 3, October-November (1977).
22. James Firebrace (with Stuart Holland), *Never Kneel Down; Drought, Development and Liberation in Eritrea* (Trenton NJ, Red Sea Press, 1985) pp. 154-61.
23. Bereket Habte Selassie, 'Eritrea and the United Nations,' p. 151.
24. Erlich, 'The Struggle over Eritrea,' p. 59.
25. Mordechai Abir, *Oil, Power and Political Conflict in Arabia, the Red Sea and the Gulf* (London, Frank Cass, 1974) p. 170.
26. *Africa Confidential* May 6 (1966).
27. Guido Bimbi, 'The National Liberation Struggle and the Liberation Fronts,' *The Eritrean Case* (Rome, Research and Information Centre on Eritrea, 1980) p. 180.
28. Patrick Gilkes, *The Dying Lion: Feudalism and Modernization in Ethiopia* (London, Julian Friedmann, 1975) p. 197.
29. Erlich, 'The Struggle over Eritrea,' pp. 60, 96.
30. Eritrean People's Liberation Front, *Political Report and National Democratic Programme* (1987) p. 163.
31. *Indian Ocean Newsletter*, 369 (1989).
32. Tom J. Farer, *War Clouds on the Horn of Africa* (Washington D.C., Carnegie Endowment for International Peace, 1976) p. 29.
33. Aryeh Yodfat, 'The Soviet Union and the Horn of Africa: Part 1,' *Northeast African Studies*, 1 3 (1979-1980) p. 11.
34. Al-Amin Mohammed Said, 'The Eritrean Case is Compatible with the OAU Charter,' *Adulis*, III, 5 (1986) p. 4.
35. Christopher Clapham, 'Ethiopia and Somalia,' *Conflicts in Africa* (London, International Institute of Strategic Studies, 1972) p. 9.
36. Taye Germaw, 'Rebellion in Eritrea—Who is behind it; What are its aims?,' *New Middle East*, 31 (1971) p. 26.
37. Erlich, 'The Struggle over Eritrea,' p. 27.
38. Erlich, 'The Struggle over Eritrea,' p. 68.

114 • ERITREA: EVEN THE STONES ARE BURNING

39. Abir, 'Oil, Power and Political Conflict,' p. 103.
40. Firebrace, 'Never Kneel Down,' p. 139.
41. A.M. Babu, 'The Eritrean Question in the Context of African Conflicts and Superpower Rivalries,' eds. Lionel Cliffe and Basil Davidson, *The Long Struggle of Eritrea for Independence and Constructive Peace.* (Nottingham, Spokesman, 1988) p. 55.
42. Abir, 'Oil, Power and Political Conflict,' p. 175.
43. *Africa Confidential*, March 13 (1970).
44. Gaim Kibreab, 'African Refugees,' p. 24.
45. Abir, 'Oil, Power and Political Conflict,' p. 192.
46. Frank Boyce, 'The Internationalizing of Internal War: Ethiopia, the Arabs, and the Case of Eritrea,' *The Journal of International and Comparative Studies*, 3 (1972) p. 64.
47. Bereket Habte Selassie, *Conflict and Intervention in the Horn of Africa* (New York, Monthly Review Press, 1980) p. 23.
48. Ryszard Kapuscinski, *The Emperor* (New York, Harcourt Brace Jovanovich, 1983) p. 87.
49. Erlich, 'The Struggle over Eritrea,' p. 103.
50. David Pool, *Eritrea: Africa's Longest War* (London, Anti-slavery Society, 1982) p. 42.
51. Erlich, 'The Struggle over Eritrea,' p. 75.
52. Dawit Wolde Giorgis, *Personal Communication* (1987).
53. Fred Halliday and Maxine Molyneux, *The Ethiopian Revolution* (London, Verso, 1981) p. 233.
54. *Ethiopian Herald*, February 10 (1978).
55. *Eritrea in Struggle*, 11, December 3 (1977).
56. Erlich, 'The Struggle over Eritrea,' p. 70.
57. *Eritrean Review*, October (1974).
58. Raman G. Bhardwaj, 'The Growing Externalization of the Eritrean Movement,' *Horn of Africa*, II, 1 (1979) p. 24.
59. *Adulis*, III, 5 (1986).
60. *Ethiopian Herald*, February 16 (1975).
61. Rene Lefort, *Ethiopia: An Heretical Revolution?*, (London, Zed Press, 1981) p. 147.
62. *Eritrean Revolution*, 1, 1, December (1975).
63. *Ethiopian Herald*, April 9 (1976).
64. *Ethiopian Herald*, May 30 (1976).
65. *Ethiopian Herald*, June 29 (1976).
66. *Ethiopian Herald*, August 1 (1976).
67. *Ethiopian Herald*, November 5 (1976).
68. *Ethiopian Herald*, November 9 (1976).
69. Erlich, 'The Struggle over Eritrea,' p. 56.
70. *Eritrea Review*, 44, July (1977).
71. David Albright, 'The Horn of Arica and the Arab-Israel Conflict,' ed. R.O. Freedman, *World Politics and the Arab Israeli Conflict* (New York, Pergamon, 1979) p. 170.
72. *Eritrean Revolution*, 2, 2. August-September (1977).
73. *Ethiopian Herald*, January 30 (1977).
74. *Addis Zemen*, February 26 (1977).
75. *Ethiopian Herald*, April 29 (1977).

76. *Vanguard,* 11, 1, February-March (1977).
77. *Eritrea Information,* 9, 4 (1987).
78. *Ethiopian Herald,* August 26 (1977).
79. *Ethiopian Herald,* September 7 (1977).
80. *Eritrean Newsletter,* 18, December 1 (1977).
81. *Ethiopian Herald,* December 20 (1977).
82. *Eritrean Newsletter,* 37, October (1979).
83. *Ethiopian Herald,* February 3 (1979).
84. *Ethiopian Herald,* March 19 (1980).
85. *Mekalih Sewrana,* 1, 3 (1979).
86. Gaim Kibreab, 'African Refugees,' p. 26.
87. United States Committee for Refugees, *World Refugee Survey: 1985 in Review* (1986) p. 46.
88. *Resistance,* 1, 4, May-June (1979).
89. *Eritrea Now,* 1, 5 (1979).
90. *Eritrea Information,* II, 9, October (1980).
91. *Liberation,* January-April (1982) p. 17.
92. *Eritrea Bulletin,* December 15 (1983) p. 1.
93. Gaim Kibreab, 'African Refugees,' p. 30.
94. Halliday and Molyneux, 'The Ethiopian Revolution,' p. 209.
95. Tesfatsion Medhanie, *Eritrea: Dynamics of a National Question* (Amsterdam, B.R. Grüner, 1986) p. 134.
96. *Ethiopian Herald,* June 1 (1982).
97. *Ethiopian Herald,* September 14 (1982).
98. *The Australian,* January 8 (1985).
99. Benjamin Rivlin and Jacques Fomerand, 'Changing Third World Perspectives and Policies towards Israel,' eds. M. Curtis and S.A. Gitelson, *Israel in the Third Word* (New Jersey, Transaction Books, 1976) p. 337.
100. Dawit Wolde Giorgis, *Personal Communication* (1987).
101. *Adulis,* VI, January (1989).
102. *Los Angeles Times,* January 22 (1990).
103. *Adulis,* 1, 2 (1984).
104. Wolde-ab Woldemariam, 'Interview,' *Intercontinental Press,* February 21 (1972) p. 184.

7

The Eritrean People's Liberation Army

In the prosecution of remote wars, the undertaking became every
day more difficult, the event more doubtful, and the possession
more precarious, and less beneficial.

—EDWARD GIBBON, *The History of the Decline and Fall of
the Roman Empire[1]*

I n spite of all the debate regarding the level of international support given to both sides in the Ethiopia/Eritrea
conflict, little attention has been given to the loss of tens
of thousands of lives and the expenditure of billions of dollars
over the past three decades. Though the conflict began with the
guerrilla actions of a handful of Eritreans, today the massive Ethiopian army faces the conventionally armed Eritrean People's Liberation Army (EPLA), the military wing of the EPLF. They are
engaged in one of the most formidable contests Africa has seen.

The armed struggle began in September 1961 when a contingent of eleven fighting men, formerly members of the Sudanese

army and police, under the leadership of Idris Hamid Awate formed the first armed forces of the Eritrean Liberation Front (ELF). In the first engagement Bereg Norai became the first Eritrean to be killed.[2] By mid-1962, some 500 men were successfully harassing Ethiopian troops around Agordat. On December 19, a group of policemen deserted to the ELF in Massawa, taking with them rifles, machine guns and several political prisoners they had freed.[3]

During the period from 1960 until 1968, the ELF claimed that it had killed over 5,000 Ethiopian troops and had liberated some two-thirds of the country. In 1962, there were four battles and engagements, in 1963, fifteen. In September 1963, the ELF was strong enough to enter Haicota to raid the army camp.[4] The village of Tokombia began to supply recruits to the ELF. In 1964, twenty-one battles took place; in 1964 and 1966 there were twenty-seven.[5] The number of trained fighters grew to some 2,000 men.[6] In that year, Ethiopian troops killed ten elders from Tokombia and destroyed the nearby village of Adi Ibrahim. Some 25,000 Eritreans fled into the Sudan.[7]

Some of these refugees joined the Eritrean Liberation Movement (ELM). The ELM sent armed units into Eritrea to fight the Ethiopians; they were liquidated by the ELF.[8] In 1965, the Supreme Council of the ELF established five military zones: zone one, the Sudanese border area; zone two, the area around Keren; zone three, Northern Sahel; zone four, Massawa and the Danakil; and zone five, Asmara and the central highlands. These zones were based upon the Algerian FLN experience.[9] They were drawn up on ethnic, regional and religious lines; the regional commanders were virtually autonomous. They were: first zone, Mahmoud Dinai; second zone, Umar Hamid Azaz; third zone, Abdulkerim Ahmed; fourth zone, Mohammed Ali Omaro and fifth zone, Woldai Kahsai.[10] The ELF confined itself to a classic, rurally-based, guerrilla strategy; it was aware that it was not strong enough for an offensive against the towns held by the Ethiopians; ELF members thought that this would come after the death of Haile Selassie, when Ethiopia was expected to fall apart.

The ELF began to attract a considerable number of recruits from highland, urban—mainly Christian—areas. Many of these young, educated men began to question the wisdom of the strategies propounded by the ELF leadership, based in Cairo, and of tactics which tended to alienate the traditionally-minded highland peasant. A revolutionary command was based in Kassala and charged with the function of coordinating the policies of the supreme council and actions of the commanders in the field, a task it appears to have discharged with incompetence.[11] Discord arose and worsened over the years to culminate in the factionalizing of the ELF and the birth of the EPLF.

ELF figures of Ethiopia casualties are probably inflated; until 1967 only one brigade of the Second Division of the Ethiopian army totalling some 3,000 men was stationed in Eritrea, with the three battalions stationed at Keren, Asmara and between Massawa and Asmara. However, the ELF was a formidable presence. Its guerrillas assassinated Asmara's Criminal Investigations Department (CID) chief in 1966, and, in 1967, blew up oil storage tanks in Assab; most roads were unsafe for traffic at night.[12] In an attempt to counter the ELF, another Ethiopian brigade was moved to Agordat and most of the Third Brigade also transferred to Eritrea, indicative of the increasing effectiveness of the Eritrean opposition. Three Saho villages in the western lowlands were destroyed by the Ethiopians in December 1966. Ethiopian troops herded the villagers into two strategic hamlets, and when this strategy failed, dispersed the population to towns. Many then fled to the Sudan.[13] In 1967, the regular army was used against the ELF forces in a concerted offensive, exploiting the ethnic rivalries between Eritreans by attacking one zone at a time.

Under Brigadier Merid Beyené, the Second Division, on the advice of the Israelis and Americans, attempted to pacify the western lowlands. Seven villages—Adfaki, Ashur, Falkat, Garabeet, Sanheet, Sawa and Tokombia—were destroyed. Plans were made to turn others into strategic hamlets. After the villagers showed their continued loyalty to the ELF, the division withdrew.[14] Abera Mekonen, a former schoolmaster who turned guerrilla, kept a diary of ELF actions; he recorded sustained action around the important Western Eritrean town of Tessenai.[15]

The army then concentrated on defending strategic targets from ELF assaults. At Halhal, on September 6-7, 1968, a battle left sixty ELF dead. Several hundred Ethiopians also died. It was the success of these tactics which caused the ELF to avoid direct confrontation with military patrols for a time.[16] Instead, the ELF carried out a number of effective ambushes and destruction of oil tankers. It made the Asmara-Addis Ababa road passable only by military convoy.[17] In 1969, there was a partial curfew in the eastern lowlands and eastern Akele Guzai; Ethiopia drafted in a battalion of airborne troops and some of the Imperial Bodyguard Brigade in an effort to counter the ELF.[18]

A special Ethiopian counterinsurgency force known as 101 commando had been formed in late 1965. By 1969, there were nine companies, based on Decamere and attached to the police; they played a major role in the fight against the ELF. The General Security Service, headed by Amde Michael Belhachaw, was in charge of intelligence.[19] In spite of the fact that all of Eritrea was under martial law, and two-thirds of the Ethiopian army was on active service in Eritrea, an American journalist was able to travel with the ELF from the Sudanese border to the outskirts of Keren.[20]

By 1970, the ELF controlled most of west and north Eritrea and part of the coast.[21] Accordingly, in March 1970, a large-scale military offensive, with the Ethiopian Second Division being reinforced with the First Division, attempted to "pacify" the coast, Sahel and the area around Keren, Eritrea's second largest city. Pacification failed; the ELF killed a district governor in Seraye.[22] In October, bridges were blown up and trains destroyed between Asmara and Keren. Maj. General Teshome Erghetu, who had been the Second Division's Commander since the mid-1960s, was killed on the Asmara-Keren road in November 1970, along with a large number of troops. By this time the forces of the ELF and People's Liberation Front (PLF), forerunner to the EPLF, were estimated to amount to 10,000 fighters.[23]

Although not formally recognized until a congress in 1977, the fighters of the EPLF and the PLF constituted a significant fighting force as early as 1970. Today, the EPLA includes twelve infantry brigades, each with three battalions having 450 fighters at full strength. There are a number of semi-regular regional armies and some 20,000 fighters in militia units. There is a heavy weapons brigade, artillery units and an engineering corps. The EPLA can mobilize over 200 tanks and armored vehicles, all captured from the Ethiopians; there are two tank battalions. Naval operations are carried out by a fleet of fast attack speedboats. The EPLA ranks eleventh in size among African armies after Angola, Egypt, Ethiopia, Mozambique, Nigeria, South Africa, Sudan, Tanzania, Zaire and Zambia. It is better equipped than any other African conventional army except those of Angola, Egypt, Ethiopia, Mozambique, Nigeria and South Africa. The Eritreans have the ability to convert the frontline regular infantry battalions into highly mobile units which can stiffen the regional armies and local militia and can now overrun Ethiopian garrisons throughout the country virtually at will. The battle experience of some of the soldiers stretches back twenty-nine years, a period of almost constant combat equalled in length only by Ethiopian soldiers. It is an entirely voluntary and literate force. And, uniquely among combat forces, some thirty-five percent of frontline troops are women.

The EPLF's aim is to end Ethiopia's occupation of Eritrea and transform Eritrean society; to these ends the role of the EPLA and the political leadership is crucial. The National Democratic Program of the EPLF was adopted in January 1977; of the eleven objectives set out in the program, the sixth reads:

Build a Strong People's Army
    A.Liberate the land and the people step-by-step

through the strategy of people's war. Build a strong land, air and naval force capable of defending the country's borders, territorial waters, air space and territorial integrity, as well as the full independence, progress, and dignity of its people in order to attain prosperity and reach the highest economic stage. The people's army shall be: politically conscious, imbued with comradely relations, steeled through revolutionary discipline; full of resoluteness, imbued with a spirit of self-sacrifice, participating in production; and equipped with modern tactics, weapons and skills. Being the defender of the interests of the workers and peasants, it serves the entire people of Eritrea irrespective of religion, nationality, or sex. The basis of this army is the revolutionary force at presently fighting for national independence and liberation.

B. Establish a people's militia to safeguard the gains of the revolution and support the people's army in the liberated and semi-liberated areas.

C. Establish a progressive and advanced military academy.[24]

At the 1977 Congress, the EPLF formally adopted a three-point strategy. Firstly: positional warfare, defending the liberated areas from enemy attack, destroying enemy bases and liberating the country step by step. Secondly, mobile warfare in the contested areas to block the enemy's maneuvers and thirdly, guerrilla warfare in the enemy occupied areas to destroy fuel, ammunition and supplies, demolish military and economic installations and prepare the ground for a general strategic war.[25] A Second Congress of the EPLF was held in March 1987; it reaffirmed the above.

There are a number of important strategic considerations in the Ethiopian-Eritrean conflict, some unique to Eritrea. In order to survive in the early years of such a protracted war members of the liberation movement had to rely upon the support of the local, mainly peasant, population. Accordingly, the EPLF stresses its political program, based on land reform measures which give land to the landless and security of tenure to the small-and medium-sized farmer. The Ethiopian regime makes similar promises, but so far, in the main, has been unable or unwilling to carry them out.[26] This issue is explored more fully in the next chapter.

The EPLA has shown its ability to capture towns and hold them for long periods at a time; in the early stages, as it could not deny the Ethiopians control of the air, it rarely attempted to maintain control of towns—not wanting to risk civilian lives or the lives of its fighters. Following several successful Eritrean raids on the Ethiopian air base in Asmara, the Ethiopians began to mount their air attacks from Ethiopia.[27] The Eritrean population living in the contested areas is defended against Ethiopian ground attacks to some extent by the EPLA's people's militias and regional armies.[28] The Second Congress of the EPLF marked the unification of the forces of the major faction of the ELF (ELF-Central Command) with the EPLA. The congress indicated that the military strategy would be the intensification of the mobile and guerrilla campaigns and the continuation of minor confrontations with the Ethiopians in frontline positions in order to drain the Ethiopians of manpower and material. The EPLA would eventually go for a major offensive.[29]

Attempts have been made to estimate the source and cost of arms used by the Eritrean fighters. It has been claimed that until the 1970s, the rebellion was supported by pro-Soviet sources and that several million dollars was required to finance it. It has also been suggested that the cost of arming the Eritreans since 1978 has been between $5 million and $7 million per year. Over fifteen years, $50 million "seems conservative" to one observer.[30] There is no evidence to support these assertions; on the contrary, first-hand observations confirm the claim that the EPLA now relies overwhelmingly on Ethiopia for its supply of weapons which are captured in battle and in guerrilla raids. The EPLA places a great premium on maintaining equipment and firepower and draining the Ethiopian Army of its supplies.[31] The EPLF repairs and maintains military equipment, feeds the army and looks after the wounded in a secure base area. The EPLA is very much smaller than the Ethiopian army and has to compensate for this by having better trained and more committed fighters; it makes the best use of surprise attacks. As far as combat forces are concerned, the ratio between the EPLA and the enemy is 1:4, and in some battles can be 1:9; in the sixth offensive in 1982 it was 1:8.[32] The battlefield mortality ratio is at least ten Ethiopians to one Eritrean.[33]

The First Congress of the EPLF held in 1977 established an organizational structure which included a central committee of thirty-seven members elected by the Congress. The central committee in turn elected a general secretary, a vice general secretary and a politburo consisting of eleven members. Each member of the politburo became head of a department. Day to day decisions were made by four men—general secretary, vice general secretary and the chairmen of the political and military committees. The chairman of the military committee was a very powerful and influential figure; until his death in action in 1986, the post was held by Ibrahim Afa. His place was taken by Ali Said Abdella, who had been head of security.[34] The departments of military supplies, signal and intelligence, and military training came under the military committee, whilst security, information and propaganda, and politicization came under the political committee.[35] Each unit of the EPLA had an EPLF political officer, who coordinated the political training of the fighters and served as a liaison officer with non-military departments.

Defects became apparent both in the military organization and in the relationship between the political and military wings; the 1987 congress abolished the position of vice secretary and the military committee, replacing them by a secretariat and general staff.[36] Isaias explained why the military committee was abolished:

> The military committee did not function effectively in the
> past ten years. When we came face to face with reality

after the First Congress, all politburo members had to be in fact part of the committee. All politburo members, whenever it was necessary, had full time work in military matters and there was no need for meetings of a special committee. After a while we had to come up with the idea of a military general staff headed by a politburo member and with other central committee members dealing exclusively with military matters.[37]

Three administrative departments are concerned exclusively with military matters: these are, ordnance, intelligence and security and the military academy.[38]

The Eritrean war of liberation is unique among African movements in that the infrastructure of the EPLF is inside the country—behind a defensive line created in the northern, mountainous third of Eritrea; this is referred to as the liberated area. The EPLF and EPLA also operate throughout the rest of this mainly rural country—an area referred to as the semi-liberated or contested area. All of the fighters are based inside the country; unlike most other liberation movements, the EPLF does not have a rear military base in a neighboring, foreign country. Neither has Arab or Soviet support been essential to the success of the Eritrean resistance. On the contrary, the Soviet Union has spearheaded the fight against the EPLF, while Arab military support has been relatively modest—insignificant compared to the support given to the PLO. The only other comparable cases of movements of such size surviving for long periods without outside aid are Mao Tse Tung's Eighth Route Army which survived for twenty years, Josip Broz Tito's Yugoslavian partisans during the Second World War and Abdul Al Krim's Republic of the Rif, which defied the French during the inter-war period in North Africa.[39] In the early years of the war, some cadres received training overseas—mainly from the PLO in Lebanon.

Until 1985, relations were good with the Tigray People's Liberation Front (TPLF); not only did the TPLF train with the EPLF, the two organizations pooled intelligence and mounted joint military operations. Ethiopian soldiers who surrendered to the TPLF were taken to prisoner of war camps in Eritrea and cared for by the ERA. In the middle of 1985, the TPLF and EPLF leaderships disagreed about the conduct of the war, appropriate responses to the famine and issues relating to the role of nationalities. And although representatives of all sections of Eritrean opinion and of other Ethiopian groups opposing the Dergue attended the 1987 Congress of the EPLF, TPLF observers were markedly absent. In 1988, the two liberation fronts buried their differences and went onto the offensive. The benefits of cooperation were quickly felt and by March 1989 the TPLF had liberated the provincial capital, Mekelle, for the first time in their fourteen year struggle. EPLF and Afar Liberation Front (ALF) units also resumed cooperation in attacks in Wollo Province in 1989.

The morale of the EPLA is extraordinarily high. The fighters are all volunteers and there is no shortage of applicants. Each recruit, male or female, is given a minimum of six month's training combining political and military education.[40] In the early years, the EPLF political training stressed Marxism; now the emphasis is very much on national and democratic issues. Female fighters are trained separately for the first six months in order to overcome the timidity of the many recruits and to accustom them to strenuous physical exercise. They then join units on the same terms as male recruits. This training in a very harsh, Spartan environment has forged a camaraderie and effectiveness rare among any fighting force. Although the forces are remarkably well disciplined, "for there is nothing in war of greater importance than obedience," there is a very friendly atmosphere in all EPLA units.[41] Insignia, medals, saluting and other conventional military distinctions are absent and commanders share the same food, accommodation and hardship as the rank and file fighters. It has been suggested that the extraordinary bravery of the EPLF fighters derives from the self-assurance that, whatever the risks, in the event of danger, a fighter in trouble can count on his or her comrades to come to the rescue.[42]

Recruits are drawn from all of the nine nationalities that comprise Eritrea; the major languages of instruction are Tigrinya, Tigré, Afar and Kunama. Defections from the EPLA have been few in number; the greatest period of stress was in 1978, when the Ethiopian government, in conjunction with Soviet, Cuban and other foreign troops, gained the upper-hand in the conflict. Three former liberation fighters were interviewed on Ethiopian television in August 1976, and claimed that many hundred others had defected or wanted to throw down their arms; such claims cannot be verified.[43] A member of the EPLF central committee with security responsibilities, Teklai Gebre Mariam, defected to the Dergue in 1980 after he could no longer reconcile his support for the Soviet Union with his membership of the EPLF. Defections from the ELF have been more numerous; the highest ranking defector being Haile Wolde Selassie, who was in charge of the ELF central security department. A field commander, Abel Gebre Mikael, defected in 1980.[44]

Since the mid-1970s, the number of troops in the Ethiopian Army, as well as the quantity and quality of their arms, has grown steadily. From 1952, the year of Eritrea's federation with Ethiopia, the real master of Eritrea was the Ethiopian Second Division, which took over responsibility for security from the departing British.[45] In 1975, the elite Imperial Brigade was disbanded and its strength distributed among the rest of the army. In 1976-1977, 6,000 members of the Territorial Army reserves were mobilized for service in Eritrea. The Ethiopian Army in Eritrea was reorganized. A northern command was created under the leadership of Col. Hailu Gebre Michael.[46] The Second Division remained as the backbone of the force and was supplemented by the Sixth (Flame) Division.

Conscription was introduced in 1978-1979, so from then onward, figures for troop strength include some forces of very low quality such as the people's militia and paramilitary forces.

By 1983-1984, there were also some 200,000 reservists who had received some form of military training. In 1988-1989, there were 150,000 members of the people's militia and 169,000 of the para-military. The tank battalions, which form the teeth of the fighting force in Eritrea, have been equipped with vastly superior weapons since 1974-1975 when there were fifty M-41 tanks.

Ethiopia has received substantial amounts of military aid from a wide variety of countries. During the period 1952-1975, United States military assistance to Ethiopia was worth some $275 million. United States Military Assistance Advisory Group (MAAG) army and air forces were based at Kagnew Air Force Base outside Asmara and naval personnel in Massawa.

In 1956, the Kagnew base was described as "the most important radio facility in the world" and from the mid-1960s until the early 1970s almost all of its operating time revolved around its roles as ground station for the United States defense satellite control system.[47] In 1964, after much hard bargaining, President Lyndon Johnson agreed to send the emperor a squadron of F-5 fighter bombers, known as the Freedom Fighters, as disguised rent for Kagnew. Ethiopia relied upon United States bombs and ammunition for use in Eritrea; in 1969, the emperor requested helicopters and M-16 rifles specifically for counterinsurgency.[48] It seems likely that, before 1974, United States and Israeli advisers were involved in intelligence and combat missions in Eritrea.[49] Assistance during the 1975 fiscal year amounted to $7 million in ammunition and spare parts; the Dergue had asked for $25 million. In 1975, $22 million was given to replace obsolete equipment, and in April, eight F-5s were delivered to Ethiopia. In 1975-1976, twelve M-60 tanks were purchased from the United States and a further twelve in 1976-1977 and 1977-1978.

In the latter year, the first delivery of tanks from the Soviet Union took place. Major maintenance of Soviet weapons was carried out in the Soviet Union.[50] The United States was still aiding the Ethiopians; during the 1977 fiscal year, $109.4 million was donated. Some $92.6 million came in the form of arms and $15.8

million was sales on credit. However, Soviet assistance became far more significant. From May to December 1977 Soviet supplies were valued at $850 million to $1 billion; these included sixty MIG-21 and twelve MIG-23 planes. A caveat should be raised here; data on arms transfers are notoriously unreliable and open to manipulation.[51] It is possible that Ethiopia took delivery of some T-62s as early as January 1978 and 100 in the last six months of 1983. In late 1986, there were also sightings of T-72s in action.

Such support enabled the Cuban- and Soviet-trained militia to defeat the armed, conservative opposition in Ethiopia, the Ethiopian Democratic Union (EDU), and roll back the TPLF in Tigray. In April 1978, napalm and cluster bombs arrived in Massawa from Israel, while in Asmara, 600 Soviet and Cuban advisers, pilots and engineers prepared for the offensive.[52] On May 15, the Ethiopians attacked. Mengistu claimed that Cubans, Soviets, South Yemenis and East Germans were dying alongside Ethiopians and that Ethiopia had already suffered 13,000 casualties. A Soviet general, Vassily Petrov, deputy commander of the ground forces of the Soviet Union, commanded the Ethiopian forces. Another Soviet general was in charge of air operations. A total of eleven Soviet lieutenant colonels also saw action including: Alexei Alexandrov, commander of the western front, Vassily on the eastern front and Eduard, commander of the northern front; the latter was killed in November 1978 during the battle for Elabored. There was an increased reliance on Soviet and Cuban training and Soviet advisers were observed at battalion level.[53]

The training and morale of the Ethiopian army is not of a particularly high standard. Portions of the army mutinied in December 1960 and discontent rumbled on for many years.[54] Morale has been particularly low since the 1974 coup. There have been successive purges of officers and men. For example, the first three leaders of the ruling Dergue were all assassinated or killed resisting Mengistu. There have also been many defections. Of the original 120-man Dergue, a mere handful were active in government by 1987.

There have been many reports of mutinies and conspiracies among officers of the Fourth Division and officers and men of the frontline divisions in the Ogaden, Tigray and Eritrea. In 1977, several units under the influence of the Ethiopian left organizations EPRP and Meison refused to obey the orders of their officers.[55] This continuing dissension was reflected in poor combat performance.

In late October 1980, the top security Kagnew Base was covered with slogans denouncing the Dergue. In December, militia from the Seventy-first Brigade in Asmara took their commanding officer hostage; army units in Adi Keih, Quazien and Adi Guadad supported them. An electric generator was blown up in Keren. In Decamere, there was a shootout between mutineers and supporters of the Dergue.[56] During the months of July-September 1981, fifty-five Ethiopian officers and men deserted to the EPLF, whilst soldiers in Afabet and Decamere fought amongst themselves with at least thirty-four killed.[57] In November, troops of the Eighteenth Brigade detained their officers and political commissars before being disarmed and transferred to Barka. Armed clashes between troops took place north of Asmara and around Keren. Some ninety-five former Dergue militiamen from Barentu and Dembelas joined the EPLF.[58]

In the first three months of 1982, 215 Ethiopian army soldiers deserted including sixty Eritreans.[59] In 1983, the head of the political education section of the Red Star Campaign in Asmara, Lt. Molla Shibesi, deserted to the EPLF; in September and October, eighty-five officers and men deserted to the EPLF whilst sixty-eight new Eritrean conscripts also joined the EPLA.[60] The Ethiopian leader, fearing that the entire northern army might rebel, executed several officers and reinforced the already formidable apparatus of political and security personnel.[61] Some of the reasons for the low morale of the Ethiopian troops and their massive rate of desertion are given by Mengesha Areda in the following interview:

> I am from Wollo and joined the army voluntarily in 1980. I trained in Alamaita, Tigray. I came to Agordat from the Nacfa front as part of the reinforcements that were sent to help the forces at Barentu who were surrounded by bandits. I defected to the EPLF. I supported the Ethiopian revolution which is why I joined the army but I then found out that a lot of things I believed were not true. I witnessed many criminal acts and had been planning for some time to leave the army. I took my chance to escape. We stole animals from the people and cooked them; we took their donkeys and camels. We were burning houses and taking away suspected people and killing them. I was always feeling guilty when I was ordered to do these things.[62]

Following the defeat of a massive Ethiopian offensive in 1985, there were reports of growing discontent and unrest in all three armed services. In January 1986, an Ethiopian Lt. Col. diverted his plane to Sudan and asked for asylum.[63] The EPLF extended an amnesty for those members of the Ethiopian forces whose salary comprises payment in kind with internationally donated grain. These men are known as the wheat militia. During August 1986, two regional administrators in Akele-Guzai province were detained on charges of instigating opposition to the Ethiopian draft constitution.[64] In November some senior officers defected, including the ideological commissioner for Decamere and Dembezan and a brigade commander.[65]

The most serious threat to the regime came in May 1989 when most of the general staff supported an unsuccessful army coup. Mengistu returned hurriedly from a trip to East Berlin and restored control with the help of foreign advisers and the presidential guard. Seven generals were executed, including the chief of staff, the air force commander, minister of defense and the commander of the Second Revolutionary Army based in Eritrea. At least thirty-four other officers were arrested including a further ten generals.

The morale of the Ethiopian army has deteriorated steadily over the past two decades and stems from dissatisfaction with dictatorial rule and inability to defeat the liberation movement. Frustration on this score resulted in the proclamation of a state of emergency in mid-December 1970 in all of Eritrea, with the exception of Asmara, Assab and Massawa. The armed forces were given a free hand in the area bordering the Sudan and the coast. All inhabitants were cleared from a six-mile wide prohibited zone on either side of the Keren-Asmara road and Keren was bombed after three bridges were blown up by liberation forces.[66] Lt. General Debebe Haile Mariam replaced the civilian Ras Asrate Kassa as governor general of Eritrea.

Another Ethiopian offensive began in December 1970, involving armor and the air force. Engineering units were brought in and roads opened into Barka, along the coast and the Sudanese border. A chain of fortified villages was constructed along the Sudanese frontier. At the same time the Ethiopians perpetrated numerous large-scale atrocities. On November 27, 112 villagers from Bascadara were shot in a mosque. Four days later, 625 people from villages near Keren were executed, while on January 27, 1971, about sixty men, women and children from a village near Elabored were murdered in a mosque.[67] In spite of these gruesome atrocities, the Bilein, probably because they were sedentary farmers, did not leave their homes for sanctuary in Sudan.[68] According to one observer, guerrilla activity died down and the bulk of fighting in the Eritrean countryside between February 1972 and October 1974 was between rival groups of Eritrean nationalists.[69]

During this period of "quiet," however, continuing military action against the Ethiopians was reported. In November 1972, serious army casualties were running about fifty per month.[70] In

June, 1973, two aircraft were shot down and four vehicles carrying troops and equipment destroyed. A number of other actions were carried out by the ELF and EPLF and by November 1973 a curfew was imposed in all Eritrean towns. A rocket attack was carried out on the army headquarters in Asmara and a number of bridges were destroyed.[71] The EPLA imposed a crushing defeat on the Ethiopian army in major battles lasting from December 1973-January 1974; the most significant engagements being at Mai Awli, twelve miles from Asmara, and at Karora.[72] On December 12, Colonel Yilma Elma, deputy commander of the Second Division, was killed in an ambush in Asmara. The ELF was also active.

One of the initial consequences of the Ethiopian military coup of February 1974, which brought the military junta, or Dergue, to power, was a diminution of army action in Eritrea. The Ethiopians claim to have suspended all military activity from July 1974 until February 1975.[73] The latter claim is an obvious fabrication: in July 1974, the colonel in charge of the brigade at Om Hager, near Eritrea's border with Tigray, was killed, leading to massive army retaliation in the area and initiating a chain of events which led to the resignation of all Eritrean members of the Ethiopian Parliament. In October 1974, 500 PLF fighters confined in their first permanent base area—on the Sahel coast near Karora—broke out from Ethiopian encirclement and reached Zagr some fifteen miles outside Asmara. The area was patrolled by ELF forces, based at Weki; initial confrontations were followed by a truce between the two fighting fronts. Following the death of General Aman Andom, the ELF made attacks inside Asmara during November and December. The Dergue built up its forces for a concerted drive against the liberation forces in the Asmara area.

In January 1975, an ELF/EPLF agreement was reached at Coazien; this led to a coordinated attack on Asmara on the night of January 31. There was heavy fighting for ten days followed by a further month of skirmishes. The Ethiopians lost major battles near Adi Nefas and Beleza and were then held under virtual siege in Asmara for many months. The fronts gathered large numbers of recruits and quantities of weapons and gained a massive increase in morale and recognition.[74]

The liberation forces sensed the weakness and lack of commitment of the Dergue's troops and switched from guerrilla tactics to conventional warfare. There were 25,000 Ethiopian troops in Eritrea—some half of their total force—but with very poor morale due to the factionalism and bloodletting following the Ethiopian revolution. Lt. Col. Berhanu and Lt. Haile Mariam Hassan were executed by the Dergue in July 1975 for leading a rebellion in Assab.[75] All Eritrean servicemen in the Ethiopian forces were withdrawn from combat duty; this halved the effectiveness of the air force.[76] The Ethiopian army began to withdraw from most of its company-sized camps and garrisons; by early 1975 it held only seventeen of sixty garrisons. Liberation forces were estimated to include 20,000-30,000 EPLF and 10,000-15,000 ELF fighters. EPLF recruits included many former Eritrean policemen and Israeli-trained commandos. In 1975, there were 110 confrontations between the EPLF and the Ethiopian army; these included fifteen operations in conjunction with the ELF. In October 1975, an oil tanker convoy en route from Assab to Addis Ababa was ambushed.

In May 1976, the Dergue, short of regular troops, hastily assembled a peasant army and sent it to rout the Eritrean "bandits;" it was defeated at Zalambesa in Tigray before it could even enter Eritrea. The 27,000 strong Ethiopian army was confined to Asmara, Keren, Massawa and a handful of smaller garrisons. In September, the EPLF launched a major offensive, encircled Nacfa and forced the Ethiopians to supply the town by air.[77] On the last day of 1976, 45 million liters of fuel were set ablaze at the fuel depot in Massawa.[78]

On January 5, 1977, the Eritrean border garrison town of Karora was captured by the EPLF. The Ethiopians had been besieged for several months but had not mined the defenses.[79] In February, 840 Ethiopians were killed during the EPLF siege of

Nacfa. On April 2, Afabet was liberated and on April 9, Elabored. Nacfa was finally overrun by the EPLF on March 23, followed by the ELF capture of Tessenai and the strategic Getachew hill overlooking the airstrip at Barentu, and the fall of Keren and Agordat. Among senior military casualties were Col. Daniel Asfaw, the command of the Fifth Division and Dergue members Col. Simi Bekele and Maj. Getachew Solomon.

The expected Ethiopian offensive in Eritrea was postponed because of the increased fighting in the Ogaden, where the army was engaged by the Western Somali Liberation Front guerrillas and regular Somali troops.

By October 13, the Eritrean offensive was still gathering momentum with the capture of the town of Dogali on the Massawa-Asmara road, followed on the next day by ELF ambushes of several Ethiopian military convoys. December 19 marked the start of the attack on Massawa. Ethiopian troops were observed taking rocket launchers on board Soviet Alligator-class support ships. The ships directed their fire at Eritrean positions and during the siege of Massawa there were at least 600 Eritrean and 4,000 Ethiopian casualties. At the beginning of 1978, liberation forces were estimated to be: 30,000 EPLF; 10,000 ELF; and 250 loyal to Osman Saleh Sabbe, who had defected from the EPLF by this time. The Eritrean forces, however, were by now spread very thinly through the country and were not able to fortify their positions. An observer wrote:

Victory in the north...still looks a chimera in any case... all the Dergue can really hope for there is to gain a position of sufficient strength from which to negotiate a political solution, or face up to an endless war that is certain to bring about their own downfall and that of the revolution as well.[80]

Following the influx of massive foreign assistance, a succession of victories followed in 1978 for the combined Soviet and Ethiopian forces. What is referred to by the EPLF as the Ethiopian First Offensive began in mid July following the EPLF withdrawal from the south; it lasted until the end of July. On July 23, Tessenai was recaptured and on July 27, Adi Ugri (Medefera); the siege of Massawa was lifted. By July 30, Decamere was in the Dergue's hands, after the EPLF was defeated at Mai Aine, south of the town. In August, Agordat, after a year under the control of the ELF, and Segeneiti and Digsa also fell. The eighteen-month long siege of Barentu was ended. But nevertheless, on July 3, Ethiopian attacks on Keren were repulsed by the EPLA and the Ethiopians driven back twenty-four miles, with some 2,000 men killed and thirteen tanks destroyed. By early August, however, ELF resistance had collapsed and four Ethiopian mechanized columns converged through Barka, Seraye and Akele-Guzai onto the EPLF highland strongholds.

A rapid EPLF withdrawal from areas south of Asmara enabled it to stall the attack for a while and, on September 22, the Dergue's main ammunition dump in Kagnew was blown up. In November 1978, the Ethiopian Tenth Division was air-lifted to Massawa, to augment the faltering offensive. The Ethiopian Second Offensive began on November 20, and lasted to the end of the month with fighting on the east and south of Keren. Soviet satellite photographs, together with intelligence gathered from sorties flown by Soviet crewed helicopters, enabled the Ethiopians to attack at weak points.[81] The most intense battles occurred on November 25-26 at Elabored, some twelve miles south of Keren, when twenty-five Ethiopian tanks were either captured or destroyed. EPLF losses were also heavy. The EPLF could clearly have defended Keren, had it so wished, but an Ethiopian landing on the northern coast and an Ethiopian breakthrough of the EPLF's defensive lines on the western approaches from Agordat raised the very great possibility of entrapment.[82] The EPLF decided upon a strategic withdrawal from Keren to the mountains of Sahel. Accordingly, the Ethiopians captured Keren on November 27 without encountering any more resistance.

The Third Offensive started in January 1979 on the Anseba, Maamide and northeast Sahel fronts, and from February 6-9 around Denden on the Nacfa Front. The EPLF constructed an elaborate network of trenches stretching some 250 miles from the mountains by the Red Sea coast through three provinces to the Barka lowlands in the east. They prepared to defend this base area. From March 30 until April 11, 1979, Ethiopia mounted its Fourth Offensive, attacking from Mersa Teklai and Afabet. Forces involved were 5,000 EPLF and 40,000 Ethiopians; there were some 8,000 Ethiopian casualties between January-May, and 25,000 during the four offensives.[83]

The offensive failed; consequently on July 8, 1979 a Fifth Offensive was initiated; this time in the form of a three-pronged attack on Nacfa. The EPLF claimed to have inflicted 15,000 casualties on the enemy including 6,000 dead. On July 18, at Agat, 10,000 men of task force 503B under the command of Seifu Wolde were crushed by the EPLA. On December 2, 1979, the Eritreans counterattacked toward Afabet after 2,000 men of the Ethiopian Third Division attempted to push north.

In the early part of 1980, 30,000 Ethiopian troops were pushed back towards Mersa Teklai, while in fighting between Afabet and Nacfa, over 100 military vehicles and seventeen T-54 tanks were captured. In June, East German GA (Tabun) nerve gas was flown in for possible use against the Eritreans, indicating once again the Dergue's desperate need to defeat the Eritrean resistance. An armored column was ambushed near Nacfa in July.

A joint ELF/EPLF force occupied the Eritrean border town of Karora, but when the ELF units were suddenly withdrawn to Barka in the summer of 1980, Ethiopian troops infiltrated the defense lines and reoccupied the town. ELF leaders held abortive peace talks with Soviet and Ethiopian representatives throughout 1980. The EPLF feared that a peace treaty would leave them in an exposed position and that ELF forces regrouping in Barka were preparing for an attack on them. EPLF intelligence had warned of an impending Ethiopian attack; the EPLF was fearful of fighting battles with both the Ethiopians and the ELF and, therefore, mounted a preemptive strike against ELF positions during October to December. It was successful in occupying Barka province, thus trebling EPLF-held areas.[84]

There were an estimated 2,000 Eritrean fighters around Nacfa; a total of eleven brigades in the Sahel and a further 15,000 militia. There were now two tank battalions. ELF strength was down to 6,600 and was diminished further by constant desertions to the EPLF. Another Ethiopian offensive was mounted on December 2, 1980. Six brigades were used to capture foothills surrounding Nacfa. Early in 1981, preparations for a major offensive were under way to use the newly trained Eighteenth Ranger Division and the Squadron of MI-24 helicopter gunships then fighting in Tigray. As is usual, the excellent Eritrean intelligence sources, both within the Ethiopian Army and at the highest levels of the civilian administration, forewarned the EPLF. They mounted preemptive strikes. An Ethiopian brigade trying to clear the area around Areza of EPLA forces lost twenty-five percent of its strength in a two-day battle in June.[85] In July 1981, Brigadier General Asrat Biru, head of military operations in Eritrea was badly wounded; while in August, the EPLF overran the garrison at Aderde, on the Agordat-Keren road in western Eritrea, killing or capturing the battalion strength force.[86]

The EPLA offensive ranged over a wide area from Tokar, twelve miles from Asmara and the lowlands of Seraye—where much action occurred around the Ethiopian-held garrison of Areza—to the outskirts of Keren and the province of Barka. In two months, more than 3,500 Ethiopian troops were killed or wounded. On December 22, units of the EPLA in the southern zone launched a surprise attack on units of the Eighteenth Division, freshly brought into Eritrea for the Dergue's planned Sixth Offensive. The Dergue attempted to mop up these guerrilla units during December, but retreated to its garrisons after six days of often intense fighting.[87]

On January 23, 1982, as the Dergue prepared for its big offensive, there was an EPLF attack on Sembel Airport in Asmara. The surrounding garrisons in Tselot and Kurba Embeito were completely destroyed, as well as the Thirty-fifth Brigade headquarters inside Asmara and the Baratollo textile factory.[88] Some 2,500 EPLF fighters were involved and parts of southeastern Asmara were attacked. Decamere, Keren and Massawa, as well as other towns were also occupied.[89]

Such actions, together with EPLA offensives on the Sahel fronts, blunted the impact of the Red Star Campaign which was launched in February 1982 with much publicity and bravado. This, the Sixth Offensive, involved 90,000 Ethiopian troops. Out of Ethiopia's twenty-two Divisions, fourteen were in Eritrea and three in Tigray. Soviet helicopter gunships were used for the first time. On March 5, the EPLF claimed that Mengistu was wounded while directing the offensive; in the period that followed, he was certainly absent from a number of state occasions. The Minister of Defense Tesfay Gebre Kidan was the operational commander; until May, the government established its base in Asmara.

The Red Star Campaign was launched on four major fronts: that in Barka—directed from Agordat—collapsed in a week, with the Twenty-first Division practically wiped out and the Twenty-fourth Division retreating to Keren and then being redeployed on the northeast second front. The commander of the Twenty-first Division, Colonel Wubishet, was executed in front of the remainder of the army in Afabet for this failure.[90] The Ethiopians directed their attack at the EPLF stationed along a line some thirty miles long parallel to the Red Sea, at an altitude of 6,500 feet and sixty miles inland from Mersa Teklai on the coast; this eventually created a seventy-five mile front of fighting.

Repeated round-the-clock bombing raids by Antonovs and helicopter gunships failed to dislodge the EPLA, prompting the opening of a third front in the northwest with troops transhipped through the Sudan, and deployed up to Aylet, three miles inside Sudan.[91] They were gradually beaten back to the lowlands. To the south, a fourth force, comprising the Twenty-third Division, tried to cut the supply lines but were beaten back with heavy losses. On the Nacfa front, the Ethiopian troops, divided into task forces 505 and 508, made initial advances over land evacuated by the EPLF, but came to a halt at the beginning of March. One observer claims that the task forces were ordered by Haile Giorgis, the Ethiopian chief of staff, to halt their advance to allow the Third Division (Mengistu's old unit) the honor of capturing Nacfa. This proved to be a monumental tactical error; the commander of the Third Division was one of the many killed when the EPLF pushed it back towards Afabet.[92] The Seventeenth Division also took heavy losses.[93] An unconfirmed source gives EPLA casualties in the Red Star offensive as 4,000 killed and wounded.[94] It is doubtful if EPLA casualties were half this number.

In the largest assault yet on the EPLA, some 33,000 Ethiopians were either killed or wounded. The Dergue used tear gas at Trukruk, Elghena and Nacfa.[95] The offensive did not daunt the EPLA which continued attacks on Asmara, Massawa and what was known as the Halhal front. After the failure of the sixth offensive, which itself involved 400 Soviet advisers in the frontline and a further 2,000 at headquarters, the Soviets became responsible for the war strategy under the direction of Field Marshal Dimitrov.

The TPLF took advantage of the Ethiopian preoccupation with Eritrea and captured four towns from the Dergue in July 1982. The Dergue had to draft troops from Eritrea to retake the towns, and dealing with the TPLF blunted the Ethiopian effort in Eritrea. In 1983, however, a Seventh (silent or stealth) Offensive which lasted from March until August brought the Dergue some gains; these were later recovered by the EPLA in a series of counterattacks on the Halhal, Barka and Nacfa fronts; the most important engagement was June 15 when they took the positions of the Twenty-ninth Mechanized Brigade at Shingray.[96]

The EPLA continued their initiative. In 200 confrontations during 1982, the EPLA claimed to have killed 15,200 Ethiopians, wounded 18,400, and taken 872 prisoners, while 165 Ethiopians had defected. Two MIG-23 and two M-24 helicopter gunships were shot down, while thirty-six tanks and armored cars were destroyed. The Soviet Union replaced these losses quickly; 100 T-62 tanks, two squadrons of MIG-23, one squadron of Sukhoi fighter planes and large quantities of ammunition were delivered in the last four months of the year.

By August 1983, the advantage seemed to be in the hands of the EPLF. It pushed the Ethiopians out of Karora, after they had held it for two years. The Ethiopians were also forced out of Kerkabet and the Barka valley area. By late August, the Ethiopians had lost key positions on the roads from Agordat-Keren-Afabet.[97] The Dergue, overstretched, and having lost so many men, enforced conscription even more rigorously. The ELF and Osman's faction claimed to be fighting; but their only verifiable actions involved the late 1983 killing of a Swedish journalist by a land mine in Barka, and attacks on EPLF militia units in Danakil.[98]

The EPLF counteroffensive, which continued into 1984, saw the liberation of Tessenai on January 15, and that of the rich farming settlement of Ali Ghidir on January 15. Some 1,200 Ethiopian troops were killed or taken prisoner, and the remainder of the garrison fled either to the Sudan or to the Ethiopian held town of Om Hager.[99] On February 22, the EPLA used its newly captured armor to attack on the northeastern Sahel front (the Ethiopian Wukaw Command); it broke through Ethiopian trenches to reach the sea. This battle marked the first time that the EPLA had won tank battles on open plains. Between March 19-23, all remaining positions were overrun, including the small port and supply depot at Mersa Teklai; 3,122 prisoners were taken, including colonel Ghirma Tessema, the assistant commander and Colonel Yihdego Okbazghi, chief of logistics and some 500 Ethiopians were killed.[100]

This action brought a further 2,500 square miles under the control of the EPLF. In May, a mobile unit attacked the airport at Asmara and destroyed ten planes while another twenty-three were damaged. One third of the Ethiopian air force was therefore incapacitated.[101] The Soviets lost two Iluysin 38 Mays long range reconnaissance aircraft and were forced to use South Yemen as a base.[102] In April 1985, a joint attack with TPLF forces resulted in the virtual destruction of the First Tank Battalion of the Eighteenth Brigade (Seventh Division) at their base at Baaker, thirty-five miles south of Humera.

On July 6, 1985, the EPLF registered one of its most impressive achievements of the war when two Ethiopian infantry divisions and two battalions of the Twenty-seventh Mechanized Brigade (one a tank battalion) were destroyed, 2,000 men killed and 400 captured at Barentu. EPLF intelligence detected a reduction in the garrison. However, the Ethiopians were well dug in and protected with 20,000 mines. The 102nd Artillery Battalion had two batteries of 122mm howitzers and two of 76mm guns, together with two batteries of ZU-223 antiaircraft guns.

The EPLA onslaught began at 0005 hours, with a series of attacks on the outer ring of forts situated sixteen miles outside Barentu. The depleted Ethiopian garrison committed most of its reserves in the north and were unable to hold back the EPLF Heavy Weapons Brigade. Heavy cloud cover prevented the Ethiopians from using their airpower. Strong Ethiopian reinforcements were sent from Agordat but were decimated by an EPLA ambush. Later that month, Mai Habar near Dongolo, a strategic garrison on the main Asmara-Massawa road, was overrun. The Ethiopians started their attempt to retake Barentu on July 15, Over the next three days, 106th Brigade losses amounted to 500, including the deputy head of operations and a battalion commander. The Eighth Brigade was caught at Konta, and almost totally destroyed during one of twelve attempts to retake the town.[103] However, when the Dergue attacked for the fourteenth time the EPLA was outnumbered at least three to one. It faced the mechanized Fifth Division rushed in from the Ogaden, the Sixth Division from Tigray and 17,000 new recruits. It decided to withdraw from positions it was no longer able to hold without suffering unacceptable losses at Barentu, Tessenai and Ali Ghidir.

The EPLA forces moved out in an orderly fashion on August 24, taking with them thirteen T-55 tanks, twelve artillery pieces and several captured armored cars.[104] Another source puts the artillery at twenty-one batteries of 122mm and 76mm guns.[105] In the battles for Barentu, the EPLF claimed to have put out of action 11,250 Ethiopian soldiers, mostly battle hardened veterans, including hundreds of officers. Their own losses were four tanks, two armored cars and seven military vehicles.[106] The Eritrean armor was clearly inadequate to deal with the threat posed by a new mechanized Ethiopian division equipped with the more heavily armed T-62 tanks. Unconfirmed Ethiopian sources claim that Eritrean casualties were 4,000—the highest ever. An independent estimate based on frontline assessment and inspections of the EPLF's base hospital is that while Eritrean casualties were not this high, they could have been close to 2,000.

Another Ethiopian offensive, named Bahri Negash (Red Sea) started on October 10 along most of the frontlines and lasted until October 25.[107] It involved sixty planes and thirty helicopter gunships; for the first time, airborne units were dropped behind EPLF lines in the northeast Sahel.[108] Having signally failed in its declared objective, the capture of Nacfa, "within five days," the Dergue commenced a second phase on November 9, concentrating on Nacfa for three days. Its forces tried to scale the Denden escarpment, and in this and other unsuccessful sorties, had 4,500 men put out of action in the first eight days of fighting. A third phase began on the Anseba front and ran for two weeks. No positional gains were made and 15,000 men were killed, wounded or captured.

The EPLF continued to operate behind enemy lines. On October 17, a garrison at Ghinda on the Asmara-Massawa road, was overrun; while on January 14, 1986, a special commando unit, armed with rocket-propelled grenade launchers and hand grenades, penetrated Asmara airport (the Dergue's second largest after Debre Zeit near Addis Ababa) destroyed over forty aircraft and set on fire the ammunition and fuel depots.[109] It is ironic to note that, following the successful EPLA attack on the base in May 1984, strengthening of the defenses and fortifications had been carried out on the personal instructions of Mengistu.

In March 1986, there was an indication of the increased Soviet presence in Eritrea, when four advisers were killed or wounded when their vehicle was destroyed by a land mine on the Asmara-Mendefera road.[110] There were reports that an additional 5,000 Soviet technicians and pilots had arrived in Asmara to supplement the 1,500-2,000 already in the country.[111] However, one must note that the Central Intelligence Agency is of the opinion that the Soviets had reduced the number of their advisers from 2,600 in 1979 to 1,700 in 1986.[112] In May, EPLA artillery units bombarded Ethiopian positions in and around Massawa, destroying fuel tanks and tankers; the EPLA also blockaded the Massawa to Asmara road.[113] Morale remained low among Ethiopian forces and the Twenty-first Division was withdrawn, leaving the entire northeastern coast once more under the control of the EPLF.[114] To commemorate the Twenty-fifth anniversary of the armed struggle, special EPLF commando forces destroyed a number of aircraft and a considerable quantity of fuel and ammunition in another attack on the Asmara airbase. The Ethiopian garrison at Om Hager was overrun in late 1986 and the beginning of 1987 saw an Ethiopian transport plane crash just outside Asmara airport with the loss of 54 military personnel.[115]

In line with the new strategy adopted at the Second Congress of the EPLF, and taking advantage of the Ethiopian failure to raise conscript battalions of sufficient battle worthy state, the EPLA began to make significant military advances. Among the key strategists were Negash Tesfatsion, deputy commander of EPLF training and Abdullah Adam, commander of the Halhal Front.[116] Regional commanders were allowed more initiative in planning attacks. This strategy began to pay off immediately. In the first six months of 1987, the EPLA engaged the Ethiopians eighty-four times throughout most of the country and put over 4,300 troops out of action. Moreover, 900 soldiers defected. The most significant action in this period was an assault on a convoy travelling between Asmara and Keren, in which eighteen trucks were destroyed. This was the first EPLA military action on the highway since 1979.[117]

In August, action continued across the Ethiopian trenches that stretched from Weki to Taba Belewi—some twelve miles west of Asmara.[118] The next month, EPLA units attacked Ethiopian forces in southern and western Eritrea and on the left flank of the Nacfa front; the Ethiopian High Command in Asmara put all its forces on full alert.[119] October saw the continuation of the offensive with regular, regional and militia forces combining in major attacks less than eighteen miles from Asmara. A communications facility was destroyed in Asmara on October 17.[120] Later that month, a convoy of thirty-four trucks (three of which contained fuel, ammunition and bombs, the rest food) was burned on the Asmara-Decamare road.[121] In early December, a surprise EPLA attack on the Nacfa Front destroyed the Fifty-first and Forty-ninth Brigades of the Twenty-second Division and the Third Brigade of the Fifteenth Division. Ten officers were captured; Maj. General Regassa Jimma, one of the few Oromo Workers Party of Ethiopia Central Committee members, was executed by Mengistu after this failure, as was General Tariku Yayene, commander of the Nadew (Nacfa) front.[122] General Kebede Begashaw of the Mekit Command was relieved of his duties.

Mengistu visited Eritrea in mid-February, shortly before his army suffered a stunning setback. On March 17 began the most comprehensive defeat of a colonial army since the French failure at Dien Bien Phu, Vietnam in 1954. Afabet, which since 1979 had been the center of Ethiopian Army intelligence, site of the strategic army reserve and supply depot, fell to the EPLA on March 19. That the war was becoming a test of intelligence capability was shown by the fact that the EPLA destroyed the Ethiopian command and control center before beginning its offensive. The Fourteenth, Nineteenth and Twenty-first Infantry Divisions and Twenty-ninth Mechanized Brigade were destroyed. Lt. Col. Afeworki Wassae, political commissar for the north and three Soviet Officers were captured, along with fifty tanks, a number of Stalin Organs and a large quantity of heavy weapons. On March 25, the Ethiopians pulled out of Tessenai, Ali Ghidir and Haicota; on March 31, Barentu, and on April 2, Agordat. On April 1, the Hal-hal front was destroyed, completing the liquidation of a front that had stood for ten years.[123] The Ethiopians had a total of 30,000 troops in Eritrea; for the first time the EPLA surpassed them in firepower.

One of the most intriguing aspects was that during this unprecedented activity, all EPLF senior commanders were also involved in the first general staff training course which was planned to last well into 1988. EPLA marine and naval comman-dos attacked the oil refinery at Assab on April 23. EPLA units took Mount Lalmba, a mere four miles from Keren, from where they could train their cannon on the city.[124] The supply depot was hit and burned for two days.[125] The Dergue put all public services on a war footing, reinstated martial law, drafted in seven new divisions (four from the Ogaden which had not fought for ten years and were the worst in Ethiopia) and frantically pressganged teenaged boys in nightly roundups known as *affassa*. Paramilitary forces referred to as the revolutionary guards were called up for combat for the first time as were civilian members of the Workers Party.[126] Mengistu assigned General Tesfay Gebre Kidan, former minister of defense and a Politburo member, to lead operations in Eritrea.[127] Twelve divisions were in Eritrea; the best paratroop and commando troops were used in May in an unsuccessful attempt to reopen the Felket and Azahara passes.

Fierce fighting continued in 1989; a major feature being com-bined operations with the TPLF and, for the first time for ten years, the ALF. In January, in the major tank battle of the war, some thirty-seven Ethiopian tanks were lost on the plains of Semenawi Bahri. EPLF/TPLF units destroyed three divisions at Enda Selassie; as a result of these losses, the Ethiopians withdrew all military forces and as many WPE cadres as they could into the town of Mai Chew on the border with Wollo province. General Addis Belachew, commander of 604 Task Force was killed and his deputy, General Berta Gomoraw captured. The EPLF continued to press Ethiopians on the road to Asmara and cleared out units in the Adi Quala area. EPLF and ALF forces entered Wollo and put a number of aircraft out of action on a state farm.[128]

The Eritrean conflict has already cost Ethiopia and Eritrea many tens of thousands of casualties and insures that the economies of both countries remain among the least developed in the world. Throughout the past fifteen years, the Eritreans have made repeated overtures to the Dergue for a negotiated peace. On a number of occasions, there have been lengthy meetings, all of which have been unsuccessful.

The Dergue reported in January 1975 that it had talked with "representatives of the people who wanted to contact the insurgents."[129] Later, the Ethiopians claimed that the real aim of these elders was to promote unity among the "bandits."[130] The first direct discussions between the Dergue and the EPLF were held at the end of 1977 in Berlin under the chairmanship of the German Democratic Republic. At that time, the Dergue held only five towns in Eritrea, and was clearly using the talks as a means of gaining time to make preparations for a major offensive; once ready, it broke off talks.

In 1980, the EPLF made proposals for an internationally sponsored referendum to try and reach a lasting peaceful resolution of the conflict. Voters would have three choices: full independence; federal association with Ethiopia; or regional autonomy. Even through the latter is in line with the Ethiopian government's own program of April 1976, the Dergue ignored the proposals and launched the Red Star campaign in early 1982. When this failed, the Dergue and the EPLF held a series of ten secret meetings, lasting from September 1982 until April 1985. These ended in failure when the Dergue refused to allow an independent third party into the talks, or to acknowledge publicly that peace talks were taking place.[131] In June 1989, the government,

shaken by the death or defection of most of the senior commanders of the defense forces, announced that it was prepared to hold
talks with the rebels in Eritrea and Tigray under a neutral chairman "without preconditions"—but at the same time would not
tolerate "talk of secession." Neither the EPLF nor the TPLF were
prepared to talk upon these conditions. In late 1989 serious talks
between the Ethiopians and Eritreans finally got underway under
the auspices of President Jimmy Carter.

For many years it was difficult to see an imminent end to the
conflict. No matter how many men and arms the Dergue threw
into Eritrea, it was unable to defeat the Eritreans. In the 1985
offensive, the Ethiopians employed new tactics—the use of surprise attacks by airborne and mechanized units. The disadvantage
of this from an Ethiopian point of view is not only that it failed,
but that in the process the Ethiopian army lost many of its most
highly trained and effective troops and thereafter was not able to
mount major offensives.

Eritrea has become a veritable graveyard of military reputations. Lt. General Debebe Haile Mariam, governor of Eritrea from
1970-1974, was executed by the Dergue in late November 1974
for counterrevolutionary activities and treason. General Aman, an
Eritrean and first head of post-imperial Ethiopia, also died in
November 1974 while fighting an execution squad sent by Mengistu. Had he not insisted on a negotiated end to the war in Eritrea
he would not have lost his life.[132] General Teferi Bante, commanded the Second Division at the time of the 1974 coup; he was
executed in February 1977 "for plotting with the ELF." [133] Brigadier Getachew Nadew succeeded Teferi as commander of the
Second Division; he was executed in 1976 "for hoarding."[134]
Teferi and Getachew were both made scapegoats for the failure of
military offensives in Eritrea. And in October 1985, another
former governor of Eritrea, Dawit Wolde Giorgis—who subsequently held a number of high-ranking positions, including that of
commissioner of relief and rehabilitation during the 1984-1985
famine—fell foul of Mengistu and was forced to defect. During

the abortive coup of May 1989, virtually all senior commanders stationed in Eritrea rose against the government. This held for those in the conventional military hierarchy, the officers in charge of political indoctrination and those in the parallel security and intelligence command. After the failure of the coup, they were imprisoned or executed and their places taken by political appointees, many of whom have little or no military experience.

The Eritreans not only have the ability to defend their continually expanding base area, but also to confound observers with their devastating surprise attacks on enemy positions and garrisons deep behind the Ethiopian lines. It is clear that one of the EPLA's greatest advantages lies in its ability to convert its frontline battalions into highly mobile units which can stiffen local militia or commando units and overrun Ethiopian garrisons throughout the country. Even with nearly 400,000 men under arms, Ethiopia lacks the ability to take territory from the Eritreans and impose a military solution in Eritrea. The chances of an Ethiopian victory have never been high; as the war enters its thirtieth year, the possibility of victory for the Eritrean forces becomes more likely.

While the Ethiopian regime looks even less secure than it did in 1974, the EPLF has not only maintained its infrastructure and army, but has extended its dominance of Eritrean politics to all areas. For all intents and purposes the EPLF is the only effective Eritrean opposition to the Dergue and commands the loyalty of the majority of Eritreans who have remained in the country. As has been the case with Switzerland and Israel, Eritrea has shown that in a multiethnic or diverse country, one way to achieve national cohesion is to have a citizens' army; all people unite under one system, one command and one objective.[135]

For as long as the Soviets continue to resupply Mengistu and train the yearly intake of conscripts (and the West continues to feed these soldiers) Ethiopia will continue to mount offensives against the Eritreans and continue to ravage the country. The key to the future of the region lies not in the viability or desirability of the constitution of the People's Democratic Republic of Ethiopia, but in the extent to which the party has entrenched itself in the Ethiopian military and in the survival of Mengistu. The removal of Mengistu from power could cause a greater upheaval in Ethiopian society than that caused by the overthrow of the emperor. The party has few deep seated roots among civilians and the rule of the Dergue is generally unpopular.[136] Not only are civil liberties almost nonexistent, but the economy—and in particular, the agricultural sector—is in a much worse state than it was in 1974. The campaigns in Eritrea and Tigray consume some two-thirds of the budget.[137] The major cause of the devastating famine of 1984-1985 was a drastic decline in agricultural productivity. The drafting into the army of 50,000 young men, mainly peasant farmers, every year since 1982 has been a major cause of this decline. The army's scorched earth policies, carried out in the north of the country regularly since 1974, has also been a major cause of famine. This topic is dealt with in detail in the next two chapters.

Ethiopia also faces more determined regional conflicts than it did in the early years of the Dergue; it appears that the government's deliberate policy is to depopulate the northern provinces and so deprive the guerrilla "fish" of the waters in which they swim. But the wars seem likely to continue for some time to come; the EPLF, TPLF, OLF and the other armed resistance groups have no difficulty in attracting high caliber recruits, who are quickly transformed into highly disciplined and effective fighters—often after training with the EPLF. The Eritreans in particular show an ability to wage guerrilla war which matches the achievements of the Chinese Red Army and the Vietnamese, and surpasses that of the liberation fighters of Mozambique, Algeria, Guinea-Bissau or Zimbabwe. As far as conventional fighting is concerned, they can be compared only to the Israelis of the 1967 and 1973 campaigns for morale, improvisation and dedication.

There is a marked lack of sustained media interest in the war in Eritrea. One reason lies in the shared belief of the two superpowers (and reporters living in these countries) that, leaving aside the wishes of the inhabitants, Ethiopia is somehow entitled to rule Eritrea. It is becoming clear, however, that the bulk of Ethiopian opposition—Amhara as well as the subject nationalities—sees the crucial importance of the military campaign in Eritrea to their own struggles. The twenty-nine year conflict has already taken the lives and destroyed the reputations of many military leaders. The hope of some members of the democratic opposition, which is forming in Ethiopia and abroad, is that the Dergue will continue to lose the struggle in Eritrea, and that another military coup will pave the way for an introduction of democracy to Ethiopia. The Ethiopian Free Soldiers Movement and the EPLF fostered relations and the movement grew very rapidly.[138] The history of many conflicts shows that a number of nationalist movements have gained their objectives in armed struggle with enemies who possess overwhelming military superiority. Many have succeeded in winning the war on the enemy's home front.[139]

Over the last twenty-nine years, the Ethiopians at one time or another have lost control of all urban areas in Eritrea, with the exception of the capital Asmara and the port city of Assab in the south. On occasions, the EPLA has occupied parts of Asmara; it has also shown its ability to penetrate Ethiopian defenses and inflict considerable damage on the Ethiopian military presence wherever it is situated. The Ethiopians are under siege in the second largest city, Keren, and also have large garrisons in several of the other major towns. Through successive waves of conscription and enormous arms transfers from the Soviet Union, Ethiopia has created the largest standing army in Africa; yet it has been unable to defeat the EPLF. And in 1990, the EPLA captured Massawa, destroying most of Ethiopia's navy.

The Dergue's lack of success in repeated actions in Eritrea is common knowledge in Ethiopia, in spite of a virtual absence of coverage in the media which is completely government-controlled. Reports circulated by wounded men and deserters, and the rare demonstrations, have led to a sharp decline in support among civilians, dissensions among the Dergue and a considerable attrition of morale among the military rank and file. The Eritreans, who have done so much to defeat the Dergue and borne so many casualties, will be the major beneficiaries of a change of government in Addis Ababa. Since 1986, there have been an even larger number of senior defections from the Dergue; two of the most notable being Ammanuel Amde Michael, one of the four vice presidents of Ethiopia and Amare Tekle, one of five most senior Eritrean public servants in Ethiopia. Although the Ethiopian government has recently made vague pronouncements that it intends to liberalize both political and economic life in the country, its ability to withstand many more military failures must be in doubt.

Notes

1. Edward Gibbon, *The History of the Decline and Fall of the Roman Empire*, Vol. 1 (first published in 1776) (London, Folio Books, 1983) p. 31.
2. Eritrean Liberation Front, *The Eritrean Revolution* (Beirut, ELF Information Centre, 1977) p. 36.
3. Tekie Fessehatzion, 'The International Dimensions of the Eritrean Question,' *Horn of Africa*, 6, 2, (1983) p. 19.
4. Robert Machida, *Eritrea: the Struggle for Independence* (Trenton NJ, Red Sea Press, 1987) p. 40.
5. Eritrean Liberation Front, *The Struggle of Eritrea* (Damascus, Eritrean Liberation Front, n.d.) p. 72.
6. Christopher Clapham, 'Ethiopia and Somalia,' *Conflicts in Africa* (London, International Institute of Strategic Studies, 1972) p. 10.
7. Gaim Kibreab, *Refugees and Development in Africa* (Trenton NJ, Red Sea Press, 1987) pp. 16-7.
8. Eritrean People's Liberation Front, *Political Report and National Democratic Programme* (1987) p. 24.
9. Eritrean Liberation Front, 'The Eritrean Revolution,' p. 43.
10. Lloyd Ellingson, 'Review of *The Struggle Over Eritrea*,' Haggai Erlich, *Northeast African Studies*, 8, 1 (1986) p. 66; Haggai Erlich, *The Struggle Over Eritrea 1962-1978* (Stanford, Hoover Institution Press, 1983) p. 23.
11. Eritrean People's Liberation Front, 'Political Report' p. 35.
12. Clapham, 'Ethiopia and Somalia,' p. 9.
13. Gaim Kibreab, 'Refugees and Development,' pp. 17-9.
14. Richard Lobban, *Eritrean Liberation Front: A Close-Up View*, Munger Africana Library Notes, 13 (1972) p. 17.
15. Jack Kramer, 'Hidden War in Eritrea,' *Venture*, 21, 5 (1969) p. 20.
16. Kramer, 'Hidden War in Eritrea,' pp. 21-2.

17. John Franklin Campbell, 'Rumblings along the Red Sea: the Eritrean Question,' *Foreign Affairs*, April (1970) p. 545.
18. Dawit Wolde Giorgis, *Personal Communication* (1987).
19. Erlich, 'The Struggle Over Eritrea,' pp. 37-8.
20. Jack Kramer, 'Africa's Hidden War,' *Evergreen Review*, 94, December (1971) p. 63.
21. Mordechai Abir, 'Red Sea Politics,' *Conflicts in Africa* (London, International Institute of Strategic Studies, 1972) p. 32.
22. Bowyer J. Bell, 'Endemic Insurgency and International Order,' *Orbis*, XVIII, 2 (1974) p. 439.
23. Mordechai Abir, *Oil, Power and Political Conflict in Arabia, the Red Sea and the Gulf* (London, Frank Cass, 1974) p. 175.
24. Bereket Habte Selassie, *Conflict and Intervention in the Horn of Africa* (New York, Monthly Review Press, 1980) pp. 188-9.
25. *Vanguard*, 11, 1, February-March (1977) pp. 15-6.
26. Dessalegn Rahmato, *Agrarian Reform in Ethiopia* (Trenton NJ, Red Sea Press, 1985) p. 68.
27. Lionel Cliffe, 'The Eritrean Liberation Struggle in Comparative Perspective,' eds. Lionel Cliffe and Basil Davidson, *The Long Struggle of Eritrea for Independence and Constructive Peace* (Nottingham, Spokesman, 1988) p. 92.
28. James Firebrace (with Stuart Holland), *Never Kneel Down: Drought Development and Liberation in Eritrea* (Trenton NJ, Red Sea Press, 1985) pp. 51-2.
29. Isaias Afwerki, 'Press Conference,' *Eritrea Information*, 9, 3, (1987) pp. 8-14; 9, 4 (1987) pp. 3-8.
30. Paul B. Henze 'Arming the Horn 1960-1980: Military Expenditure, Arms, Imports and Military Aid in Ethiopia, Kenya, Somalia and Sudan, with Statistics on Economic Growth and Governmental Expenditures,' ed. Sven Rubenson, *Proceedings of the Seventh International Conference of Ethiopian Studies* (Addis Ababa, Institute of Ethiopian Studies, 1984) p. 655.
31. Cliffe, 'The Eritrean Liberation Struggle,' p. 89.
32. *Adulis*, III, 5 (1986).
33. Dawit Wolde Giorgis, *Red Tears: War, Famine and Revolution in Ethiopia* (Trenton NJ, Red Sea Press, 1989) p. 113.
34. *Indian Ocean Newsletter*, 277, April 11 (1987).
35. Firebrace, 'Never Kneel Down,' p. 43.
36. Isaias Afwerki, 'Press Conference.'
37. Isaias Afwerki, *Interview*, December 12 (1987).
38. Richard Leonard, 'Popular Participation in Liberation and Revolution,' eds. Lionel Cliffe and Basil Davidson, *The Long Struggle of Eritrea for Independence and Constructive Peace* (Nottingham, Spokesman, 1988) p. 117.
39. Leonard, 'Popular Participation,' p. 111.
40. Roy Pateman, 'Eritrea's Struggle for Independence,' *Current Affairs Bulletin*, 60, 11 (1984) p. 28.
41. Carl von Clausewitz, ed. Anatol Rapoport, *On War* (Harmondsworth, Penguin Books, 1968) p. 259.

154 • ERITREA: EVEN THE STONES ARE BURNING

42. Robert D. Kaplan, *Surrender or Starve: the Wars behind the Famine* (Boulder CO, Westview, 1988) p. 71.
43. *Ethiopian Herald,* August 21 (1976).
44. *Ethiopian Herald,* October 6 (1979); December 24 (1980).
45. Haggai Erlich, *Ethiopia and the Challenge of Independence* (Boulder CO, Lynne Rienner, 1986) p. 217.
46. *Ethiopian Herald,* July 13 (1977).
47. Jeffrey A. Lefebvre, 'Donor Dependency and African Arms Transfers to the Horn of Africa: the F5 Legacy,' *The Journal of Modern African Studies,* 25, 3 (1987) pp. 472-3.
48. Robert A. Diamond and David Fouquet, 'American Military Aid to Ethiopia—and Eritrean Insurgency,' *Africa Today,* 19, 1 (1972) p. 41.
49. Georgie Anne Geyer, 'Eritrea—a Name to Remember,' *The Progressive,* June (1970) p. 25.
50. Dawit Wolde Giorgis, 'Red Tears,' p. 47.
51. Michael Brzoska, 'Arms Transfer Data Sources,' *Journal of Conflict Resolution,* 26, 1 (1982) p. 77.
52. *Sudan News Agency,* April 16 (1978).
53. John Keegan, *World Armies* (Michigan, Gale Research, 1983) p. 179.
54. Richard Greenfield, *Ethiopia. A New Political History* (London, Pall Mall, 1965) pp. 375-418.
55. Dawit Wolde Giorgis, 'Red Tears,' p. 38.
56. *Eritrea Information,* II, 11, December (1980).
57. *Liberation,* August-September (1981).
58. *Liberation,* November-December (1981).
59. *Liberation,* January-April (1982).
60. *Eritrea Bulletin,* December 15 (1983).
61. Dawit Wolde Giorgis, 'Red Tears,' p. 358.
62. Mengesha Areda, *Interview,* July 21 (1985).
63. *Adulis,* III, 2 (1986).
64. Eritrean Relief Association, *Informational Bulletin* 18 (1986).
65. *Adulis,* III, 11 (1986).
66. David Pool, *Eritrea: Africa's Longest War* (London, Anti-Slavery Society, 1982) p. 46.
67. Geoffrey Morrison, *Eritrea and the Southern Sudan. Aspects of Some Wider African Problems* (London, Minority Rights Group, 1976) p. 6.
68. Gaim Kibreab, 'Refugees and Development,' p. 20.
69. Richard Sherman, *Eritrea: the Unfinished Revolution* (New York, Praeger, 1980) pp. 80-1.
70. Bell, 'Endemic Insurgency,' p. 442.
71. Eritrean Liberation Front/Popular Liberation Front, *Communique,* November 28 (1973).
72. Machida, 'Eritrea,' p. 59.
73. *Ethiopian Herald,* July 28 (1976).
74. *Vanguard,* 1, 13, January (1976). 12.
75. Machida, 'Eritrea,' p. 66.
76. Peter Robbs, 'Battle for the Red Sea,' *Africa Report,* March-April (1975) p. 15.

The Eritrean People's Liberation Army • 155

77. Lloyd Ellingson, 'The Origins of the Eritrean Liberation Movement,' ed. R.L. Hess, *Proceedings of the 5th International Conference of Ethiopian Studies* (Session B) (Chicago, University of Illinois Press, 1979) p. 624.
78. Linda Heiden, 'The Eritrean Struggle for Independence,' *Monthly Review,* 30 (1978) p. 13.
79. Edward Hoagland, *African Calliope: A Journey to the Sudan* (New York, Penguin, 1984) p. 150.
80. Mesfin Gabriel, *New African,* April (1978) pp. 23-4.
81. *Horn of Africa,* 'Eritrea: War and Drought,' 4, 1 (1981) p. 22.
82. Firebrace, 'Never Kneel Down,' p. 54.
83. EPLF, 'Political Report,' p. 115.
84. Frits N. Eisenloeffel, 'With the EPLF in Barka,' *Eritrea Information,* 3, 2 (1981) p. 7.
85. *Eritrea Information,* 3, 5 May-June (1981).
86. *Eritrea Information,* 3, 7 (1981).
87. *Liberation,* November-December (1981).
88. *Eritrea Information,* 3, 10 (1981).
89. Christian Sabatier, 'Interview,' *Eritrea Information,* 4, 2 (1982) p. 5.
90. Lord Avebury, 'Question, The Horn of Africa: Policy,' *House of Lords Official Report,* 431, 98 (1982) p. 8; Dawit Wolde Giorgis, 'Red Tears,' p. 108.
91. *Liberation,* January-April (1982) p. 33.
92. Dawit Wolde Giorgis, *Personal Communication* (1987).
93. Sabatier, 'Interview,' pp. 3-6.
94. Keegan, 'World Armies,' p. 177.
95. *Eritrea Information,* 5 (1981).
96. *Eritrea Information,* 5, 5 (1983).
97. Frits N. Eisenloeffel and Inge Rönnbäck, *The Eritrean Durrah Odyssey: 1983* (Utrecht, Dutch Interchurch Aid, 1983) pp. 50-1.
98. *Resistance,* III, 6 (1983) p. 23.
99. Isaias Afwerki, *Press Conference* (Rome, 1984) January 18.
100. *Eritrea Information,* 6, 2 (1984).
101. Firebrace, 'Never Kneel Down,' pp. 57-8.
102. Kaplan, 'Surrender or Starve,' pp. 79-80.
103. *Africa Events,* I, 11 (1985).
104. *Adulis,* III, 5 (1986).
105. *Eritrea Information,* 7, 7 (1985).
106. *Adulis,* III, 1 (1986).
107. Eritrean People's Liberation Front, Central Bureau, *Communique,* October 21 (1985).
108. *Adulis,* III, 1 (1986).
109. Eritrean People's Liberation Front, *Press Release* January 16 (1986).
110. *Adulis,* III, 4 (1986).
111. *Adulis,* III, 7 (1986).
112. *Indian Ocean Newsletter,* 347 (1988).
113. *Adulis,* III, 6 (1986).
114. *Adulis,* III, 8-9 (1986).
115. *New York Times,* January 14 (1987).
116. Carol Berger, 'Eritrea: the Longest War,' *Africa Report,* 32, 2 (1987) p. 32.

117. Eritrean People's Liberation Front, General Staff. *Military Communique,* July 3 (1987).
118. Eritrean People's Liberation Front, Foreign Relations. *Military Communique,* August 31 (1987).
119. Eritrean People's Liberation Front, Foreign Relations, *Military Communique,* September 15 (1987).
120. Eritrean People's Liberation Front, *Press Release.* October 22 (1987).
121. Eritrean People's Liberation Front, *Press Release,* October 26 (1987).
122. *Adulis,* V. 3 (1988).
123. *Adulis,* V. 4 (1988).
124. *Adulis,* V, 4 (1988).
125. Eritrean People's Liberation Front, *Press Release,* April 4 (1988).
126. *Adulis,* V, 9 (1988).
127. Dawit Wolde Giorgis, 'Red Tears,' p. 367.
128. *Indian Ocean Newsletter.* 369, February 11 (1989); 371, February 25 (1989).
129. *Ethiopian Herald,* January 7 (1975).
130. *Ethiopian Herald,* September 3 (1975).
131. *Adulis,* III, 1 (1986).
132. Bereket Habte Selassie, 'Conflict and Intervention', p. x.
133. *Ethiopian Herald,* February 4 (1977).
134. *Ethiopian Herald,* July 13 (1976).
135. Talukder Maniruzzaman, *Military Withdrawal from Politics: A Comparative Study* (Cambridge Mass, Ballinger, 1987) p. 124.
136. Paul B. Henze, *Encounter,* June (1986) pp. 5-17.
137. Dawit Wolde Giorgis, 'Personal Communication' (1986).
138. *Adulis,* V, 10 (1988).
139. Andrew Mack, 'Why Big Nations Lose Small Wars: the Politics of Asymmetric Conflict,' *World Politics,* 27, 2 (1974) p. 184.

8

The Impact of Land Reform

Property should be defended...even an inch shall never be surrendered.

—AMBAYE ZEKARIAS, *Land Tenure in Eritrea*[1]

The passionate attachment of Eritrea's peasants and nomads to the land is legendary. Some eighty percent of all Eritreans live in rural areas. Disputes over land ownership have been a recurrent theme in Eritrean history.

Ancient systems of land holding have contributed greatly to the underdevelopment of the country. In the settled areas of the central plateau, there are three main systems of land tenure. They include: *tsilmi* (family); *diesa* or *shehena* (communal) and *domeniale* (government).[2] In the nineteenth century, before the Italian conquest, the Tigrinya speakers on the central plateau were organized into some 800 villages.[3]

Under *tsilmi* ownership, the major form of land tenure in highland Eritrea before 1952, land was held freehold and was handed down either from father to sons or through the family and kinship (*enda*) structure.[4] The first form was more common in Seraye, Hamasien and around Keren.[5] As the average holding was only five acres in size, and the land usually of poor quality due to the ravages of drought, and the lack of fertilizers and good seed, such fragmentation inevitably lead to reduced production. As a result, many families did not produce enough to feed themselves. Under the *tsilmi* tenure system, large sections of the population (including virtually all women) were excluded from land ownership and, therefore, participation in the administration of their communities; they were kept in a permanent state of insecurity and economic dependence.[6] All transactions of sale, lease and mortgage were based solely on oral tradition and no deeds existed.[7]

Collective ownership is possibly the oldest institution throughout the highland villages; under *diesa* tenure in Hamasien and Seraye Provinces or *shehena* tenure in Akele-Guzai Province, every married man who could establish his right of residence in the community was entitled to an equal share of land (*gibri*). Generally, daughters were not allowed to share land except on humanitarian grounds, while immigrants may have waited forty years before being admitted into membership.[8] Married women shared with their husbands while widows, older unmarried women and orphans were also entitled to half a share. It was possible for young married couples waiting for their share to rent the land.[9] Land should be redistributed every five or seven years; for a number of decades, however, this practice fell into disuse.

Because of incessant, disruptive disputes that arose as a result of failings of the family land tenure system, the Italian administration attempted by decree to convert *tslimi* holdings into *diesa*.[10] But, in spite of this declared policy, it was almost impossible for a small peasant to increase his holding to allow for the needs of a growing family. During the Italian, British and imperial Ethiopian occupations, feudal landlords increased their holdings; as a consequence, some forty percent of families in a village may have become landless.[11] Moreover, large landowners, retired officials, army officers and clergy were given the right, by the emperor, to appropriate any surplus produce from the peasants.

Land held under *domeniale* tenure was land alienated by the Italian government through laws enacted in 1909 and 1926. Some of it was land that had been occupied and claimed by Ethiopian armies on their temporary raids into Eritrea in the nineteenth century.[12] By 1907, some 27,301 acres had been expropriated (including over 5,000 acres held by the Bezien Monastery) and granted as concessions to Italian citizens. Before the Italian occupation of Eritrea, the Ethiopian Orthodox Church owned significant tracts of land, acquired through grants made by kings and rulers and also donated by highland peasants, most of whom were adherents of the church; some of it was rented to local peasants.[13] The most significant landholder was the Bezien Monastery, founded near present-day Asmara between 1350-1360 by Filipos of Sera. Land was given to Father Filipos by Dawit in 1407; further grants were given by Zara Yaqob in 1433-1468, and by Galawdewos after 1546.[14] There are also other forms of land tenure and several forms of leasing.[15]

In the western lowlands and the northern coast as far down as Massawa, where Beni Amir pastoralists predominate, each kinship group held the land collectively.[16] Most of their lands, as well as the lands of the Saho and Afar pastoralists in the Danakil, were claimed as state property by the Italian government. The settled agriculturalists of the western lowlands, the Kunama and Baria peoples, held land collectively before the Italian conquest; they were then forced to accept a system of chiefs.[17]

Under the 1909 statute, all land held under traditional systems of tenure, and land left fallow for more than three years, reverted to the state. This state property eventually comprised at least one half of Eritrea, including over 3.7 million acres of wood and forest, as well as vast areas of fertile arable and pasture land.[18] The British and Ethiopian administrations increased the amount of *domeniale* land and gave some—either freehold or leasehold (usufruct)—as a reward for Eritrean collaborators. From 1946 onwards, some of this land was sold back to the villages or individuals, but was the cause of endless disputes.[19]

From 1962-1974, the emperor (in theory at least) owned all land in Eritrea. The position remained the same as in the days of Italian colonization. A group of Eritrean elders declared: "The statement that the land belongs to the government is made in order to affirm that the earth belongs to the king in the same way as the heavens belong to God. We allude to this statement when we wish to enhance the power of the government, but we do not thereby intend to refer to the ownership of the fields.... No one can take away our lands."[20]

It will be seen from the above brief description of systems of land tenure in Eritrea, that there are some significant differences between Eritrea and Ethiopia; note that the major work on land tenure in Ethiopia which covers the period until 1974 does not mention Eritrea at all.[21]

After such a history of oppressive land tenure. it is not surprising to find that poor peasants—i.e., those who farm less than eight *tsimdi* (approximately five acres) of land and who own at most one ox—form sixty percent of the rural population, and own less than ten percent of the land. Middle peasants are those who own at least eight *tsimdi* of land, a pair of oxen and some domestic animals. Rich peasants form twelve percent of the population and own forty percent of the land; these are defined as those who own at least eight *tsimdi* and two pair of oxen.[22]

It is not surprising that a major priority of the EPLF lies in land redistribution. However, the EPLF is faced with something of a dilemma in as much as peasant demands are primarily for land redistribution. rather than far-reaching reform of the land holding system which could include the giving of rights to women and newcomers and for cooperative farming.[23] So, before redistributing land, the EPLF attempts to politicize the peasants; cadres from the Department of Public Administration form clandestine cells in the villages (village committees) and carry out a thorough survey of the area, establishing who is a poor, middle or rich peasant. After a period of time ranging from six to twelve months the traditional *enda* administration, headed by village chiefs, is abolished and replaced by overt cells comprising around fifteen particularly receptive peasants, and armed militias. The cells (challenge or resistance committees) are controlled by poor and middle peasants. Training is given to the villagers by the Education Department of the EPLF. This includes: instruction on the aims of the EPLF; the nature of the class struggle and the meaning of land redistribution and cooperative farming. Adult literacy campaigns are commenced. Since 1981, resistance committees consisting of four to five members have been formed in areas recently liberated from Ethiopia.[24]

The third stage of EPLF village development is known as the People's Assembly; the liberated village of Janni took six years to reach this stage.[25] In plenary sessions of all villagers, an executive committee is elected for a six-month term. If a proposed candidate faces strong and determined opposition, he or she will be prevented from running for election, to ensure that the committee is acceptable to all villagers. This follows a long tradition of consensus democracy in Africa.[26] The ballot, however, is secret. Assemblies are divided into units, each unit being led by a *kom*.[27] All land is placed in the hands of the people's assembly and redistributed to all adult, married men and women. In pre-revolutionary Eritrea, women did not usually own land; women now play an increasing role in all parts of the EPLF and are "gradually liberating themselves from three oppressors—landlords, men and the church or mosque."[28] There are also people's assemblies at district and town level.[29] In 1988, six percent of Eritrea's villages had an EPLF people's assembly; thirty-two percent had challenge committees; forty-seven percent village committees and only fifteen percent had no EPLF infrastructure.[30]

The EPLF began to implement its agrarian policies in 1974. The village of Azen—a few miles north of Asmara, and with a population of 5,000—was under the *diesa* system, and, typically, land had not been redistributed since 1922.[31] Consequently, much of the land had become the *de facto* private property of a few people. The *diesa* system was revived and 1,200 people, including fifty priests, benefited from the redistribution. The Ethiopian Orthodox Church owned most of the land of the neighboring village of Medri-Zen. EPLF pressure caused many monks to side with the villagers and eventually return the land to the *diesa* system.

During the 1976-1981 period, land redistribution took place in 162 Eritrean villages—half of the cases occurring in the first two years; of these, 138, were formerly under *diesa* tenure and twenty-four, *domeniale* tenure.[32] Members of the village militia usually received land adjacent to one another, facilitating the pooling of land, implements, animals and labor into small farming cooperatives; these holdings were used by the EPLF to demonstrate the potential benefits of cooperation to the peasants. The small agricultural town of Afabet was brought under EPLF control in 1977. In this mainly Muslim area, there were many landless peasants and tenant farmers. The newly elected people's assembly, overwhelmingly poor peasants and women, confiscated the land of the largest landlords.

One of the best documented case studies is the village of Zagr, whose population of 300 was divided into three *endas* and operated under the *diesa* system.[33] The EPLF began to organize in Zagr in 1974; a people's assembly was established in 1976. Eventually, the assembly redistributed land to 120 landless peasants, while former *domeniale* land was also shared out. Some fifty people were barred from the process as "undeserving," they were regarded as being either too rich or uncommitted to the revolution. Some fifteen percent of the land, that belonging to absentee landlords and collaborators with the Dergue, was expropriated and worked on a cooperative basis. An attempt was also made to amalgamate fragmented holdings.[34] In September 1978, the villagers were working the land cooperatively; however, by 1979 they were under constant harassment by Ethiopian bombers and the land was left untilled.[35]

The task of the EPLF was complicated by the fact that only under the Italians was some form of land measurement carried out. Between 1942 and 1966, no land surveys were undertaken in Eritrea.[36] Had it not been for determined offensives by the Ethiopian army when the EPLF temporarily lost control of some areas much more redistribution would have occurred. After the military situation had stabilized toward the end of 1981, however, land in the Hazemo area in the southern highlands was redistributed to some 168 landless and poor peasants.[37] In August 1981, it was announced that a people's assembly had been established in the village of Era in Senhit. Land was also distributed to sixty-two landless men and women in the village of Mai-Zila in Akele-Guzai.[38] On December 2, 1981, residents of Afta, a village on the shores of the Red Sea, demanded the implementation of the EPLF land reform measures, while residents of Adi Shekha, a village to the north of Asmara—after training sessions in the EPLF agricultural school in Semenawi Bahri—established a cooperative farm.[39] In January 1982, five communities in Akele-Guzai carried out a redistribution, as a result of which 275 formerly landless peasants received land.[40] By 1987, land reform had been undertaken in a third of Eritrea's villages.[41]

The EPLF's land reform policy is unique in Africa but there are two areas of concern. Firstly, it is not enough for the EPLF to provide services and establish democratic structures, the material lot of the peasants must improve or their support for the EPLF might be jeopardized.[42] Secondly, the pastoralists have been relatively neglected, possibly, it has been suggested, because there is no suitable model for social transformation of such people.[43] Pastoralists have not been very interested in forming a state; what they have felt since the Dergue has destroyed their herds and grazing grounds is lack of access to power. The EPLF could offer an opportunity for them to rechart their lives.[44]

One of the EPLF's main priorities is increased food production. The Agriculture Department clears virgin land for mechanized production and grazes its own herds for breeding, milk and beef production using modern techniques. It also runs an agricultural school and demonstrates improved crop production methods. At the beginning of 1982, the headquarters of the Agricultural Department was moved to the fertile and thinly populated Gash-Setit area of southern Eritrea close to the border with Tigray. In 1983, the main EPLF farm grew between 12,000-15,000 acres of durrah, sesame and chickpeas.[45] Durrah is a grain crop similar to sorghum. The Agriculture Department works closely with ERA.

> We do our utmost to help the peasants improve their livelihood by discarding old methods and the use of modern tools, new seedlings, etc. We have established an extension scheme whereby villagers go for two to three month training. When they go back to their villages they train their neighbors and have refresher courses or call the extension officer. We develop projects with the Agriculture Department experts.[46]

Agricultural production is carried out by the EPLF wherever water can be found. Even in the bombed town of Nacfa, there are some surprisingly healthy cows and flourishing gardens. According to the regional director of the EPLF Agriculture Department, the purpose of this is "to feed ourselves and show the people around what can be done: we grow lettuce, cabbage, peppers, onions, eggplant, melon, cucumbers, etc. Many vegetables can grow here. We have some disease and pest problems. The water is salty which is another problem."[47]

A settlement camp for members of the Hedareb nationality, who had lost all of their livestock, was established by ERA at Mehar in 1985. In 1986, a diversion canal from a seasonal stream was used to irrigate some sixty-nine acres, yielding some thirty-seven tons of sorghum. In 1987, there were plans to expand the area to 100 acres.[48] A lot of effort has been put into the Rora-Habab integrated community development project. Over 500 acres have been terraced; two nurseries have been established to form the basis of a twenty-acre reforestation scheme. A small dam has also been built, together with a four-mile access road.[49]

The most ambitious EPLF project was carried out at the Ali Ghidir 20,250 acre irrigation area. At one time Ali Ghidir was the site of the largest cotton plantation in the Horn of Africa. In 1984, the first year of operation by the EPLF, some 7,500 acres of cereal crops were harvested—almost entirely sorghum. Some 2,300 landless local peasants were given land; in fact, most of the land was given over to be farmed privately in plots ranging from two acres to that sufficient for one family to handle. According to the director of the EPLF Agriculture Department, some 750 acres was farmed collectively by members of the National Union of Eritrean Peasants and 320 acres was set aside for a settlement for refugees from Zohar in the Sudan. The seed was provided on a service cooperative basis by ERA. Some 12,350 acres was planted between May and August 1985, when the area was overrun by the Ethiopian army.[50]

Building upon a more equitable and rational redistribution of land and better food production, the EPLF then encourages and supports villagers in the formation of local shops and consumer cooperatives. These are financed initially through loans and grants from the EPLF and from village income. The EPLF subsidizes transport costs to enable the villagers to attend markets and also trains them in elementary bookkeeping. The aim is to reduce the villagers' exploitation by private traders and money lenders and prevent them from running into debt. Some cooperatives have now become self-financing.

ELF land reform policy was outlined in its policy statement, "Building a Democratic Eritrean Liberation Front," of May 1975. The ELF acknowledged that the country: "cannot over-leap the stage of non-capitalist development" and pledged that: "land ownership in the *Dessa, Risty,* etc...areas shall be democratized and organized for the realization of social justice and greater productivity." Moreover, "the revolutionary state shall settle those sections of the Eritrean population who have been condemned to a life-time of nomadism."[51] However, very little is documented on ELF land reform practice. There are vague references to: "land reform proclamations with full participation of the peasants."[52] Land was confiscated from: "agricultural capitalists, certain religious institutions and other large landholders.... It [ELF] set up farm co-operatives which became quite successful."[53] It is known that during 1977, the ELF controlled Ali Ghidir and reportedly cultivated 4,000 acres of Sorghum there.[54] However, some eye-witnesses paint a different picture; the ELF attempts at land reform in Seraye in 1979 were a "complete failure."[55]

In 1975, all rural land in Ethiopia was placed in the hands of peasant associations; the sale, lease and mortgage of land was prohibited and holdings of more than twenty-five acres in size expropriated without compensation. The law (known as Proclamation 31) applied to Eritrea and the other thirteen provinces of Ethiopia. The destruction of the immense power wielded by private landlords was universally welcomed, but by no means has it ushered in an era of prosperity in the small portion of rural Eritrea controlled by the Dergue. The distribution process excluded oxen and implements; the position of the mass of peasants, who did not own these essential tools of production, has worsened since land reform. Moreover, as each peasant association is faced with a fixed area of land (approximately 2,000 acres) to administer and a growing rural population, fragmentation of holdings has been aggravated further.[56] The area is based on the feudal Ethiopian social institution, the *Golmassa*. Although Article 19 of the proclamation gave peasants in the communal areas of the north rights over the land they tilled, and pastoralists possessory rights over the land they grazed or used for agriculture, Article 20 prohibited land litigation and Article 23 indicated the main purpose of land reform—the inducement and organization of peasants into cooperative or collective farms.[57] Most peasants are aware that the land belongs to the government and not to them.[58]

All peasants—former tenants and owner-occupiers alike—have to pay a multiplicity of taxes, such as land use tax, levied irrespective of the size of the holding. In 1977, this was assessed at seven *birr* but jumped to twenty *birr* in 1978; it climbed to thirty *birr* in 1980 and reached fifty *birr* in 1984.[59] There were approximately two *birr*, the standard Ethiopian currency, to a United States dollar. Agricultural income tax was also payable; initially, this was assessed at ten *birr* for income of 600 *birr* and less per year, and on a progressive scale above this. Peasants also have to make "voluntary" payments in cash and labor to public fund-raising campaigns (such as to aid drought victims, the literacy campaign and the "call to the Motherland" which helped to pay for the government's military activities in Tigray and Eritrea), together with contributions to peasant associations and youth and women's associations. By 1984, taxes had risen to such an extent that farmers were forced to sell livestock in order to satisfy the government.[60] When combined with the time spent at ideological seminars and political meetings, it is not surprising that peasants feel "over burdened and resentful."[61]

The leadership of the government-sponsored peasant associations that exist in the north, including Eritrea, has been taken over fully by the rich peasant class.[62] It has been argued that this is because of the state's need to have access to the maximum amount of agricultural surplus.[63] The peasant associations' executive function consists, in the main, in the carrying out of government directives. Although election of officers should occur every two years, this is not adhered to in practice. Moreover, county and district peasant association officials and political cadres have the major say in the election and removal of officials.[64] The Dergue resists giving peasant associations more autonomy.[65] One reason (but by no means the only one) for the lack of participation in the peasant associations is the persistence of kinship relationships in communities where communal land tenure was practiced. Strong ties between local officials and the community often prevent action against the wealthier members.[66] In a number of instances, a majority of registered members of a peasant association are criminal or antisocial elements from nearby urban areas.[67]

In June 1979, peasant association officials from Ethiopia came to Eritrea "to guide them in ways to flush out separatists."[68] It was admitted that Eritrea's cooperatives faced slow progress and shortcomings through the lack of proper implementation of the government's rural land proclamation. Although the Dergue claimed that large masses of peasants enthusiastically supported its every directive and that the "days of bandits lurking in bushes are numbered," it is evident that it had great difficulty in getting Eritrean peasants to accept leadership positions. Some Soviet writers were less sanguine over the government's ability to overcome the "inescapable psychological barrier" that arises in connection with a seeming contradiction between the 1975 agrarian reform, which gave land to the tillers, and the 1979 plan which took it back from them, and collectivized it under state control.[69] It has also been suggested that forced collectivization may "endanger forever the prospects of a transition to socialism."[70]

As a result of the Dergue's land reform, most peasants have been net losers. Not only has the size of their holdings decreased, but their living conditions have worsened. The reasons for this lack of success are varied. The government has a monopoly on distribution of fertilizer and controls its price.[71] It increased the price so much in the 1974-1978 period that it was beyond the reach of most peasants. Moreover, fertilizer is only available to peasants if they sell their crops to the Agricultural Marketing Corporation (AMC), which is controlled by the state. Peasants are also starved of other farm necessities. For example, seventy percent of seed goes to state farms.[72] The AMC pays peasants much less than the market price; moreover, in a period of acute inflation, such as 1980-1984, it actually decreased prices in real terms.[73] Credit is not available for a producer who wants to expand production. Land reform abolished the traditional money lender, but was not accompanied by the provision of alternative credit sources. The main reason, however, for the disastrous agricultural record has been the imposition of low producer prices, coupled with a spectacularly inefficient marketing system; two-thirds of storage centers are inadequate.[74] And without adequate incentives such as reasonable prices, credit and marketing facilities and cheaper inputs, appreciable and sustained growth in agricultural production is clearly an unrealistic expectation. The very poor performance of agriculture was the main reason for Ethiopia's marked economic decline in the decade ended 1982-1983.[75]

The government has adopted the dubious strategy of attempting to improve agricultural production through the collectivization of peasant holdings. This is in spite of the less than successful record of societies which have adopted the Stalinist model, and clear indications that peasants are in favor of individual holdings.[76] It is unfortunate that Marx's view that the concentration of land into larger holdings would lead to greater efficiency has become the basis of a dogmatic and intolerant agrarian policy.

The tragic consequences of forced collectivization of Soviet agriculture are well known; but this has not prevented the Dergue from replicating the disaster. The analogies with the first twelve years of the Bolshevik revolution are indeed remarkable. One of the reasons for the revolution was the uncertainty caused by constant conflict between small peasants and landless farm laborers on the one hand and landowners and rich peasants (*kulaks*) on the other. As was the case in Russia, the peasants and farm workers' cause was eventually taken up by industrial workers and students. A revolution occurred in both countries and land was distributed to the tiller. In the Soviet Union, rapid urban and industrial growth then occurred; agrarian cooperation was enforced, leading to the liquidation of the peasant class and the establishment of a large scale collectivized system.[77]

The peasant associations are the medium through which the Workers Party ideologues envisage that the transformation of agriculture will be carried out in Ethiopia. Peasant associations are the government's major means of control; they combine the functions of tax collector, policemen and judge and possess wider powers than the landlords of Haile Selassie. In fact, the leadership of the peasant associations is dominated by former landlords or well-to-do peasants, some of whom affect the worst mannerisms of civil service bureaucrats.[78] While peasant associations are in theory responsible for development work, they have so far been inactive in this regard. One of the greatest failures of peasant associations has been that in many cases they have perpetuated the subordinate role of women—they have not distributed land to women and have not allowed the development of effective women's associations.[79]

Official statistics show a growth in agricultural production during the seven year period from 1975-1983 of 5.2 percent. This growth, however, is almost entirely accounted for by increases in output in the peasant sector; yields remained unchanged in the cooperative sector and declined quite sharply in the state sector.[80] These statistics probably mask a real decline in output. Peasant output may not have risen. One source says that since 1980, there has been a sharp decline in some regions.[81] It could well be that a larger proportion of peasants' output, has been sold through the AMC and therefore included in official statistics for the fist time. As service cooperatives acting as agents of AMC purchased more of the peasant sector's marketed output, while private traders were forced to sell part of their purchases to the AMC, the statistics almost certainly reflect an increase in coverage rather than increase in production. Also, Ethiopian statistics should be treated with extreme caution, as the method of collection, as well as the quality of data has deteriorated over the years.[82] Almost all sources agree that the performance of the collectivized sector has been most disappointing.[83] Fassika Sidelil, alternate member of the WPE Politburo and head of its Economic and Social Affairs Department, called for state farms to be run on a cost-effective basis.[84.]

The leadership of the Dergue, however, still places a great deal of emphasis on the 1979 decree which stressed collectivization. Collectivization has, so far, proven ineffective in improving the lot of the peasants. In 1979-1980. mean yields of major crops was 0.5 tons per acre for peasant holdings and only 0.4 tons for cooperative groups.[85] In 1982-1983. there were 94,000 peasant families enrolled in cooperatives—covering 1.9 percent of the total area of Ethiopia under annual crops. There are many fewer producer cooperatives in Eritrea than in any other province. It has been said of producer cooperatives: "labor and land productivity are low, the marketable surplus is small. non-agricultural activities are poorly developed and the rate of accumulation is distressingly modest."[86]

Ethiopia has also established state and settlement farms. In 1982-1983 there were 213 state farms covering 3.6 percent of the area of Ethiopia under annual crops. None of these were in Eritrea. The Dergue's ten-year perspective plan envisaged that by 1993, Eritrea alone would have state farms of 10,000 acres in Sebar Guma, Agordat and Elabored, growing cereals. fruits, vegetables and fiber crops, mainly under irrigation.[87] Plans were underway to use the Ali Ghidir irrigation area as a resettlement farm. State farms in Ethiopia include the few, large, commercial enterprises existing under the emperor, farms created from existing fallow (and usually marginal) land and land expropriated from peasants.[88] They are highly mechanized, large units (covering from 10.000 to 25.000 acres) and all, apart from the farms in the Awash Agricultural Area, operate at a substantial loss, in spite of employing labor under what can be reasonably termed slave conditions. Losses in 1979-1980 amounted to seventeen million *birr* and rose to forty-seven million *birr* in 1980-1981.[89] The main reasons for losses are: low output prices imposed by the government; inadequate management; low productivity on capital and an excessively centralized control structure which requires that even routine decisions have to be referred to a central planning council.[90]

The Dergue faces almost insurmountable contradictions in its attempts to socialize agriculture. State farms are confronted with several conflicts of interest, i.e. between management and workers; management and the central planning council and financial institutions; and between central, provincial and local needs, interests and priorities in both the short and long term. A cautious approach and a democratic organization of the planning mechanism is necessary; there should be bargain and compromise rather than coercion.[91] In Ethiopia, centrally planned decision making has led to lack of power at the enterprise level and falls in production as managers have concentrated on a passive implementation of central policy. The "correct" line is constantly dictated to the workers through constant meetings; the workers become alienated and terrorized. The state exhorts the workers to increase production but offers them no incentives and can provide no consumer goods for them to buy with extra earnings. There is no benefit from increased productivity.[92]

Statistics on the development of peasant associations in Eritrea are very sketchy. One of the few concrete references to Ethiopian-sponsored land reform in the last decade indicates that in June 1983, in three districts of southern Hamasien, close to Asmara, "the peasant leadership faced a challenging task" of allocating plots.[93] As peasants have to belong to a peasant association in order to farm without excessive harassment from the government, the slow growth of peasant associations in Eritrea is a sure sign of the resistance of the Eritreans to Ethiopian institutions and attests to the lack of control by the Dergue. One example of the dubious value of official Ethiopian statistics is that in May 1982 the Dergue claimed that there were sixty-six peasant associations in Seraye; when elections were held later in the month, it transpired that there were only thirty-five.[94] The poor showing of the peasant associations has been ascribed to the pernicious influence of the "bandits."[95] Certainly the EPLA destroyed the infrastructure of a number of peasant associations in 1981, including four in Seraye and two in Akele-Guzai, and arrested all officials appointed by the Dergue.[96]

In 1982, the Dergue announced that it aimed to have 1.000 peasant associations in Eritrea.[97] By 1990, the Dergue expected that the peasant associations would have "voluntarily" converted themselves into producers' cooperatives.[98] All this is totally impracticable. Over the 1953-1980 period, agricultural production in Ethiopia has grown at a slowly decreasing rate. Ethiopia lacks the basic infrastructure and incentive system to create conditions in which technological innovations, applicable to small-scale, labor-intensive production, will be possible.[99]

There are no peasant associations in Barka or Sahel Provinces; moreover, none of the cooperatives in Eritrea have full legal status.[100] For comparison, note that in March 1982, there were 834 producer cooperatives in Ethiopia. It is by no means obvious that cooperatives are the answer to Ethiopia's declining agricultural production; Arsi Province has by far the highest number of service cooperatives in the country but in spite of the resources lavished on the province, almost half of the members find the services to be unsatisfactory.[101] Attempts have been made to revitalize the Elabored agroindustrial complex, which employed thousands of people in imperial times. Under the wing of the Dergue, it employed 350 workers.

The Ethiopian model of imposing socialism is most unlikely to succeed in the other provinces let alone Eritrea; it has been said that the revolution has "done little to change the technical or social basis of production in the rural north."[102] The EPLF approach seems much more promising; however, the problems it faces would daunt the most optimistic outsider. The record of the EPLF's land reform measures, particularly the large-scale pro-

gram carried out during the 1970s, however, gives good reason to
believe that it would be able to face up to this immense challenge.
Moreover, the very great efforts the Eritreans have made since
1975 to cope with ever more devastating droughts, has shown that
they can handle short-term as well as long-term developmental
needs.

Notes

1. Ambaye Zekarias, *Land Tenure in Eritrea (Ethiopia)* (Addis Ababa, Institute of Ethiopian Studies, 1966) p. 7.
2. S.F. Nadel, 'Land Tenure on the Eritrean Plateau,' *Africa,* XVI, 1 (1946) p. 6.
3. Tekeste Negash, *Italian Colonialism in Eritrea, 1882-1941: Policies, Praxis and Impact* (Uppsala, University Press, 1987) p. 4.
4. Nadel, 'Land Tenure,' p. 7.
5. John M. Cohen and Dov Weintraub, *Land and Peasants in Imperial Ethiopia: the Social Background to a Revolution* (The Netherlands, Van Gorcum, 1975) p. 64.
6. S.F. Nadel, 'Land Tenure on the Eritrean Plateau,' *Africa,* XVI, 2 (1946) p. 108.
7. Ambaye Zekarias, 'Land Tenure in Eritrea,' p. 12.
8. Ambaye Zekarias, 'Land Tenure in Eritrea,' pp. 15-6.
9. Kidane Mengisteab, 'The Political Economy of Land Reform: An Exploratory Study of Structural Changes in Ethiopia's Agriculture, 1975-1981' (University of Denver, Unpublished Thesis, 1985) pp. 70-73.
10. Jordan Gebre-Mednin, 'Eritrea: Pre-capitalist Social Formation,' *Horn of Africa,* 3, 4 (1980/81) p. 25.
11. Richard Leonard, 'European Colonization and the Socio-Economic Integration of Eritrea,' *Eritrea Information,* 3, 3 (1981) pp. 7-10.
12. Ambaye Zekarias, 'Land Tenure in Eritrea,' p. 33.
13. Jordan Gebre-Medhin, 'Eritrea,' p. 26.
14. G.W.B. Huntingford, *The Land Charters of Northern Ethiopia* (Addis Ababa, Institute of Ethiopian Studies, 1965) pp. 34, 36, 54-5, 98.
15. Jordan Gebre-Medhin, *Peasants and Nationalism in Eritrea: A Critique of Ethiopian Studies* (Trenton NJ, Red Sea Press, 1989) p. 45.
16. Jordan Gebre-Medhin, 'Eritrea,' p. 29.
17. Tekeste Negash, 'Italian Colonialism,' p. 6.
18. Jordan Gebre-Medhin, 'European Colonial Rule and the Transformation of Eritrean Rural Society,' *Horn of Africa,* VI, 2 (1983) p. 50.
19. Ambaye Zekarias, 'Land Tenure in Eritrea,' p. 24.
20. Aster Akalu, *The Process of Land Nationalization in Ethiopia: Land Nationalization and the Peasants* (Lund, G.W.K. Glerrup, 1982) p. 49,

citing Carlo Conti Rossini, *Principipii di Diritto Consuetudinario Dell'Eritrea* (Roma, Ministero delle Colonie, 1916) pp. 111-2.

21. Joanna Mantel-Niecko, *The Role of Land Tenure in the System of Ethiopian Imperial Government in Modern Times* trans. K.A. Bobinski (Warsaw, Wydawnictwa University, 1980).

22. Eritrean Relief Association, *Social and Economic Services in Eritrea* (Khartoum, Eritrean Relief Association, 1983) p. 5

23. *Resistance,* III, 6 (1983) p. 8.

24. Richard Leonard, 'Popular Participation in Liberation and Revolution,' eds. Lionel Cliffe and Basil Davidson, *The Long Struggle of Eritrea for Independence and Constructive Peace* (Nottingham, Spokesman, 1988) p. 119.

25. *Eritrea Information,* 10, 4 (1988).

26. Paul Nursey-Bray, 'Consensus and Community: the Theory of African One-Party Democracy,' ed. Grahame Duncan, *Democratic Theory and Practice* (Cambridge, Cambridge University Press, 1983) p. 100.

27. *Eritrea: Food and Agricultural Production Assessment Study,* 'Final Report' (Leeds University, Agricultural and Rural Development Unit, 1988) p. 138.

28. Tensai, *Interview with Author,* August 28 (1983).

29. Eritrean Relief Association, *Revised Emergency Relief Budget for 1988* (Khartoum, Eritrean Relief Association, 1988).

30. 'Eritrea: Food and Agricultural Production Assessment Study,' p. 22.

31. Tony Barnett, 'Agriculture in the Eritrean Revolution,' eds. Basil Davidson et. al., *Behind the War in Eritrea* (Nottingham, Spokesman, 1980) pp. 113-4.

32. *Liberation,* January-April (1982) p. 13; Peter With, *Politics and Liberation: the Eritrea Struggle, 1961-1986* (Denmark, University of Aarhus, 1987) p. 108.

33. *Resistance,* III 6 (1983) p. 17.

34. *Resistance,* III 6 (1983) p. 19.

35. Barnett, 'Agriculture,' p. 114.

36. Cohen and Weintraub 'Land and Peasants,' p. 94.

37. *Eritrea Information,* 3, 6, July (1981).

38. *Liberation,* August-September (1981).

39. *Liberation,* November-December (1981).

40. *Liberation,* January-April (1982) p. 11.

41. Leonard, 'Popular Participation,' p. 125.

42. With, 'Politics and Liberation,' p. 21.

43. Leonard, 'Popular Participation,' p. 132; Lionel Cliffe, 'The Eritrean Liberation Struggle in Comparative Perspective,' eds. Lionel Cliffe and Basil Davidson, *The Long Struggle of Eritrea for Independence and Constructive Peace* (Nottingham, Spokesman, 1988) pp. 101, 96.

44. John Markakis, *National and Class Conflict in the Horn of Africa* (Cambridge, Cambridge University Press, 1987) pp. 274-5.

45. Peter With and Maria Kibaek, 'Agriculture in Eritrea,' *Eritrea Information,* 6, 1 (1984) pp. 10-11.

46. Yonas Debassai, *Interview,* August 29 (1983).

47. Andom, *Interview,* August 28 (1983).

48. *Eritrea in Relief,* December (1986).

176 • ERITREA: EVEN THE STONES ARE BURNING

49. Eritrean Relief Association, *Informational Bulletin*, 20 (1986).
50. Mahari, *Interview*, July 21 (1985).
51. Volker Mathies, *Der Eritrea—Konflikt: Ein "Vergessener Krieg" am Horn von Afrika* (Hamburg, Institut Für Afrika-Kunde, 1981) p. 168.
52. Mekalih Harnet, 'Reflections on the Eritrean Revolution,' *Horn of Africa*, VI, 3 (1983/84) p. 11.
53. Tesfatsion Medhanie, *Eritrea: Dynamics of a National Question* (Amsterdam, B.F. Grüner, 1986) p. 64.
54. Richard Sherman, *Eritrea: the Unfinished Revolution* (New York, Praeger, 1980) p. 126.
55. With, 'Politics and Liberation,' p. 82.
56. Dessalegn Rahmato, *Agrarian Reform in Ethiopia* (Trenton NJ, Red Sea Press, 1985) pp. 30-1; Alemneh Dejene, *Peasants, Agrarian Socialism, and Rural Development in Ethiopia* (Bolder CO, Westview, 1987) p. 24.
57. Allen Hoben, *Social Soundness Analysis of Agrarian Reform in Ethiopia* (Ethiopia, USAID, 1976) pp. 73-4.
58. Alemneh Dejene, 'Peasants,' p. 38.
59. Jason W. Clay and Bonnie K. Holcomb, *Politics and the Ethiopian Famine: 1984-1985* (Cambridge MA, Cultural Survival Inc., 1985) p. 139.
60. Clay and Holcomb, 'Politics and the Ethiopian Famine,' p. 140.
61. Dessalegn Rahmato, 'Agrarian Reform,' p. 68.
62. Dawit Bekele, 'Peasant Associations and Agrarian Reform in Ethiopia,' *Bulletin*, Institute of Development Studies, Sussex (1982) p. 63.
63. Paul Keleman, 'Ethiopia: Heretical Socialism or Orthodox State Capitalism?,' *Horn of Africa*, 6,5 (1983-84) p. 35.
64. Dessalegn Rahmato, 'Agrarian Reform,' p. 84-5.
65. Alemneh Dejene, 'Peasants,' p. 35.
66. Aster Akalu, 'The Process of Land Nationalization,' p. 212.
67. Alula Abate, 'Peasant Associations and Collective Agriculture in Ethiopia: Promise and Performance,' *Journal of African Studies*, 10, 3, Fall (1983) p. 99.
68. *Ethiopian Herald*, June 1 (1979).
69. Georgi Galperin, *Ethiopia: Population, Resources, Economy*, trans. J. Shapiro (Moscow, Progress Publishers, 1981) p. 164.
70. Alula Abate, 'Peasant Associations,' p. 108.
71. Ajit Kumar Ghose, 'Transforming Feudal Agriculture: Agrarian Change in Ethiopia Since 1974,' *The Journal of Development Studies*, 22, 1 (1985) p. 139.
72. Alemneh Dejene, 'Peasants,' p. 103.
73. The World Bank, *Ethiopia: Recent Economic Developments and Future Prospects*, Vol 1 (Washington DC, 1984) p. iii.
74. Alemneh Dejene, 'Peasants,' p. 91.
75. The World Bank, 'Ethiopia,' pp. i, 22.
76. Aster Akalu, 'The Process of Land Nationalization,' p. 156; Alemneh Dejene, 'Peasants,' p. 80.
77. David Mitrany, *Marx Against the Peasants* (London, Weidenfeld and Nicolson, 1951) p. 187.
78. Dessalegn Rahmato, 'Agrarian Reform,' p. 90.
79. Alemneh Dejene, 'Peasants,' pp. 62-4.
80. Ghose, 'Transforming Feudal Agriculture,' p. 134.

81. Alemneh Dejene, 'Peasants,' p. 35.
82. Dessalegn Rahmato, 'Agrarian Reform,' p. 73.
83. V.V. Sokolov et. al., *Considerations on the Economic Policy of Ethiopia for the Next Few Years* (Addis Ababa, 1985) p. 14.
84. John Clarke, *Resettlement and Rehabilitation: Ethiopia's Campaign against Famine* (London, Harney and Jones, n.d.) p. 132.
85. Dessalegn Rahmato, 'Agrarian Reform,' p. 72.
86. Keith Griffin and Roger Hay, 'Problems of Agricultural Development in Socialist Ethiopia: An Overview and a Suggested Strategy,' *Journal of Peasant Studies*, 13, 1 (1985) p. 54.
87. Government of Socialist Ethiopia, Ministry of State Farms Development, *Report* (Addis Ababa, 1983) annex 6.
88. Ghose, 'Transforming Feudal Agriculture,' p. 130.
89. The World Bank, *Ethiopia: Recent Economic Developments and Future Prospects*, Vol 2 (Washington DC, 1984) p. 15.
90. Griffin and Hay, 'Problems of Agricultural Development,' p. 56.
91. Haile Yesus Abegaz, *The Organization of State Farms in Ethiopia after the Land Reform of 1975* (Saarbrücken, Verlag Breitenbach, 1982) p. 234.
92. Mulatu Wubneh and Yohannis Abate, *Ethiopia: Transition and Development in the Horn of Africa* (Boulder CO, Westview, 1988) p. 199.
93. *Ethiopian Herald*, June 4 (1983).
94. *Ethiopian Herald*, May 22, May 29 (1982).
95. *Ethiopian Herald*, October 31 (1980).
96. *Liberation*, August-September (1981).
97. *Ethiopian Herald*, April 14 (1982).
98. Clay and Holcomb, 'Politics and the Ethiopian Famine,' p. 19.
99. Warren C. Robinson and Fumiko Yamazaki, 'Agriculture, Population, and Economic Planning in Ethiopia, 1953-1980,' *Journal of Developing Areas*, 20, April (1986) p. 335.
100. Government of Socialist Ethiopia, Ministry of Agriculture, *Statistics*, June (1981).
101. Alemneh Dejene, 'Peasants,' p. 55.
102. James C. McCann, *From Poverty to Famine in Northeast Ethiopia: A Rural History 1900-1935* (Philadelphia, University of Pennsylvania Press, 1987) p. 206.

9

Drought, Famine and Development

You've seen our country. Now you know why we want to be free. The Ethiopians came, they bombed our villages, they slaughtered our cattle and burned our children. Everything is burning now. Even the stones are burning.

—Mama Zeinab[1]

Eritrea is a predominantly agrarian society, with about eighty percent of the population living in the countryside and farming in a traditional manner. According to an extensive survey of two-thirds of Eritrea's 182 districts, carried out in late 1987 with the cooperation of the EPLF, some sixty-one percent of the rural population are agriculturalists who grow food for their own needs and also supply it to other groups. One-third are agropastoralists who grow some of their own food, but who are also dependent on their animals. The rest of the rural population are pastoralists, some of whom are nomadic; they rely on the sale of goats, camels and cattle to buy food.[2]

There are four major agricultural regions: the eastern coastal area—which is suitable only for livestock raising; the western lowlands, mainly flat land up to 2,000 feet in elevation and potentially very fertile; the highlands comprising about one-third of the total area; and the Sahel lowlands, a narrow, fertile strip of land running between the highlands and the coastal area. The eastern coastal areas receive the unpredictable, "little rains (*belg*)" during October to March, while the other areas get "main rains (*kiremti*)" from June-September. In good years, the Sahel lowlands experience two rainy seasons, which enables the cultivation of a wide variety of crops such as fruit, vegetables and coffee. The principal crops in the western lowlands are durrah, corn, pulses, sesame for seed, cotton and bullrush millet. The latter, along with durrah, is relatively tolerant of drought. At an average height of 5,000 feet above sea level, the highlands are cool enough to grow barley, teff (a staple grain crop indigenous to the Horn of Africa) and wheat—providing the rains come. These crops are seriously affected by drought.

To some extent Eritrea's peasants have developed traditional measures to cope with predictable fluctuations in climatic conditions, and in the past were able to maintain physical reserves to cope with a bad year. These measures included stockpiling surplus grain from one year for consumption during subsequent poor harvests, working seasonally for wages in towns and the Sudan, and maintaining herds of livestock as an insurance against low crop yields. Such measures enabled Eritrea's peasants to survive serious droughts from 1913 to 1914 and again in the 1940s.[3] The poor performance of agriculture in the Horn of Africa was evident in the 1950s, but over the past fifteen years there has been a significant decrease in rainfall in the area; this can be seen by looking at records of levels of lakes in the region.[4] Fifteen years ago Lake Rudolf in northern Kenya was six feet higher than it is today. The worst may be yet to come; geological records indicate that in the past the lakes may have dried up almost completely. A drop of a further twelve feet over the next years is possible; if this occurs an even worse disaster than 1983-1985 could be in store.[5]

Eritrea's present problems, however, are by no means entirely due to climate; by and large they are man-made, and as such amenable to solution. Throughout the long period of the liberation struggle, the recurrent famines have been caused, in large part, by the action or inaction of the imperial and revolutionary Ethiopian governments, other governments and international organizations. Moreover, in the period from 1970-1984, rains were poor in nine years; i.e. 1970, 1973, 1974, 1977, 1980, 1981, 1982, 1983, and 1984. Traditional measures proved totally inadequate to deal with such a cumulation of disasters. Even though band-aid assistance during 1984-1986 saved thousands of lives and some rains fell, giving farmers the chance to rebuild food supplies, there is little hope of a long term solution to Eritrea's recurrent famines unless the conflict is stopped and the Ethiopian military occupation is ended. The 1987 food and agricultural assessment survey disclosed that yields of grain in Eritrea were poor, even by African standards, and were only one-third to one-half of Ethiopian yields—sure indicators of very abnormal conditions.[6]

An inequitable land tenure system, as discussed in the last chapter, has been a major factor contributing to Eritrea's plight. Moreover, ever since Eritrea's federation with Ethiopia in 1952, and particularly over the past twenty-five years, its economy has been in recession, and many people simply do not have the money or goods to barter for food; they are almost completely destitute and increasingly reliant on the EPLF, the Eritrean Relief Association (ERA) and the uncertain generosity of international donors, who allocate most of their resources to the Ethiopian government.[7] ERA operates throughout rural Eritrea, and in 1987, conducted some twenty-five percent of its operations in territory technically under the control of the Ethiopian government. During the past thirteen years, ERA has increased its role to such a degree that in the crisis of 1988, when by the end of February, almost all food reserves had been exhausted, it was capable of transporting nearly 200,000 tons of supplies into Eritrea.[8]

In spite of the daunting problems they have faced since 1961, the Eritreans have made an encouraging start on the road to self-sufficiency. ERA was founded in 1975 after widespread bombing by the Ethiopian military had destroyed the homes and livelihoods of thousands of people within Eritrea, and precipitated an exodus of 4000,000 refugees into the Sudan. In August 1975, the Ethiopian government ordered all international relief agencies to stop their work in Eritrea—compounding the plight of the people.[9] The EPLF opened a camp for some of the displaced people in the heart of the liberated base area, and, after some initial setbacks, succeeded in efforts to make the inhabitants self-sufficient and engaged in productive work.[10] The EPLF's strategy contrasts favorably with the Dergue's policy of burn and destroy, the deliberate creation of a refugee population and a land without a people. As Tibebu Bekele, Ethiopia's acting foreign minister said in December 1984, "food is a major element in our strategy against the secessionists."[11]

ERA's role was fourfold: to mobilize international agencies for support; to feed displaced people and refugees; to curb the flow of refugees; to rehabilitate the population.[12] By 1983, 120 international agencies were cooperating with ERA, even though the policy of most agencies is to follow the lead of their governments, which entails dealing only with nations recognized by the UN and the OAU. ERA did not oppose aid to Ethiopians; however, because of the probability of misappropriation, it advocated a policy of bypassing the Dergue.

That Ethiopian government aid was ineffective or non-existent is indicated by strident claims of the Dergue that "bandits" were hindering relief and that "bandits" driving Red Cross vans were crossing from the Sudan. A particularly inspired claim was made in late 1975, that "bandits" wearing government uniforms were preparing to burn crops and poison wells and then blame the Dergue.[13]

The years 1978 and 1979 experienced relatively good rains, but intense fighting in Eritrea; increasing calls were made on EPLF and ERA resources. ERA undertook a harvest survey every year to assess the crop situation, and in 1981, reported on the failure of the winter rains on the eastern coastal lowlands. This drought led to over 100,000 people becoming totally dependent on the EPLF and ERA.[14] During the year, three new camps for displaced people were opened and ERA extended its activities throughout Eritrea. However, international donations to ERA showed a decline; durrah shipments, the mainstay of the diet, dropped from 5,700 tons in 1979 to 5,280 in 1980. Food donations accounted for less than thirty percent of need.[15]

ERA carried out a drought survey of some sixty percent of the country during July-October 1982 and found a very grim situation, with some 600,000 people in need of assistance.[16] In the eastern coastal areas and in Barka there had been drought for three successive years, while in the other areas of Eritrea, there had been virtually no harvest for two years. The price of durrah doubled in 1982, and many people were forced to subsist on cactus fruit and grass. The Ethiopian Red Star offensive during the planting months of July-August, and forced conscription into the militia, severely disrupted agricultural activity and further decimated the dwindling herds of livestock in Barka and Sahel.

Aid continued to be administered effectively in the liberated areas. Dutch journalist Frits Eisenloeffel spent a month during the most demanding period of the year (July-August) monitoring the distribution of 13,000 sacks of durrah—twenty-five percent of the total international food aid for Eritrea for the year—from Kassala to the western, southern and central parts of Eritrea. He was the first foreigner since 1978 to travel deep behind the Ethiopian front line, and established the substantial truth of the EPLF's claim to control some eighty-five to ninety percent of Eritrea. Only ten minutes' drive from Asmara, he found territory effectively administered by the EPLF, with relief and development activities in full swing. While visiting six provinces, he found that in most villages controlled by the EPLF, the elected village council had a register of people in need of aid; this was used as a guide for distribution. Unlike Dergue-held areas, where whole families are often compelled to trek many arduous miles to feeding centers in order to obtain rations, aid was distributed directly to the villages. Farmers are encouraged to remain on their land and cultivate for the next year's crop; in this way it is possible to minimize the large-scale displacement which plays havoc with future food production.

Transport was a major bottleneck; ERA had a maximum of fifty trucks available, and the driving conditions were probably the most demanding in the world. Eisenloeffel commented that the relief aid made available to ERA was pathetically little—the international community has never met more than a meager proportion of the need. With the development of the EPLF into the major political and military force in Eritrea, ERA could be assured of safe and regular access to the vast majority of Eritrea's inhabitants; however, he found no evidence that any relief aid supplies were diverted to EPLF combatants, nor any other signs of abuse of aid.[17]

As a result of positive reports on conditions in the liberated areas by this observer and by delegations from bodies such as Christian Aid, Lutheran World Relief, and many others, more international aid was received in the latter part of 1983. ERA distributed 16,113 tons of durrah (or its equivalent) to 600,000 people during the year.[18] ERA ran ten camps in Eritrea, holding some 65,000 people—50,000 of these were victims of the 1982 drought.[19] But in spite of its excellent record, ERA received funds amounting to only eight percent of its emergency budget in the first four months of 1984.[20] Ethiopia received thirty times this amount.[21]

Yonas Debessai, the field coordinator of ERA gave a graphic picture of the problems faced:

For the last three years it has been very hard. The farmers lack seeds so this rain will not alleviate, but next year *inshallah*, if we can get money to buy seeds...the next stage will be rehabilitation. There is no problem from the Sudanese authorities and we clear it very smoothly through the port of Sudan...where trucks cannot go we use camels and donkeys, in some places this is on a basis of rent; for example, one Sudanese pound per quintal. The local people are often willing to help us and do freely. We do not face problems of waste.[22]

Between mid-June and the beginning of August 1983, i.e., the crucial period of planting, there was no rain to speak of in virtually the whole Eritrea. According to ERA, some 1.25 million people, mostly women and children, were affected by the drought which entered its fourth consecutive year.[23] The health of the population was very grave; they were susceptible to many kinds of disease. A survey by an Australian doctor showed that over forty percent of children under five years of age were undernourished.[24] The rains, which normally fall in Sahel in the early part of year, failed again in 1984, leading to a very serious water shortage. Some wells dried up for the first time in twenty-five years; it was decided to give special attention to the digging of deeper wells. By April 1984, durrah had doubled in price following a severe harvest shortfall in the Sudan.[25]

In 1984, only ten percent of food aid requirements reached the liberated areas. The situation improved somewhat, however, in early 1985. In May 1985, when an Australian delegation visited Eritrea to monitor the distribution of some 3,000 tons of wheat, ERA was receiving about half of its needs. Australian aid reached nearly two hundred villages; the team also saw developmental work among 3,000 resettled families on the restored irrigation system at Ali Ghidir.[26]

The light rains that began to fall in Eritrea in the spring of 1985 brought hope of recovery after five years of drought. The harvest produced surpluses in several small pockets of the country. Meanwhile, relief supplies continued to pile up and spoil at the port of Massawa as the Dergue appropriated most civilian transport for its military activities.[27] The Dergue also bombed refugees returning from the Sudan and trucks carrying relief supplies into Barka.[28] Increased military activity in Barka led to a further rise in the number of displaced people dependent upon ERA's assistance in thirty-one camps. The primary emphasis was on food production and a major campaign was started to purchase quantities of seed and farm implements; in 1985, ERA distributed enough seed for the cultivation of 320, 000 acres.[29]

Some of the 3,500 people who fled the Ali Ghidir settlement in advance of the invading Ethiopian army returned to Eritrea during December, and were assisted by ERA. A key part in the agricultural rehabilitation program was played by a water drilling rig with a capacity to dig up to 100 meters. The Eritreans' tasks were made easier through the generosity of United States based private organizations, which enabled ERA to purchase seventy-five new trucks in 1985.[30]

In April 1985, ERA estimated that some 1.5 million people (some 1 million less than the previous year) were still affected by drought and 650,000 of these were faced with starvation. It was clear that the vast quantities of food aid sent to the Dergue had not been distributed in Eritrea. During a distribution of grain by ERA in Senhit Province, 14,000 out of 17,000 people came from Ethiopian-controlled areas; the Dergue had mined their fields and cultivation was impossible.[31] ERA's immediate priorities for 1985 were for seeds, tools and other farming materials to reach Eritrea by early January to enable optimum planting.

In July 1986, ERA estimated that there had been a short-fall in emergency food supplies in 1986. With late rains and the imminent danger of locust infestation—locusts had been sighted in four provinces and were threatening durrah, corn and millet—

yields were likely to fall below expectations.[32] ERA and the EPLF made an international appeal for aid and a large shipment was unloaded in September. Aid given to ERA and distributed in the liberated areas has had a very marked impact; a survey carried out by the International Committee of the Red Cross (ICRC) in Senhit Province in 1986 showed that the incidence of severe child malnutrition had decreased from fourteen percent to four percent during the year.[33]

In the wake of the Ethiopian army's withdrawal from Barka in early summer of 1986, ERA distributed seeds and agricultural tools to people in the town of Shilalo and the districts of Medri-Wedisebera, Zadekolom, Deqotsinea and Mereb.[34] During the first six months of 1986, ERA distributed seeds, oxen and tools to villages throughout Eritrea.[35] In December, some 13,000 people around Agordat who could not plant crops because of constant Ethiopian harassment were given emergency assistance.[36] It was estimated that 600,000 people would continue to need humanitarian assistance in 1987.[37] With a return to a better rainfall pattern, however, EPLF staff could turn their attention to other pressing matters; for example, the Veterinary Commission of Eritrea vaccinated over 800,000 cattle, sheep and goats against rinderpest and other animal diseases during 1986.[38] Unfortunately, 1987 turned out to be another drought year; the response of ERA and the Ethiopian government to this crisis is discussed in greater depth in the following sections.

The situation in the liberated areas of Eritrea contrasts very sharply with that in the portion of Eritrea under Ethiopian military occupation. The imperial government of Haile Selassie and the military government of the Dergue share at least one characteristic—they receive the lion's share of aid and development assistance, but are unable, or unwilling, to relieve famine in Eritrea. Drought is not unusual in Eritrea, nor is government neglect. During the 1958-1959 famine—which followed drought and locust swarms—plenty of food was available at the ports, but not transported inland to relieve the famine.[39] During the famine in Ethiopia in 1976, donated grain was diverted to Assab and sent to the USSR to pay for arms.[40] Monsignor Bomers, Bishop of Haarlem in the Netherlands, relates that in 1982 and again in 1983 (drought and famine years in Eritrea), he witnessed the export to the USSR of hundreds of thousands of bags of grain from Nekemte in West Ethiopia.[41]

It is instructive to compare the progress of the 1973-1975 and 1983-1985 famines. In late 1973, the Ethiopian Relief and Rehabilitation Commission (RRC) claimed that a negligible proportion of the Eritrean population was affected by drought. Although less than half of the country was surveyed, the RRC felt confident enough to claim that eighty-two percent of districts had normal, or above normal crop production, and only nine percent were substantially below normal.[42] After the partial failure of the little rains and the complete failure of the summer rains in 1974, the newly proclaimed provisional military government appealed belatedly for aid for Eritrea.[43] By August, 80,000 were affected and in late October, famine was reported throughout Eritrea.[44] Between November 1974 and January 1975, 9,357 tons of grain were allocated to Eritrea but only 4,500 distributed—sure indication that the Dergue did not control much of the country.[45] In December, relief was said to have been distributed as far north as Afabet.[46] The after effects of the drought persisted into 1975; the RRC estimated that 500,000 people were still affected. Some 187,521.53 *birr* was allocated by RRC for relief in Eritrea during the year, but there is no indication that any of this was actually spent on relief assistance.[47]

In the middle of the next bad drought year, 1977, it was announced that wheat had been distributed in drought affected areas around Barentu.[48] As the ELF had the town under siege, this was, to say the least, somewhat implausible. There was no independent confirmation of the Dergue's claims—a state of affairs which became commonplace.

In 1980, the drought in Assab was said to be the worst ever; this was exacerbated by the Dergue's policy of forcibly resettling Afar pastoralists, so depriving them of their seasonal grazing grounds.[49] RRC head Shimelis Adugna, claimed that one million people in Eritrea were affected by drought and appealed for aid.[50] As the government's area of operations was limited to the urban areas and main roads, this can be regarded as a ploy, and a partially successful one, to coax aid from donors. Some rations were distributed by Ethiopian officials, the army and "some white visitors" to the village of Hadamo, a suburb of the government held town of Decamere in 1980.[51] Some aid was also given for the assistance of refugees said by the Dergue to be returning from the Sudan. In fact, very few returned, and 15,000 more Eritreans crossed into the Sudan during 1980-1981.

In August 1983, the RRC reported that Eritrea was in as critical a drought condition as in 1974, but "that prompt action by the Government has forestalled a potentially calamitous situation." During the period 1979-1983, the Dergue claimed to have distributed 12.5 million *birr* for rehabilitation and resettlement.[52] But whatever the claims of the Dergue, the fact is that since it assumed power in 1974, it had carried out no effective famine planning in Eritrea. At no point during Eisenloeffel's mission to Eritrea in 1983 did he find any evidence that the Ethiopian government, agencies working through it, or agencies working out of government held areas, had distributed food in the eighty-five to ninety percent of Eritrea controlled by the EPLF. Nevertheless, the RRC claimed that it had distributed grain to two districts in Hamasien and in the vicinity of Asmara; "bandits" were blamed for compounding difficulties in drought relief.[53]

It was the actions of the Dergue, however, which ensured that the famine would be harsh: for example, no food supplies entered the port of Assab from November 1983 until April 1984. The port was closed to allow military and military related equipment to enter in preparation for military offensives and the lavish celebrations to mark the tenth anniversary of the revolution.[54] At these festivities no mention was made of the famine which had already killed tens of thousands of people.

The major responsibility for handling the famine was taken by the RRC. The RRC has been widely praised by many visitors to the country. On the other hand, it has also been described as "almost totally paralyzed by political meddling, sloth and over management."[55] It has been said that the RRC "has set a shining example of inefficiency over the years.[56] Even sympathetic observers comment that as the RRC has no formal accounting procedures, it is not possible to account for all of the supplies channeled through the Ethiopian government.[57] As no minutes were ever taken at meetings between RRC officials and donors, an objective appraisal of the organization is impossible.[58]

At the onset of the famine, for unspecified reasons, substantial quantities of grain remained in government warehouses and were not distributed to victims in the south of the country; moreover, minders from the Ministry of Foreign Affairs often prevented inspection.[59] Bureaucracy is so pervasive that forty-two pieces of paper had to be signed in Assab before any grain could be loaded for distribution; moreover, 40,000 tons rotted in the state farm in Humera.[60] The RRC met in Asmara and claimed to be distributing food grains in Massawa and Ghinda to people from Hamasien, Seraye, Akele-Guzai, Danakil and Sahel; but on a subsequent five day tour of drought areas, the Commission did not visit any part of Eritrea, apart from Assab.[61] There were conflicting views as to the seriousness of the problem. On one occasion, Mengistu claimed that transport problems were the reason for lack of distribution throughout the country. [62] On another, he stated that there was no place in Eritrea where "terrorists" impeded Ethiopian aid.[63] On a visit to Asmara a few days after making this assertion, however, and after being informed that "secessionist groups were disrupting relief operations," he again changed his tune.[64] The Dergue continued to make contradictory claims leading to the conclusion that it either did not know, or did not care, what happened to the majority of the drought victims in Eritrea. It was admitted that the RRC did not serve forty percent of the highland areas, and the president of the aid agency World Vision attempted to negotiate an agreement with the Dergue by which aid could reach EPLF-held areas.[65]

There has also been conclusive evidence of Ethiopian misuse of aid. Food, mainly the gift of the EEC, has been found in a number of army stores. In November 1982, the European Parliament suspended food aid to Ethiopia after it was alleged that EC grain had been hoarded, or sent to the USSR in partial payment of a huge arms bill.[66] On April 14, 1983, Edgar Pisani, EC Third World Aid Commissioner, denied the charges, quoting denials by the Ethiopian government and investigations by the World Food Program (WFP). It seems likely, however, that the removal of Shimelis Adugna from his post as RRC head in April 1983 was related to these charges. Moreover, evidence given to the Australian government's enquiry into the provision of aid showed that, "the World Food Program, on which Australia relies for monitoring food aid [in Ethiopia] is ill-equipped with the necessary skills or facilities to efficiently carry out this function."[67] During the critical months of March to October 1984, WFP statistics were "dangerously misleading," and an "unconvincing presentation of food aid statistics at a...meeting was greeted with ridicule."[68] In December 1983, documents smuggled out of Ethiopia confirmed the allegations made in the British *Sunday Times*, and showed the great lengths to which the RRC went to cover up such abuses. The documents, leaked by Abraha Haile Mikael, a RRC official defecting from the Dergue, contained a directive by Shimelis Adugna instructing officials to falsify and destroy records which showed how food aid was diverted to the Dergue's marketing agency, the AMC.[69]

When the EPLF captured the Ethiopian garrison of Mersa Teklai in early 1984, it found large quantities of butter oil which had been donated by the EC; this donation to the civilian population of Ethiopia had been used as rations regularly for the previous five years. EC powered milk was also used until it became rancid and caused outbreaks of dysentery; and in Decamere, EC flour was used to make army biscuits. In spite of EC Commission attempts to cover up these scandals, there can be no real doubt that such misappropriation also occurs in other operational areas.[70] For example, during 1985, a British aid monitor discovered that 4,000 tons of grain had been transferred from an RRC regional warehouse to an army depot.[71] It is obvious that the large armies which the Dergue used in Tigray and Eritrea, could not find food in the war-devastated and drought-ridden countryside.

EC donations are invariably transported in Ethiopian army trucks or government owned trucks, under military convoy, to storehouses located in military garrisons. Although most Western agencies strenuously and tediously denied the charges, the senior American diplomat in Addis Ababa reported, "there are persistent reports from credible sources of a system whereby RRC transferred to the army stock from warehouses where donated food is kept."[72] Conclusive proof was given by former RRC head, Dawit Wolde Giorgis. In March 1984, Mengistu ordered him to divert RRC grain (the gift of Western governments) to the armed forces and the Addis Ababa kebeles. Dawit states that food had been diverted as a matter of course to the peasant militias and also to the Sudan People's Liberation Army, whose headquarters is in Ethiopia.[73] During the 1984-1986 emergency, the entire transport operation was under the control of the Soviets, and Dawit claims that Soviet crews pilfered food.[74]

The great increase in the number of unproductive workers, few of whom return to their villages after "temporary" military service, has contributed markedly to the food shortages in Ethiopia and Eritrea.[75] When the great flood of international aid arrived in Ethiopia in late 1984, the Dergue launched a "food for arms" campaign; military recruits were given 200 lbs. of wheat a month with an extra 112 lbs. for combat missions, and more if they were wounded. Thousands of workers in Asmara were paid in emergency grain intended for drought victims.[76] When a number of foreign aid personnel and journalists visited Barentu a few days after its capture by the EPLF in July 1985, they saw in the garrison sacks of grain and high protein biscuits (in unopened and open containers) donated by the EC and Norway. Numerous POWs told how these formed part of their regular rations.

The Dergue set up food distribution centers in some of its garrisons and flew in Western aid workers, press and sundry visitors to witness distribution. The casual visitor did not see the army screening supplicants and refusing aid to anyone suspected of EPLF support, which happened to people of the Baria nationality in Barentu in November 1984.[77] Ethiopian lack of concern for people beyond its reach was shown in the confiscation of $1.7 million supplies collected in Australia and bound for Port Sudan for distribution by ERA and the Relief Society of Tigray (REST), a humanitarian organization which operates in the TPLF controlled areas of Tigray.

In spite of the Dergue's protests that it was in complete control of the country, and following an exhaustive parliamentary enquiry into the provision of humanitarian aid to the Horn of Africa, the Australian government concluded that "aid channeled through Sudan to the Eritrean Relief Association is an effective way of ensuring that aid reaches those in pressing need in Eritrea."[78] The Australian government replaced the shipment in full. The Australians were also influenced by an assessment made by a mission of the Australian Development Assistance Bureau, which visited Ethiopia from November 29-December 9, 1984 and reported that it had been informed that the Dergue was "deliberately refusing to allow relief supplies into certain areas in order to starve the people there into submission."[79] The International Committee of the Red Cross claimed that the Ethiopian government was deliberately keeping aid from Tigray and Eritrea.[80]

The Dergue profited greatly from the famine. In 1985, it collected at least $30 million in foreign currency by levying extortionate port and handling charges on grain donations. It charged rates twenty-five times as high as those at Port Sudan.[81] Dawit

Wolde Giorgis continued his indefatigable efforts to put pressure on groups such as Oxfam, which worked both in Ethiopia and Eritrea, to prevent aid from reaching Eritrea through ERA. He complained that "there is a discrepancy between the funds collected [in London] and the funds received in Ethiopia."[82]

As a matter of course, donated food aid and transport has been diverted to the Dergue's resettlement and villagization programs. The RRC revealed that it had plans, to be financed by the United Nations, to resettle 45,000 Eritreans throughout Ethiopia in a ten-year period.[83] It appears, however, that the government has not yet seriously attempted to resettle Eritreans in the malarial and tsetse fly-infested "empty or underused lands" of the South and West, as has been the fate of many thousands of unwilling and unhappy people from Tigray, Wollo and Gondar. On one occasion when the Dergue's representatives tried in Eritrea at Ghinda in October 1985, peasants resisted fiercely and successfully.[84]

Even though numerous articles were published confidently proclaiming that the famine was over, it was clear that there was still famine in government-held areas.[85] In March 1986, people from Mendefera, Debaroa and Areza had to abandon their homes.[86] By June 1987, only 13,000 tons had been committed to Eritrea by the RRC; Asmara's water supply had been out of action for several weeks and rationing begun.[87]

Much of the blame for the disasters which have visited Eritrea in the past fifteen years must be laid on some of the larger international aid agencies and donor countries; indeed a senior official of the League of Red Cross Societies said of Ethiopia in late 1984, "already the disaster has begun. It started with the arrival of the first foreign aid."[88] The role of the government of Haile Selassie in the perpetuation of the 1972-1975 famine is widely known; that of the international relief agencies and donor nations—who kept quiet so they would not embarrass the government or jeopardize established working relationships, is less publicized. In June 1973, a Red Sea missionary reported that "the situation south of

Massawa has been overlooked and omitted from all records, in spite of very serious famine in that area."[89]

The Dergue made concerted (and successful) efforts to get Western development and humanitarian aid in 1982. In June, ambassadors from Belgium, Great Britain and Italy, together with John Valder, EC representative in Ethiopia, briefly visited Eritrea. They expressed satisfaction with soil and water conservation efforts, were impressed by the "enthusiastic involvement" of the peasants and called for vast international assistance to the Dergue.[90] Dawit Wolde Giorgis, who was governor of Eritrea at the time, shows how visitors were misled about the peasants' "enthusiastic involvement." Cadres of the Workers Party were briefed before the visits and dressed as peasants. They not only began to work vigorously as soon as the Land Rover carrying the distinguished guests was sighted, but also ensured that they would be interviewed. The visitors could well be impressed by the knowledge and motivation of such government servants.[91]

In 1983, the Dergue sent a team from the Catholic Relief Services (CRS) to study the drought situation; they did not venture outside of Asmara "due to communication problems." In June 1983, Count Pontiatowski, EC Commissioner for Development and Cooperation, said that aid was monitored effectively and efficiently and that he was impressed with the food for work scheme.[92] It seems that 317,000 people were involved in this program, working on dams, terraces and afforestation as so-called "volunteer free labor." The scheme was clearly a failure, however, as it was closed down completely in late 1983 for unknown reasons.[93] The failure of the Dergue's afforestation scheme is also shown in data from the Ethiopian province of Arsi; even though the Dergue claims to have distributed over 1.7 million seedlings in ten years, sixty percent of farmers surveyed said that they thought that there were fewer trees than before the revolution.[94]

In September 1983, there was some evidence of relief agency activity in government-held areas; the ICRC distributed some 542 tons of food to 28,000 people. However, the ICRC also said in its

Bulletin that "insecurity in many areas and the logistical problem of moving large amounts of food around a mountainous and underdeveloped country have left large sections of the civilian population...on the brink of starvation."[95] It is noticeable that ERA and the EPLF are not intimidated by such "logistical problems," nor are the numerous agencies who work with them to deliver aid.

As soon as the famine in Ethiopia had attracted the frenzied, genuine, but unfortunately, ephemeral, attention of the world's media, the EPLF called for a truce to allow ERA to distribute food more speedily and safely to the 1 million people in need. The Dergue refused; it used the substantial Western aid donations which were flown into Massawa and Asmara to pay off members of urban kebeles (270 lbs. of grain a month), members of armed militias (200 lbs.) and informers (112 lbs.). Large amounts of milk powder and oil given by USAID were sold in the open market and transported to Sudan; in November 1984 alone, some $400,000 worth of Western donations passed through Girmaica and out of Eritrea.[96] The largest donors—USAID, the EC and Canada—exerted minimal control over distribution and turned a blind eye to the allocation of food on political grounds. They used their generosity as a way of regaining influence with the Dergue. That this policy has been remarkably ineffective will be discussed later. It was also fortunate that the famine occurred at a time when there was a record world grain harvest of 509 million tons, the EC had a surplus of 8.7 million tons and the major suppliers were beginning to subsidize sales in an effort to boost their flagging economies.

In February 1985, the United Nations reported that Ethiopia had stopped sending food into Eritrea and Tigray.[97] And in May, it was estimated that only forty percent of the grain shipped to Ethiopia had been distributed, ostensibly because of lack of transport.[98] All available transport was being used in the war against the Tigrayans and Eritreans; nevertheless, the UN launched a $50 million appeal for money, new trucks, parts and tires to aid Ethiopia.

By July 1985, the media's view was that the famine was a thing of the past (or at least a story of the past). Particularly gullible reporters chorused enthusiastically on the "voluntary" resettlement scheme as the permanent solution of the cycle of crisis.[99] Their enthusiasm was based on an erroneous view that vast areas of the north are uninhabitable wastelands on the verge of total, irreversible economic collapse. These attitudes were fostered by the Ethiopian government when its inability or unwillingness to prevent and alleviate famine in Ethiopia and Eritrea was becoming an acute embarrassment, and too noticeable for all but the most naive to miss. Kurt G. Jansson, director of relief operations in Ethiopia for the UN, commented, after a day spent in government-held areas of Eritrea, that seventy-five percent of famine victims were receiving aid from Ethiopia and that ERA's cross border operation from the Sudan was "insignificant" (less than ten percent of the total).[100]

ERA's claims to have distributed 65,000 tons in the first six months of 1985 have been independently verified by numerous monitors. The ICRC estimates that ninety percent of food aid distributed in Eritrea comes from Ethiopian sources, indicating that 585,000 tons would have been distributed by the Ethiopian Government in Eritrea from January-June 1985. In the whole of Ethiopia and Eritrea statistics of RRC and non-governmental organization deliveries cite 154,000 tons as being distributed during January and February and 171,000 tons during March-May.[101] The half-yearly total claimed by the Dergue would be of the order of 400,000 tons for all Ethiopia and Eritrea—i.e., still considerably less than the ICRC estimate for government relief in Eritrea! The Dergue's claims cannot be substantiated; no reliable monitoring of aid emanating from government areas has been carried out. In fact, foreign aid workers estimated in May 1985, that the final destination of at least 30,000 tons of food donations per month could not be accounted for by the Dergue.[102] It also appears that the Dergue deliberately inflated the numbers of "people in need" in order to secure food to replace production disrupted in the course of its massive resettlement program. The Addis Ababa director of the Irish aid agency Concern indicated that there had been doctoring of facts on resettlement.[103]

In June 1985, the UN Assistant Secretary General for emergency assistance to Ethiopia claimed that out of an Eritrean population of 827,000 in need, 644,000 were being reached by the government (i.e., seventy-eight percent).[104] These figures, taken from official Ethiopian sources, are remarkable not least for claiming that Ethiopian coverage was greater in contested areas than in quiet areas such as Showa, where sixty-three percent were reached, and Gemu Goffa, fifty-five percent. They also claim that seventy-nine percent of people were reached in Tigray. The estimates of people in need were also far below ERA's which range from 1.75 million to 2.5 million. The Dergue also estimated Eritrea's population at only 2,704,000, while ERA and EPLF figures gave 3.0 million.

Such claims presumably influenced the United States government, which appears to have made a decision to support Mengistu. It abandoned firm commitments made by George Bush and United States AID chief Peter McPherson during their visit to Sudan in March 1985 to support REST and ERA.[105] USAID's background information on Eritrea seems particularly bad; officials drew up lists of areas in Eritrea where they were told by the United States' intelligence sources that the Dergue was not operating. These included Barentu, Areza and Keren, all held by the Dergue at that time. They asked Dawit Wolde Giorgis if the RRC could distribute food from these centers; when he said that he could, the USAID people jumped to the totally erroneous conclusion that the Dergue could handle the whole of Eritrea, and therefore, that ERA needed no support.[106]

Consequently, in September, after the recapture of the towns it had lost in Barka Province, the Dergue, together with USAID's agent in Ethiopia, CRS reportedly began "a northern initiative." CRS collected $50 million for Ethiopia famine relief, but by August 1985 had spent only $5.9 million of it in Ethiopia (at the same time, $100,000 was given as an interest-free loan to its executive director).[107] An eyewitness reported on a scheme in a Keren Roman Catholic Mission under which "those who sign up in advance are allowed through the gates.... Hungry people try to force their way in.... Mission guards scream and threaten them with whiplike sticks.[108] CRS claimed to have expanded its activities in "Koren [sic], Akordat, Areeza, Barentu and Afabet."[109] However, it appears from testimony given by William E. Schaufele, CRS African director, that CRS had not actually been at these centers, "we have been assured that people are coming in from other [non-government] areas to pick up food."[110] As these centers were all in the middle of heavily fortified garrisons, and access was through surrounding fields which had all been extensively mined, these people would indeed be few in number. In any event, CRS claims to have fed a mere 14,000 people in Tigray and Eritrea—hardly "an effective stop gap measure."[111]

CRS has come in for some even harsher criticism; it appears its representatives ask recipients of "free" food, donated by the United States, for payment. These sums—totaling $11 million in 1985—disappear in the organization. Those unable to pay their so-called "mother's contributions" are often refused food. Moreover, food unfit for human consumption is sold by CRS and the proceeds are not remitted to the government.[112] CRS took title of the grain from the silos in Kansas through the customs clearing agent at Massawa and Assab. For the duration of the famine, CRS contracted with a private Kenya trucking firm to deliver the grain to the feeding centers. RRC took title on the trucks and managed to make a tidy profit on the deal, charging the United States government, $165 per ton handling and trucking charges.[113] RRC also made money out of food recipients; any Eritrean wanting food had to pay a registration fee.[114] Another shipload of medicine and relief supplies bound for Eritrea, some fifty-one tons in all, gift of the British aid agency started by rock musicians, Band Aid, was confiscated by the Ethiopian authorities in Assab in May 1985.

There was increasing evidence of a potential catastrophe which could have been even more dangerous than the 1984-1985 famine—and one from which the Dergue again tried to profit. Locust hatchlings destroyed 10,000 acres in Danakil in January 1986. Bureaucrats close to the Ethiopian government discounted such on-the-spot reports by EPLF or ERA workers. In August, a United Nations official, Andre Auciert, said that the situation "was not yet dangerous."[115] By the end of 1986, 200,000 acres were damaged by these pests, affecting over a quarter of a million people.[116] The Dergue refused to allow any international team to spray near its front line; however, the EPLF mobilized twelve ground control teams—who also worked in areas normally out of the EPLF's reach.[117] Prompt and concert action on 330,000 acres of land killed some ninety percent of locusts; however, the locust and army worm infestations were accompanied by a very dry summer.[118] By November 1987, it became clear that there had been an eighty-five percent crop failure in Eritrea and numerous families began to leave home in search of food. It was expected that some 1.5 million people would need emergency food assistance. The highland provinces were hit particularly hard.

On October 23, 1987, EPLA forces burned a convoy of Ethiopian trucks containing bombs, ammunition, fuel and food supplies. The EPLF regretted the loss of food and instructed all units to take precautions that relief supplies and vehicles were not attacked in the future. The EPLF received bad publicity, but more percipient observers noted that the relief question could not be treated effectively without also taking into account the fact that Eritrea had been fighting for independence for over two decades.[119]

Over the past twenty-nine years, the Eritreans have not only been fighting a numerically superior and better armed Ethiopian army, but also a war against disinformation. The Dergue's capital, Addis Ababa, is the most important diplomatic city in Africa. It is the headquarters of both the OAU and the Economic Commission for Africa, and the center of the most expensive aid program in

African history. Little information emanates from the area, unless it is passed through the filter of the Dergue, the RRC or other government organizations. Moreover, United Nations agencies work only with sovereign nations and "recognized" liberation groups; they refuse to deal with the EPLF, even though it controls eighty-five percent of Eritrea. The UN must take the blame for the many deaths in Eritrea over the past years. If its member states and agencies had possessed the courage they could, in cooperation with the EPLF and ERA, have saved many thousands of people from hunger and starvation.

Since the establishment of ERA, however, an increasing number of outside observers have visited the areas of Eritrea controlled by the EPLF, and many voluntary agencies have started to operate in Eritrea. In cooperation with ERA's cross-border operation from Sudan, they have distributed humanitarian aid and development assistance to all corners of Eritrea. Unfortunately, food supplies received by ERA over the past years have invariably been less than needed.

The EPLF and ERA are extraordinarily sensitive to the implications of their actions. For example, during the 1985 drought, EPLF leaders debated long over the consequences of engaging in military action during such a crisis. But, as the then vice secretary general observed, "we had to go to the military venture to check the offensives of the regime, which were aimed at destabilizing our development projects. They were determined to not allow agencies to be active in our area... so we attacked, and Barentu was the position we chose for many reasons, not least because our development projects are mainly located in the western lowlands.[120]

Every conceivable aspect of the work of ERA has been investigated by a host of visitors to the field; in some cases monitoring operations have accounted for virtually every sack of grain donated by the international community. On the other hand, relief agencies working in Ethiopian government-held areas regularly budget for losses of thirty to forty percent.[121] By the time the

Army and other agents of the Dergue have taken their cut and some of the rest has been sold on the open market and taken to the Sudan, very little reaches the starving. It is clear that the Ethiopian military government "played a significant role in the creation, maintenance and expansion of the [1980s] famine," and used it "to undermine agricultural production" with the intention of making peasants dependent upon the central state. Such dependence has been facilitated by massive shipments of international food assistance; these have enabled the Dergue to coerce large numbers of dissidents and also feed a large conscript army.[122]

The Ethiopian government is becoming very sensitive to criticism—so dependent has it become on Western governments for food supplies and constant diplomatic support—that it devotes a great deal of energy and resources to cover up evidence which would bring to light its manifold abuse of aid. Most governments are reluctant to apply sanctions on the Dergue for fear of losing the little influence they have in this strategically important area of the world. Most representatives of non-governmental agencies also refrain from criticism for a variety of reasons, the most important being that if they offend the Dergue they risk expulsion from Ethiopia. The case of the French agency, Médecins sans Frontières (Doctors Without Borders), which was expelled after reporting that up to 100,000 Ethiopians had died during the forced resettlement scheme, is an ever present warning. Even though aid workers are aware of the rampant waste and misappropriation of aid in Ethiopia, they are also fearful of voicing their disquiet, for fear that adverse publicity will reduce international assistance and force a scaling down of the assistance program.

Such adverse publicity has already had an affect. Oxfam was under a great deal of pressure to reduce its work in Ethiopia after its Ethiopian drivers were beaten by government officials for refusing to transport people to resettlement areas.[123] A Protestant church linked to the Lutheran World Federation had its senior relief headquarters staff imprisoned by the Dergue.[124] Other charities are also under pressure. In the United States, donations to

World Vision fell forty percent in 1986, while the UNICEF appeal for Africa netted only $13 million in 1986, against $102 million in 1985.[125] The UN Office of Emergency Operations in Africa, which oversaw the 1984 famine relief effort, was closed in October 1986.[126]

Punitive government policies have also been a major reason why farmers in areas controlled by the Dergue have steadily reduced their production. The Dergue has prevented planting by stealing oxen and mining fields. It has conscripted thousands of farmers into the militia and destroyed hundreds of homes and villages. It has burned and confiscated harvests. Because of the continuing uncertainty under which they live, farmers—even on the infrequent occasions when they are left in peace—have adopted the strategy of producing for their own needs. If they produce a surplus, they are compelled to sell a major proportion of it to the Agricultural Marketing Corporation at prices far below those paid by private merchants. In 1985, for example, whilst the market price of 220 lbs. of barley was $50, the official price was only $14. As shown in the previous chapter, the bulk of government investment in agriculture has been diverted to state and collective farms, which have proved a signal failure. A former RRC head admitted that even before Ethiopia was affected by a serious lack of rainfall, Dergue policies were responsible for much hunger and malnutrition.[127] Peasant farmers are discriminated against in many ways; for example, state farms, which produce only two percent of crop output, nevertheless consume over half the fertilizer used in Ethiopia.[128] The government doubled the price of fertilizer for peasants in 1980, putting it further from their reach.[129] The military government's response to declining food production has been to increase coercion—fines, jailing, beatings and replacement of the leadership of peasant associations. Peasant association leaders can transfer land from one peasant to another (this is used as a major disciplinary measure) so there is little incentive for farmers to improve the land and productivity.

While the Dergue continues its war against the Eritrean people, Eritrea will continue to rely on international assistance. Just as the Dergue and the EPLF will fight for political dominance, so will the Dergue and ERA continue to appeal for humanitarian assistance and development aid. From 1945-1984, Ethiopia received $390 million aid from the United States; in the 1985 fiscal year it topped $279 million.[130] Even with this level of aid, Ethiopia's economic development remained stagnant.[131] The Dergue will continue to use this aid to try to defeat the EPLF and to make the Eritrean peasant dependent on the colonial Ethiopian power; the EPLF—with the necessary assistance of ERA—will use the aid to rescue the starving, build up the self-reliance of the Eritrean people and lay the groundwork for an independent, viable, democratic Eritrea.

As long as the war persists, there will be Eritrean refugees and displaced people, reliant on the EPLF, ERA and international aid. Clearly the major medium-term priority is to stop the war through political and diplomatic initiatives, and then allow the Eritrean people to exercise their right of self-determination. The EPLF could improve its efforts to broaden its base of international support; it is possible for more Western governments and parties to be persuaded to support the right of the Eritrean people to self-determination along the lines of the resolution first passed by the Australian Labor Party at its national conference in July 1986.[132] From late 1986, the prospects for a negotiated end to the conflict seemed more promising with the defection of a number of members of the Central Committee of the Workers Party of Ethiopia, heralding an abortive military coup in 1989 and the disintegration of the Dergue into several factions.

But irrespective of the urgent need for negotiations to end the conflict, the short-term priority remains to ensure that the basic needs of the Eritrean refugees and malnourished people are met. In Eritrea there exist efficient, national organizations such as EPLF and ERA with the skill, experience and infrastructure to meet these needs—would international bodies only match them.

There are now encouraging signs that significant members of the international aid community are gradually coming round to the view that in order to aid Ethiopians and Eritreans in an effective and humane manner, they must try to bypass Ethiopian government channels and deal with domestic agencies on a bilateral basis. The EPLF has recognized that it would be more efficient if some drought assistance could come from the government side: the General Secretary said in December 1987: "One has to make a demographic study of the distribution of the population and the infrastructure that exists and accordingly work out a plan where distribution centers should be publicly declared. Neither the EPLF nor the Ethiopian government should be active in those areas in any way; and all roads leading to this should be free to everyone and all donor agencies should have the right to be active in these areas."[133]

Donors wishing to continue massive aid shipments to the Dergue must rid themselves of many illusions, the most damaging of which is that Western aid, amounting to $1 billion from 1978-1982 and a further $1 billion in 1985 alone, does not support a military government in its wars against liberation movements and in ill-conceived and counter-productive mass resettlement and villagization schemes. Even an otherwise totally uncritical supporter of the Dergue admits that production in the resettlement areas is insufficient to sustain the population without relief aid.[134] Convincing evidence has come from resettlement areas in Pawe (in Gojjam) and also in Illubar of abuses of human rights and rates of mortality some three or five times the average.[135] The Berliner Missionwerk of West Berlin Maryknoll Fathers also criticized the schemes.[136]

Without the "band-aid relief" contributed from 1984-1986, the Dergue could not have trained and fed the conscript army it unleashed in Tigray and Eritrea. Many well-meaning aid workers, politicians and journalists were so overwhelmed by the magnitude of the 1984-1985 famine, and so obsessed by the imperative need to assist in alleviating the disaster, that they not only suspended moral and political judgment on the Dergue and its servants, but devoted much time and energy in trying to argue that misappropriation did not occur.[137] Agencies and governments must consider very seriously the proven case against the Dergue and reallocate aid and development assistance through independent agencies such as ERA and REST.

The 1988-1990 crisis tested the Eritreans to the limit. The Dergue expelled the few relief agency workers active in Government-held areas. The ports were closed to relief shipments and Eritrea's starving became totally dependent on ERA's activities.[138] ERA was forced to keep open settlement camps it had hoped to be able to close in order to support people who had returned to their homes.[139] The three-year recovery program, started in 1985, also had to be curtailed.

The long-term priorities are to assist Eritrea to become self-sufficient in food production and, therefore, lay the foundations of a viable state. The EPLF has already trained a number of farmers in more modern farming techniques and has sent teachers, nurses and other technical staff into the field to tackle the large problems of an underdeveloped country which has been rent by war for the past thirty years. A very sustained effort must be made to attract expatriate Eritreans, as well as development assistance from a plurality of sources. A start has also been made in remedying an inequitable land tenure system; a coordinated plan can only be put into operation when farmers are free from the constant fear of Ethiopian attacks. More land can also be brought into use if the underground water supply is tapped with modern drilling techniques and fuller use made of river water by constructing dams and irrigation schemes.[140] More could be done to aid the many thousand Eritrean refugees in the Sudan and assist those who desire to return home to farm under the protection of the liberation movement.

There are many problems to be overcome on the way to freedom, but Eritrea possesses a priceless asset—the dedication of hundreds of thousands of patriots. They have built up an organization against tremendous odds, which has been described by Médecins sans Frontières as, "the only [one] in the whole region of the Horn with which one feels confident to leave alone with their distribution network... it always reaches the affected people wherever they are." This is a fitting tribute.

Notes

1. Mama Zeinab cited in Stephen Levett and Fiona Douglas, *Even the Stones are Burning* (Film) (Sydney, Freedom From Hunger Campaign, 1985).
2. *Eritrea: Food and Agricultural Production Assessment Study, Preliminary Report* (Leeds, Agricultural and Rural Development Unit, 1987) p. 11.
3. *Eritrea: Food and Agricultural Production Assessment Study, Final Report* (Leeds, Agricultural and Rural Development Unit, 1988) p. 31.
4. James C. McCann, *A Great Agrarian Cycle? A History of Agricultural Change in Highland Ethiopia, 1900-1987* (Boston, Boston University Press, 1988) p. 1.
5. Preston King, *An African Winter* (Harmondsworth, Penguin, 1986) pp. 17-8.
6. Assessment Study, 'Final Report,' p. vii.
7. Eritrean Relief Association, *Annual Report 1987* (Khartoum, Eritrean Relief Association, 1987) p. 10.
8. Eritrean Relief Association, 'Annual Report 1987,' p. 13.
9. Jack Shepherd, *The Politics of Starvation* (New York, Carnegie Foundation, 1980) p. vi.
10. Eritrean Relief Association, *Report on Drought in Eritrea* (Khartoum, 1983) p. 12.
11. David A. Korn, *Ethiopia, the United States and the Soviet Union* (London, Croom Helm, 1986) p. 137.
12. Gebre Michael Mengistu (Lelo), *Interview*, August 22 (1983).
13. *Ethiopian Herald*, December 3 (1975).
14. *Eritrea Information*, 3, 2, February (1981).
15. *Horn of Africa*, 'Eritrea: War and Drought,' 4, 2 (1981) p. 25.
16. Eritrean Relief Association, 'Report on Drought.'
17. Frits N. Eisenloeffel and Inge Rönnbäck, *The Eritrean Durrah Odyssey* (Utrecht, Interchurch Aid, 1983) pp. 57, 69-70.
18. *Eritrea in Relief*, I, 1, January (1984).
19. Gebre Michael Mengistu, 'Interview.'
20. James Firebrace, with Stuart Holland, *Never Kneel Down: Drought, Development and Liberation in Eritrea* (Trenton NJ, Red Sea Press, 1985) pp. 99-100.
21. *Christian Science Monitor*, July 20 (1984).
22. Yonas Debessai, *Interview*, August 29 (1983).

208 • ERITREA: EVEN THE STONES ARE BURNING

23. *Eritrea in Relief,* I, 1, January (1984).
24. Michael Toole, 'Health Services in Eritrea,' *New Doctor,* 32 (1984) p. 15.
25. Firebrace, 'Never Kneel Down,' p. 92.
26. Eritrean Relief Committee (Australia), *Newsletter* (1985).
27. *Eritrea in Relief,* March (1986).
28. *Human Rights and Food Aid in Ethiopia,* Hearing Before the Subcommittees on Human Rights and International Organizations and Africa of the Committee on Foreign Affairs, House of Representatives, Ninety-ninth Congress, October 16 (Washington D.C., United States Government Printing Office, 1985) pp. 36-7, 43.
29. Eritrean Relief Association, *Informational Bulletin.* 4 (1986).
30. Eritrean Relief Association (New York), *Press Release,* July 21 (1986).
31. Eritrean Relief Association, *Informational Bulletin.* 9 (1986).
32. Eritrean Relief Association (New York), *Press Release,* July 7 (1986).
33. Eritrean Relief Association (New York), *Press Release,* August 4 (1986).
34. Eritrean Relief Association, *Informational Bulletin,* 14 (1986).
35. Eritrean Relief Association, *Informational Bulletin,* 19 (1986).
36. Eritrean Relief Association, *Informational Bulletin,* 20 (1986).
37. Eritrean Relief Association, *Informational Bulletin,* 28 (1987).
38. Eritrean Relief Association, *Informational Bulletin,* 29, 30, (1987).
39. Richard Greenfield, *Ethiopia, A New Political History* (London, Pall Mall, 1965) pp. 305-6.
40. Myles F. Harris, *Breakfast in Hell: A Doctor's Eyewitness Account of the Politics of Hunger in Ethiopia* (New York, Poseidon Press, 1986) p. 60.
41. *The Australian,* December 15 (1987).
42. Abdul Mejid Hussein ed. *Rehab: Drought and Famine in Ethiopia* (London, International African Institute, 1976) p. 36.
43. *Ethiopian Herald,* October 5 (1974).
44. *Ethiopian Herald,* October 20 (1974).
45. Hussein, 'Rehab: Drought,' pp. 47-8.
46. *Ethiopian Herald,* December 1 (1974).
47. Hussein, 'Rehab: Drought,' pp. 47.
48. *Ethiopian Herald,* May 6 (1977).
49. *Ethiopian Herald,* April 30 (1980).
50. Ibid.
51. Eisenloeffel, 'The Eritrean Durrah Odyssey,' p. 65.
52. *Ethiopian Herald,* August 23, September 3 (1983).
53. *Ethiopian Herald,* March 6, 24 (1983).
54. Human Rights and Food Aid, p. 178.
55. Harris, 'Breakfast in Hell,' p. 48.
56. *Indian Ocean Newsletter,* 154, November 3 (1984).
57. Peter Gill, *A Year in the Death of Africa: Politics, Bureaucracy and the Famine* (London, Paladin, 1986) pp. 141, 75.
58. Kurt Jansson, 'The Emergency Relief Operation—an Inside View,' eds. K. Jansson et. al., *The Ethiopian Famine* (London, Zed Books, 1987) p. 9.
59. Jansson, 'The Emergency Relief Operation,' p. 14.
60. Dawit Wolde Giorgis, *Red Tears: War, Famine and Revolution in Ethiopia* (Trenton NJ, Red Sea Press, 1989) p. 231.
61. *Ethiopian Herald,* December 16, 20 (1984).
62. *Ethiopian Herald,* September 17, 18 (1984).

63. *Ethiopian Herald*, November 7, 20 (1984).
64. *Ethiopian Herald*, December 2 (1984).
65. Dawit Wolde Giorgis, 'Red Tears,' pp. 238, 225.
66. *Sunday Times*, March 27 (1983).
67. Parliament of the Commonwealth of Australia, *The Provision of Development Assistance and Humanitarian Aid to the Horn of Africa* (Canberra, Australian Government Publishing Service, 1983) pp. 106-7.
68. Angela Penrose, 'Before and After,' eds. K. Jansson et. al., *The Ethiopian Famine* (London, Zed Books, 1987) pp. 146-7.
69. *Eritrean Information*, 5, 9 (1983).
70. *Eritrea in Relief*, I, 1, January (1984).
71. Jansson, 'The Emergency Relief Operation,' p. 56.
72. Korn, 'Ethiopia,' p. 150.
73. Dawit Wolde Giorgis, *Personal Communication* (1987).
74. Dawit Wolde Giorgis, 'Red Tears,' pp. 232-7.
75. Jason W. Clay and Bonnie K. Holcomb, *Politics and the Ethiopian Famine* (Trenton NJ, Red Sea Press, 1986), p. 135.
76. *Eritrea Information*, 6, 9 (1984).
77. *The Australian*, December 13 (1984).
78. Commonwealth of Australia, 'The Provision of Development Assistance,' p. 129.
79. *The Australian*, January 8 (1985).
80. Gill, 'A Year in the Death of Africa,' p. 140.
81. *Christian Science Monitor*, October 17 (1985).
82. *Manchester Guardian Weekly*, November 17 (1985).
83. *Ethiopian Herald*, October 5 (1982).
84. Eritrean Relief Association, *Informational Bulletin*, 7 (1986).
85. Theodore M. Vestal, 'Famine in Ethiopia: Crisis of Many Dimensions, *Africa Today*, 4th Quarter (1985) p. 7.
86. Eritrean Relief Association, *Informational Bulletin*, 8 (1986).
87. Eritrea: Assessment Study, 'Final Report,' p. 150.
88. Harris, 'Breakfast in Hell,' p. 215.
89. Shepherd, 'The Politics of Starvation,' pp. x, 44, 20.
90. *Ethiopian Herald*, June 30 (1982).
91. Dawit Wolde Giorgis, 'Personal Communication.'
92. *Ethiopian Herald*, June 23 (1983).
93. Eisenloeffel, 'The Eritrean Durrah Odyssey,' p. 63.
94. Alemneh Dejene, *Peasants, Agrarian Socialism, and Rural Development in Ethiopia* (Boulder CO, Westview, 1987) p. 116.
95. International Committee of the Red Cross, *Bulletin*, May (1984).
96. James Firebrace, 'Food as Military Aid,' *New Statesman*, December 20 (1984) p. 20.
97. *San Francisco Chronicle*, February 6 (1985).
98. *Manchester Guardian Weekly*, May 12 (1985).
99. John Clarke, *Resettlement and Rehabilitation: Ethiopia's Campaign against Famine* (London, Harney and Jones, n.d.) P. 65; Graham Hancock, *Ethiopia: the Challenge of Hunger* (London, Victor Gollancz, 1985) pp. 110-11.
100. Eritrean Relief Committee (New York), *Newsletter*, August (1985).
101. *Adulis*, II, 12 (1985); Human Rights and Food Aid, 'Hearing,' p. 181.

102. *Le Monde*, May 25 (1985).
103. Robert D. Kaplan, *Surrender or Starve: the Wars Behind the Famine* (Boulder CO, Westview, 1988) p. 110.
104. Human Rights and Food Aid, 'Hearing,' p. 145.
105. *San Francisco Chronicle*, July 1 (1985).
106. Dawit Wolde Giorgis, 'Personal Communication.'
107. *New York Times*, January 14 (1986).
108. Anthony Suau, 'Region in Rebellion: Eritrea,' *National Geographic*, 168, 3 (1985) pp. 390-1.
109. Human Rights and Food Aid, 'Hearing,' p. 31
110. Human Rights and Food Aid, 'Hearing,' p. 156.
111. Gill, 'A Year in the Death,' p. 59.
112. *New York Times*, October 21 (1986).
113. Vestal, 'Famine in Ethiopia,' p. 18.
114. Assessment Study, 'Final Report,' p. 112.
115. *Manchester Guardian Weekly*, August 31 (1986).
116. Eritrean Relief Association, *Informational Bulletin*, 26 (1986).
117. Eritrean Relief Association, *Informational Bulletin*, 32 (1987); Eritrean Relief Association, Press Release, July 4 (1986).
118. Eritrean Relief Association, *Informational Bulletin*, 35 (1987).
119. *Washington Post*, January 3 (1988).
120. Isaias Afwerki, *Interview*, July 18 (1985).
121. *New African*, December (1984).
122. Clay and Holcomb, 'Politics,' p. v.
123. *New Statesman*, April 18 (1986).
124. Penrose, 'Before and After,' p. 152.
125. *New York Times*, August 17 (1986).
126. *New York Times*, November 2 (1986).
127. *New York Times*, May 21 (1986).
128. Keith Griffin and Roger Hay, 'Problems of Agricultural Development in Socialist Ethiopia: An Overview and a Suggested Strategy,' *Journal of Peasant Studies*, 13, 1 (1985) p. 51.
129. Joseph Collins, *Statement* Submitted to the Committee on Foreign Affairs, United States House of Representatives, Subcommittees on Africa and Human Rights (1985).
130. Korn, 'Ethiopia,' p. 189.
131. Vestal, 'Famine in Ethiopia,' p. 22.
132. *Adulis*, III, 8-9 (1986).
133. Isaias Afwerki, *Interview by Author*, December 12 (1987).
134. Clarke, 'Resettlement,' p. 103.
135. Giordana Sivin, 'Famine and the Resettlement Program in Ethiopia,' *Africa* (Roma) 41 2 (1986) p. 222.
136. *Africa News*, XXVII, 1 (1986).
137. Gill, 'A Year in the Death,' p. 60.
138. Eritrean Relief Association, *Briefing*, May 26 (1988).
139. Eritrean Relief Association, *Report* (1989).
140. Araia Tseggai, 'Independent Eritrea: Economically Viable?,' *Horn of Africa*, VI, 2 (1983) p. 41.

10

Transformation and Independence

It seems better to have compact, viable states than sprawling
empires that are incapable of governance and vulnerable to protracted internal strife.

—ROSS K. BAKER, *Biafra: Balkanization or Nation-Building*[1]

P revious chapters have argued that Eritrea and Ethiopia
have never formed a politically integrated society. The
various ethnic groups that comprise Eritrea are not integrated with the diverse peoples that make up Ethiopia. The great
majority of Eritreans regard the rule of the Amhara elite as illegit-
imate. There is no cohesive political interaction between Eritrea, a
territory at the periphery, and the core Ethiopian Empire. The
debate over the political and economic viability of an independent
Eritrea, however, still needs to be addressed.

In the post-war years, when the major powers were deciding
upon the fate of Eritrea, the argument was repeatedly made that
Eritrea, because of its small size and underdeveloped economy,
could not become a viable nation-state. Since then, over fifty

countries with a smaller population and many with much fewer resources than Eritrea have become independent. In Africa, there are eighteen member states of the OAU with smaller populations than Eritrea; moreover some twenty micro states have been created in the Pacific and Caribbean. There is no correlation between size, economic viability and political survival.[2] A brief sketch of Eritrea's political economy will indicate that it could indeed stand alone.

The most recent Ethiopian statistics show that in Eritrea, in 1980, land use was as follows: 1,477,307 acres of crops; 496,717 acres fallow and 9,504,313 acres pasture, i.e. total 11,478,337 acres. The World Bank statistics derive from these Ethiopian estimates.[3] These figures are somewhat surprising; in 1950, the United Nations Commission estimated that only 781,000 acres was used for crops or fallow and 22,301,630 acres pasture—i.e., total crops and pastures was 23,082,150 acres; therefore Eritrea's agricultural land halved in thirty-four years.[4] It must be noted that until 1987 the only other data readily available, from the Eritrean Chamber of Commerce, showed that in 1976, only 674,801 acres of crops was grown.[5] There is no accounting for an apparent doubling of crop area in four years. The most recent, as well as the most reliable, statistics on cultivated land and fallow land in Eritrea derive from the independent 1987 Assessment Study. Arable land amounts totals 1,204,372 acres and follow 802,915 acres; cultivated land amounts to 2,007,287 acres. The survey team did not attempt to assess the extent of pasture land.[6]

However unreliable the statistics, it can be said with confidence that a wide variety of crops can be grown in Eritrea. Even tea was grown experimentally by the Italians.[7] With irrigation, equitable land reform and adequate materials and prices, Eritrea could not only feed its population, but continue to export to Ethiopia and other countries. Even during the severe drought of 1983 the 3,000 acre Elabored agro-industrial complex produced 689,000 cans of tomato paste for export.[8]

In normal years, i.e., before the massive Ethiopian military offensives, there were ample numbers of livestock in Eritrea. With peace, herds could be replenished in a relatively short time. Red Sea marine and mineral resources have great potential.[9] The EPLF program recognizes this by including among its objectives a commitment to "exploit marine resources, expand the production of salt and other minerals, develop the fish industry, explore oil and other minerals."[10]

The highland plateau is of considerable geological age and has been subjected intensely to the processes that lead to mineralization.[11] Although considerable exploration took place under the Italians, Eritrea's mineral resources were by no means fully exploited in this period. Since 1941, mineral production has been of even less importance to the Eritrean economy; however, Eritrea's potential is considerable. Iron ore with a fifty percent ferrous content was discovered in Ghedem, some nine miles south of Massawa.[12] Later prospecting revealed that some deposits had a ferrous content of sixty percent.[13] The Agametta area in Semhar Province has the most readily available deposits; possible as much as 20 million tons.[14] The Debarua copper mines, located twenty-two miles southwest of Asmara are of 7.8 percent grade ore and are, therefore, probably the richest in the world.[15] They were mined during 1973-1975 by a joint company in which Japan had an eighty percent equity.[16] Production was halted after ELF raids in 1975. One estimate of potential production is 160,000 tons.[17]

Gold is another mineral found in significant quantities. It has been mined in Eritrea from ancient times; the richest sites are in the Hamasien highlands.[18] There are also outcrop veins of from nine to twelve feet thick and yielding gold values of 9 grams per ton in the southwestern plains. Production reached 17,000 ounces in 1941.[19] Marine salt is mined in Assab and Massawa. In the early 1970s production was about 200,000-220,000 tons per year.[20] More recent production figures, however, show that production has declined; in 1977-1978, Assab produced 70,000 tons and plans were to double the output (even though the plant, set up in 1922, is designed for a maximum of 125,000 tons). Massawa produced 37,000 tons in 1980-1981—again much less than in pre-revolutionary times.[21]

Potash was mined at Dallul in Danakil province on the border with Ethiopia; reserves are among the richest in the world and there is a possibility of mining up to 1 million tons per year. Nickel and chromites have been located in Barka Province near the junction of the Barka and Anseba rivers.[22] Kaolin is found in several parts of Hamasien province and is used by a ceramics plant in Asmara.[23] White asbestos and feldspar of good quality is known to exist. Traces of manganese, titanium and magnesium have also been found. Mica and vermiculite occur in small quantities.[24]

There is a distinct possibility that the Red Sea off Massawa contains accessible deposits of petroleum and natural gas.[25] Before 1929, there were signs that petroleum was present near Massawa.[26] Extensive drilling on the Dahlak Islands was carried out from 1938-1940 but no drilling records have survived.[27] A well drilled by the Mobil oil company in the Red Sea in 1969 blew out with gas and condensate.[28] The escalation of war has prevented any further systematic exploration. Ethiopia's only oil refinery is located in Assab. As far as other fuels are concerned, there are scattered deposits of lignite coal.[29]

Eritrea has large numbers of skilled workers. In 1980-1981, according to Ethiopian statistics, there were 13,855 Eritreans working in some ninety-five establishments employing more than ten persons. Some indication of the greater productivity of Eritrean compared to Ethiopian workers is that, although Eritreans comprised only 17.5 percent of the labor force, they nevertheless produced 24.2 percent of total gross value of industrial production.[30] These figures also indicate that deindustrialization has taken place in Eritrea. Ten years before (in 1970) 14,000 Eritreans were employed in 165 establishments and were responsible for thirty-five percent of Ethiopia's total industrial production.[31] Eritrea's contribution to the economy of Ethiopia can be seen by comparing export figures before and after federation in 1952. During the seven years prior to federation, Ethiopian exports averaged 81.5 million *birr* per year. During the first three years of federation, they averaged 164 million *birr*, i.e., they doubled in value.[32] It is expected that with peace and independence, many thousand skilled workers would return to Eritrea, just as many trained Zimbabwean exiles have returned to their own country since independence was won in 1980.

In 1976, the Ethiopian government nationalized the commanding heights of the economy; twenty-five Eritrean factories were taken over. Twenty were in Asmara, two each in Decamere and Massawa and one in Assab. These factories produced batteries, beer and other beverages, canned meat and fish, cement, edible oils, glass, kitchen utensils, leather goods, matches and textiles. The program of the EPLF indicates that, under its administration, some industries would probably remain under public ownership. One big difference from the centrally directed dictatorship of the Dergue is that under the policy of the EPLF, workers would participate in the management of industry. Small factories and workshops would remain in private hands while the emphasis (and a mistaken one) would be on heavy industry.[33] The 1987 program indicates that there would be both private and public sectors in industry, as well as in trade and agriculture; the EPLF would also rescind the Dergue's nationalization of urban land.[34]

The economic prospects are promising.[35] A great deal of comment has been made over the inability of colonial Eritrea to balance its budget. In fact, the Italians managed to achieve a balanced budget for the first time in 1927-1928.[36] By careful efforts, the British emulated the Italians in 1944.[37] Leaving aside the fact that the richest and most powerful economy in the world, the United States, has also been unable to balance its budget in recent years, there is no reason to accept a stereotypic view that an independent Eritrea would be weak economically and politically. It would certainly not be weak militarily, as to be independent it would have either have defeated the Ethiopian army or forced the Ethiopians to negotiate a settlement; they would be a major power in the region. However, the fact that Ethiopia is economically dependent on Eritrea must be discussed. In 1974, forty-six percent of Ethiopia's trade was handled by the port of Massawa, thirty-one percent through Assab and only twenty-three percent through Djibouti.[38] There is no reason to doubt an independent Eritrea's willingness to allow this to continue; the EPLF program of 1977 says it will "establish trade relations with all countries that respect Eritrean sovereignty irrespective of political systems."[39] Ethiopia and Eritrea could take advantage of peace and build two sovereign nations which would be economically interdependent.

There is a well developed network of roads in Eritrea, including 300 miles of asphalt and several thousand miles of all weather roads. The EPLF has built roads in virtually all parts of Eritrea: during the past few years alone, over 1,000 miles have been constructed with the help of a few pieces of heavy equipment but mostly through manual labor.[40] One of the most impressive sights in Eritrea is the Challenge Road, linking the mountainous Sahel Province, long a base area for the EPLF, with the fertile lowland province of Barka, once a stronghold of the ELF, but securely in EPLF hands since 1980. A railway, some 180 miles in length, connects the major port of Massawa with the capital and continues east to the second city, Keren and on to Agordat, near the Sudanese border; because of guerrilla activities it has not operated since 1975.

The main factors limiting increased production are the shortage of raw materials and inadequate technical knowledge. Self-sufficiency is the guiding principle behind EPLF economic activity. The second objective of the National Democratic Programme calls for the building of "an independent, self-reliant and planned national economy."[41] All units of the EPLF see themselves as providing the groundwork of an independent Eritrean industrial economy.[42] Not all projects met their targets, but as Fekadu Ghebre Medhin of the construction department commented, "problems teach people."[43] During 1977-1978, when the liberation fronts controlled most of Eritrea's urban areas, it was estimated that they could provide for more than eighty percent of civilian needs.[44] Since 1978, large numbers of skilled workers have joined the EPLF or have been trained by specialist fighters; industrial production in the liberated areas has increased greatly. For instance, the EPLF is now able to manufacture petrol tankers and make major modifications to captured Soviet and Western vehicles and machinery. There are also many acknowledged deficiencies. Transport is a problem area; efforts to expand transport, particularly pack animals, have not been successful. There has been a leakage of skilled people from the department of transportation and little has been accomplished in sea transport.[45]

The EPLF emphasizes self-sufficiency not only for political reasons but also because it is the only way, given the virtual absence of any imported raw materials and finished goods, for the Eritreans to develop their economic potential. Through voluntary, collective work, EPLF cadres try to encourage innovativeness, perseverance and pride in work and struggle. Hundreds of visitors to the EPLF-held areas will attest to their success. The EPLF is also aware that in conditions of peace, volunteerism may not suffice; experience has shown that in the transitional stage, material incentives are more likely to increase productivity.[46] The EPLF also realizes that one of its greatest difficulties will be in controlling prices.[47]

Sherman has argued that self-sufficiency was forced upon the EPLF in the field, as the foreign mission under the external leadership of Osman Saleh Sabbe, during 1972-1974, deliberately deprived units in Eritrea of finance.[48] Since this period, the major external source of support has certainly been that given by Eritreans (clandestinely) in the towns under Ethiopian military rule, and by the tens of thousands of Eritreans dispersed in many countries around the world. Equipment needed for large and small scale industries, schools, hospitals and farms in the liberated area is continually being taken out of the cities by workers sympathetic to the EPLF.[49] Many of the materials used by the EPLF are also captured from the Ethiopians. Every available item is used and recycled in a most ingenious way. External purchases are limited to fuel oil some categories of heavy ammunition and food for the fighters.[50]

The experiences of Nigeria, Zimbabwe and a number of the more economically developed Latin American countries show that a period of involuntary self-reliance—perhaps brought about through civil war or prolonged depression—can be the spur to developing an industrial economy; Eritrea has also passed through this period of trial.[51] The Eritreans are aware that the experience of other small socialist nations with regard to building a self-sufficient economy is not particularly encouraging. A number of socialist countries have tried very hard to break away from the capitalist world economy in an effort to curb the power of the international and domestic actors who benefit from the dependency relationship with the West. In the well documented case of Tanzania, this attempt at self-reliance led in the end to marked distortions to the economy, the need for even more external support and an even greater dependency.[52] So pressing will be the need of Eritreans for external finance for development, they will probably cultivate trade and financial links with a diversified group of third world and small social democratic countries. They will use competitive currency and commodity markets, private banks and non-governmental organizations as a source of development funds.[53]

All too many Eritreans and Ethiopians have died in the course of the independence struggle. It has been said that "death is inevitable and, therefore, it is better to die with one's honor without giving cause to the future generation to curse."[54] The Eritreans who have died have given no reason for the future generation to curse them; on the contrary they have left a legacy which could be the inspiration for the Horn of Africa. Their achievements in the areas of education and health have been particularly impressive.

The EPLF is vitally involved in all aspects of Eritrean life and nowhere more so than in education. Colonial rule left an appalling legacy of neglect and illiteracy. Under the Italians, the highest level an Eritrean could reach in public schools was the fourth grade; the main objective of Italian education seems to have been to teach him (girls being denied education) to be able to recite in Italian "the names of those who had made Italy great."[55] The Italians were alarmed that a more liberal education would create, "misunderstanding among the natives whose aspirations were many times in excess of their status."[56] The British quadrupled the number of primary schools, from twenty-four to 100, and also introduced fourteen middle schools with 1,200 students and two secondary schools with 167 pupils.[57]

During the federation period, education was extended for the first time to the rural areas and to girls. The two sexes were segregated and the curriculum emphasized a narrow theoretical view. After the Ethiopian annexation of Eritrea in 1962, educational standards worsened. Students resented the forced introduction of the Amharic language—just as Black children in South Africa in 1976 opposed the introduction of Afrikaans as the compulsory language of education. All over the country, schools became the center of opposition to Ethiopian rule; in consequence many were burned down by the men of the Second Division and thousands of students imprisoned or driven to exile.[58] For many years education in the rural areas came virtually to a standstill. The little education offered was substandard. The EPLF has noticed a general distaste for education among all age groups; under the Dergue, a generation has been raised which has rejected a colonial education system and has not been able to find an adequate replacement.

The EPLF examined curricula used by British and Ethiopian administrations and found them totally unsuitable. The distinguishing feature of the newly developed EPLF system is the integration of theory with practice. All students participate in productive work; they learn through doing and take part in the struggle for social and economic justice. In 1976, the EPLF opened a revolutionary school, named "Zero," in the north of Eritrea. This school was designed as a teaching laboratory and started with ninety children, mostly orphans, the children of fighters, refugees and nomads. By 1983, the school had over 3,000 students and remarkable progress had been made, in spite of the shortage of all equipment, materials and even nutritious food.[59] In 1986, the school had 3,270 boarding students.

In the Zero School, there are five years of elementary education and two years of middle school. The subjects taught are: the history of Eritrea and world civilization; geography of Eritrea, Africa and the world; general science; arithmetic; Tigrinya; Tigré; English; Arabic; arts, music and sports. Handicrafts are taught at elementary level and technical education at the middle level. All of the mass organizations, i.e., those involving workers, peasants, women and youth, take an active part in deciding the curriculum and organization of the school. The graduating students have already played a vital role in opening up schools in other parts of the country and in teaching peasants to read and write; until recently, ninety percent of the rural population was illiterate. In 1985, a new vocational school was opened at Wina with 100 students; it offers a two-year course in some seven skills including auto mechanics, electrical engineering, metal work, carpentry and civil engineering.[60]

Before the strategic retreat of 1978, the EPLF had opened over 150 schools with 30,000 students. These schools were closed in 1978. Since then the EPLF has concentrated upon a mass literacy and basic mathematics campaign in parts of the highland provinces and in Barka, where the children of nomads begin full-time work from an early age and consequently never attend school. After the expulsion of the ELF and Ethiopian forces from rural Barka, the EPLF resumed its primary educational program. An elementary school was opened at Agraa. Another was launched in 1986 at Rora Habab with an enrollment of 225.[61] Three new day schools were opened for the population of the Solomuna camp; 1,280 children were enrolled in grades one through three, while 1,120 people, mostly women, started adult primary education courses.[62] By 1987, 25,000 students were enrolled in 125 schools.[63] The literacy campaign among adults has been going on for quite a time and has picked up, particularly since 1981 and the departure of the ELF from Barka.[64] The number and competence of teachers, however, is inadequate even for the EPLF's initial schemes.[65] Refugees in the Sudan have not received attention until recent years. During the 1986-1987 year, almost 1,000 students were enrolled in Kassala, half of them girls. This figure represents a thirty percent increase on the previous year; moreover, 300 students were turned away because of lack of space. In 1986, adult education classes started in Kassala with 180 students.[66] Another primary school was opened in Khartoum in 1987, making it the tenth for refugees in the Sudan.[67] The EPLF also regards it as its duty to teach the Ethiopian prisoners of war to read and write.[68]

Not only has the EPLF inherited a totally inadequate education system but, in common with the rest of the colonized third world, has inherited a health delivery system which is totally unsuited to its needs. During the colonial period, most of the rural population was excluded from the system. The EPLF Medical Department has been trying to redress this imbalance for over fourteen years and has developed a medically sound preventative and curative Primary Health Care Scheme, but health services are still at a low level.[69]

The EPLF health service began in 1970 with a single mobile health clinic. The training of barefoot doctors was started in 1972 and the present health service in 1975.[70] The core of the scheme is the village health worker, who is trained close to the community where he or she works and lives. As of early 1986, there were 418 village health workers operating in most highland areas. There were also 150 traditional birth attendants, trained by the EPLF in six to eight week courses.[71] Less than the required number have been trained so far because of the increased intensity of the war. The priorities of the health worker, in order of importance, are: proper nutrition; adequate and safe water supplies; basic sanitation; immunization; the prevention and control of endemic disease; health education and curative services.[72]

Proper nutrition is placed at the head of priorities because, even in a good year, some farms produce insufficient food for the proper nutrition of the peasant's family. Moreover, as shown in Chapter Nine, some parts of Eritrea have been ravaged by drought in nine of the past twelve years, each year more serious than the one preceding it. Malnutrition is the most important direct or associated cause of death. For example, in the Solomuna displaced people's camp, over eighty percent of children's deaths are related to malnutrition. And, in Barka Province, over fifty percent of newborn babies die before their first birthday.

The EPLF is very concerned about the lack of an adequate and safe water supply for nomads and settled farmers. To improve their living conditions priority has been given to the digging of deep wells. Sanitation is almost non-existent, and unsanitary practices have contributed to a pattern of infectious diseases similar to England of 200 years ago. This area of Africa was the last to be declared free from smallpox.

There are thirty functioning health service stations, each of which serves a group of ten villages. There are twenty-two functioning health centers which cover some thirty percent of the population of liberated rural Eritrea. They deal with maternal and child health and also function as polyclinics; they are the base for forty-one mobile units of barefoot doctors, midwives, medical and health assistants who also operate in contested areas.[73] By the beginning of 1985, some 1,600 barefoot doctors and forty-one barefoot midwives had been trained in six-month courses.[74] The barefoot doctors not only treat common diseases and give health education, they also teach self-defense. It appears that some of these trained staff have a primary military role, as at the end of 1987 the establishment of barefoot doctors stood at 800, village health workers 320, laboratory and radio technicians 41, midwives 28, dental assistants 18 and nurses 151.[75]

There are six regional hospitals, which care for referral cases and also carry out training and prepare publications. They are situated in Sahel and Danakil provinces; at Filfil in the northern highlands, one in the southern highlands and another on the Mareb border between Tigray and Eritrea. The hospitals behind the enemy lines have mobile operation tents and wards—capacity is from 150-200 beds.[76]

There is also a central hospital at Orota in Barka, where eleven out of the twenty-nine Eritrean doctors who work in liberated Eritrea are stationed. Some 328 paramedics also work in the Central Hospital.[77] Many of the patients are victims of Ethiopian attacks. In 1985, more than 1,000 civilians were wounded, eighty-five of them napalm burn cases.

The twenty-two member pharmacy unit works hard to produce essential drugs. By the end of 1987, it was producing fourteen types of tablets and capsules—two million per month—and hoping to provide soon for sixty percent of the population's needs. Already it has the makings of a national drug manufacturing program, the envy of most of the third world.[78] Throughout the health system, the EPLF strives to ensure adequate involvement of the local communities in the implementation and evaluation of health care. Once again, the effectiveness of the scheme is limited by a shortage of the most elementary supplies. Large numbers of medically trained personnel have joined the EPLF and there are sufficient numbers to staff the district hospitals throughout the liberated areas; over twenty years of ferocious warfare have stretched them to the limit.

The trials of the EPLF fighters have both toughened and humanized them. The EPLF has begun to build a democratic egalitarian society even though its political structure has been developed under conditions of intense armed struggle. That the symbols of rank between commanders, platoon and squad leaders, and other fighters are absent is a good pointer to the future.[79] The EPLF emphasizes internal debate, discussion and persuasion. The National Democratic Programme was adopted by the First Congress of the EPLF meeting inside liberated Eritrea in 1977; one third of the membership of the congress was drawn from mass organizations established by the EPLF, but operating under their own leadership. At the Second Congress the ratio of civilian to military delegates was 3:1. There was a secret ballot for the election of the seventy-one members (and seven alternate members) of the central committee. The members of the central committee, six of whom were women, then elected the nine member political bureau (Politburo)—all of whom are men.

Most foreign observers who visit Eritrea comment on the self-discipline and self-reliance of the EPLF as well as the open democratic nature of liberated Eritrean society. They also note its sophisticated organization and the depth of the social reforms it has been able to institute.[80] A veteran observer of liberation movements compared the Eritrean revolution in 1977 to the Vietnam revolution in terms of liberated territory and ability to hold towns.[81] The EPLF held Keren, with a population of over 30,000, for over a year and learned that they needed to broaden the political base of the movement. They ran the town in an efficient and democratic manner and were still able to control the prices of basic goods, to nationalize housing and to redistribute food.

The Eritrean liberation movement already holds a unique place among African revolutionary groups but there are some parallels with the revolution in Guinea-Bissau. In Guinea-Bissau, according to the leader of the African Party for the Independence of Guinea-Bissau and Cape Verde (PAIGC), the largely petty bourgeois leadership of the movement became radicalized when it became dependent upon and, therefore, responsive to, the peasants.[82] The ELF and EPLF, the bulk of whose leadership was not from the working class and peasantry, could not have survived the hardships of the early years without the support of the bulk of the peasants.

Some writers have deplored the dependent development path taken by the leadership of many independent African countries who initially claimed to be socialist. They claim that this is due to the fact that liberation was achieved without the full proletarianization of the revolutionary leadership.[83] They fear that Eritrea could follow the same path. There is probably little need for this concern; the EPLF has proceeded very circumspectly. In recent years, it has had to guide the traditional, patriarchal and mainly Muslim population of Barka Province carefully through the necessary steps of social and political transformation. There are already encouraging signs that the EPLF is succeeding in this task; many sons and daughters of Barka peasants have joined the EPLF. There seems little danger that the EPLF will fall into the trap of theorizing without action.[84]

The EPLF's policy and practice on women's rights also gives hope for a fully democratic independent Eritrea. The National Democratic Program assures women full rights of equality with men in politics, economy and social life as well as equal pay for equal work.[85] Women have had greater success than men on the many literacy courses.[86] The former chairwoman of the National Union of Eritrean Women, Luul Ghebreab, indicated the gradual approach that is taken saying, "We work with women on different levels, according to their level of consciousness. We raise issues very slowly. As time goes by the women from the village take up new concepts themselves, and they become those who are working for change."[87]

Women have frequently played central roles in revolutionary warfare—the examples of Guinea-Bissau and Zimbabwe come to mind—only to return to domestic life and an unequal position after liberation. For a long period, women have been involved in the EPLF at all levels from doctor to truck driver and front line fighter, to leader of mass organizations; one hopes that Eritrean women will not be forced to take a back seat once liberation is obtained.

In other areas, EPLF practice also leads one to hope that post-revolutionary society in Eritrea will be unauthoritarian to a marked degree. Its practices of voluntary recruitment of literate fighters, internal democracy in all wings of the EPLF, and the fostering of cooperation between the peasants and fighters, will all lead to this end. Political analysts warn against predicting either the course of events, or the likely outcome of a revolution, solely on the interests, outlook or ideology of revolutionary leaders, writers or theorists; and also that "the causes of revolutions could only be understood by looking at the specific interpretations of class and state structures and the complex interplay over time of domestic and international developments.[88] But one reason for predicting the ultimate success of the EPLF lies in the firm relationship between the peasants and the movement. Peasants have been as important as technology in transforming societies. Those societies with an agrarian bureaucracy and a central authority which extracts surplus from the peasants, and consequently inhibits the growth of a commercial and manufacturing class, have proved the most susceptible to revolution. Peasants are most likely to revolt if faced with a new or sudden imposition which breaks with accepted rules and customs.[89] Eritrean peasants swung their support behind the liberation fronts in 1975 and 1976 following the Dergue's attempt at forced collectivization and its repression of traditional life with massacre, torture and rape. Peasant acceptance of the EPLF's land reform policy has been a major reason for the EPLF's continued ability to mobilize popular support.[90]

The future development of the Eritrean revolution will be largely determined by the degree to which the Ethiopian conscript army can continue its costly campaign against the Eritrean people. If the Ethiopian army lost its will to fight, the independence of Eritrea would soon follow, an independence that could be safeguarded by the EPLA, already a better equipped army than that of many independent African states.

The form of an independent Eritrean state will depend upon a number of factors. The most important of these are: the domestic and international economic constraints faced by the new state; the relations of Eritrea with Ethiopia and the major powers, none of whom have assisted Eritrea, and some of whom have tried to destroy the revolution; and the relation of the new state to class forces. If the style of Eritrean administration in the liberated areas is any guide, the state will be strengthened but will not be as bureaucratized as other socialist states. The EPLF style of administration can be aptly categorized as coordinated decentralization.

No matter what the beliefs of the new revolutionary leadership, some of the old state structures are inevitably carried over into the new state and may come to exert a great deal of influence over the transitional institutions. In Eritrea, however, the old structures have been so transformed by twenty-nine years of war that one could venture an observation that the old slogan may hold good, "the new society will be built within the shell of the old." The EPLF has had to start every service and industry virtually from scratch using its own resources.

Clearly, the independence of Eritrea and its recognition by the major powers, would deal a severe, probably mortal blow to the Ethiopian empire. Ethiopia has been in turmoil for over fifteen years. The Dergue seized power and was supported initially by workers, students and various subject nationalities.[91] The army consolidated its power; strikes were declared illegal and trade unions made subservient to the wishes of the military. Some left-wing students organized into the Ethiopian People's Revolutionary Party (EPRP) took the disastrous decision to mount an urban guerrilla campaign against the Dergue. In a bloody reaction, the Ethiopian Army killed tens of thousands of innocent people and suspected EPRP sympathizers and imprisoned hundreds of thousands of others. The Dergue is a very narrowly based regime, comprising in the main Amharic speaking army officers, and even among the army its hold is slackening; not a week goes by without desertions to the EPLF, TPLF, OLF, the Somali liberation movement, or other opposition forces.

But although the Dergue has lost most of its initial support among Ethiopians, it is still given massive aid and support by all major powers. The Soviet Union and its allies give considerable military assistance. In 1984, Mengistu formed a Workers Party, organized on similar lines to the Soviet party. The United States and the Western powers, on the other hand, not only continue to supply significant levels of arms, but also give considerable humanitarian aid to Ethiopia and, through their influence in the World Bank and International Monetary Fund, see that Ethiopia receives constant support for its bankrupt economy. The Western nations presumably hoped that, if Mengistu defeated the Eritrean and Tigrayan revolts, he would send the Soviet troops home and return to the western fold—as did Egypt's Anwar Sadat, Sudan's Jaafer Nimeri and Somalia's Siad Barre before him.

The Ethiopians, with or without military aid from whatever source, have not been able to defeat the Eritreans. The success of the Eritrean revolution would see the accompanying success of the other liberation struggles. Apart from the Eritreans—who would presumably opt for full independence if given the chance in a referendum—the other movements would probably settle for a democratic federated Ethiopia. The Somalis in the Ogaden would also be able to press for independence. Such change in the third largest country in Africa would have profound effects on liberation and secessionist groups throughout the continent.

The "balkanization" of the Horn of Africa is a nightmare for centralists, who claim that a united Ethiopia will do far more to aid the political and economic advancement of all nationalities than the formation of an Ethiopian federation or confederation and the independence of Eritrea. An examination of the recent history of the Horn of Africa shows, however, that the actions of the Dergue have caused economic disaster and some of the world's most severe repression. This has led to one of the world's most disastrous and persistent famines and the highest proportion of refugees.[92]

On the other hand, the Eritrean revolution has already transformed the lives of hundreds of thousands of people and brought about political and social betterment to a degree rare anywhere in the world.

Notes

1. Ross K. Baker, 'Biafra: Balkanization or Nation-Building,' *Orbis*, XII, 2, (1968) p. 523.
2. Robert A. Dahl and Edward R. Tufte, *Size and Democracy* (Stanford, Stanford University Press, 1973) p. 122.
3. World Bank, *Ethiopia: Recent Economic Developments and Future Prospects*, Vol. 2 (Washington, D.C., 1984) p. 131.
4. Araia Tseggai, 'Independent Eritrea: Economically Viable?' *Horn of Africa*, VI, 2 (1983) p. 41.
5. Araia Tseggai, 'Independent Eritrea,' p. 40.
6. *Eritrea: Food and Agricultural Production Assessment Study*, Final Report (Leeds University, Agricultural and Rural Development Unit, 1988) pp. 168-9.
7. Ferdinando Quaranta, *Ethiopia: an Empire in the Making* (London, P. S. King, 1939) p. 24.
8. *Ethiopian Herald*, May 19 (1983).
9. Araia Tseggai, 'Independent Eritrea,' pp. 42-6.
10. James Firebrace with Stuart Holland, *Never Kneel Down: Drought, Development and Liberation in Eritrea* (Trenton NJ, Red Sea Press, 1985) p. 154.
11. Giotto Dainelli, 'The Italian Colonies,' *Geographical Review*, 19, July (1929) p. 415.
12. Quaranta, 'Ethiopia,' p. 69.
13. United Nations, General Assembly, *Official Records, Supplement 8* (1950) p. 77.
14. Georgi Galperin, *Ethiopia: Population, Resources, Economy*, trans. J. Shapiro (Moscow, Progress, 1981) p. 213.
15. Araia Tseggai, 'Independent Eritrea,' p. 44.
16. Galperin, 'Ethiopia,' p. 214.
17. Patrick Gilkes, 'Eritrea Could Stand Alone,' *African Development*, 9, April (1975) p. 18.
18. Araia Tseggai, 'Independent Eritrea,' p. 44.
19. United Nations, 'Official Records,' pp. 15, 77.
20. Galperin, 'Ethiopia,' p. 214.
21. *Ethiopian Herald*, October 26 (1978); August 20 (1981).
22. Galperin, 'Ethiopia,' p. 214, 30.

23. Richard Sherman, *Eritrea: the Unfinished Revolution* (New York, Praeger, 1980) p. 120.
24. United Nations, 'Official Records,' p. 77.
25. Araia Tseggai, 'Independent Eritrea,' p. 45.
26. Dainelli, 'The Italian Colonies,' p. 416.
27. United Nations, 'Official Records,' p. 77.
28. World Bank, *Ethiopia: Recent Economic Developments and Future Prospects*, vol 1 (Washington, D.C., 1984) p. 45.
29. World Bank, 'Vol 1,' p. 55.
30. World Bank, 'Vol 2,' p. 136.
31. Sherman, 'Eritrea,' p. 119.
32. Gilkes, 'Eritrea Could Stand Alone,' p. 18.
33. Firebrace 'Never Kneel Down,' p. 157.
34. Eritrean People's Liberation Front, *Political Report and National Democratic Programme* (1987) p. 167.
35. Sherman, 'Eritrea,' p. 111.
36. Stephen H. Longrigg, *A Short History of Eritrea* (Oxford, Clarendon Press, 1945) p. 132.
37. Sylvia E. Pankhurst and Richard K.P. Pankhurst, *Ethiopia and Eritrea: the Last Phase of the Reunion 1941-1952* (Essex, Lalibela House, 1953) p. 106.
38. *Ethiopian Herald*, June 8 (1975).
39. Firebrace, 'Never Kneel Down,' p. 155.
40. *Eritrea Information*, 5,4 (1983).
41. Firebrace, 'Never Kneel Down,' p. 153.
42. *Eritrea Information*, 5, 7 (1983).
43. Nicholas Mottern, *Suffering Strong: the Journal of a Westerner in Ethiopia, the Sudan, Eritrea and Chad* (Trenton NJ, Red Sea Press, 1988) p. 63.
44. Firebrace, 'Never Kneel Down,' p. 71.
45. Eritrean People's Liberation Front, 'Political Report,' p. 83.
46. Carmelo Mesa-Lago, *The Economy of Socialist Cuba: a Two-Decade Appraisal* (Albuquerque, University of New Mexico Press, 1981) p. 21.
47. Eritrean People's Liberation Front, 'Political Report,' p. 84.
48. Sherman, 'Eritrea,' p. 46.
49. Francois Houtart, 'The Social Revolution in Eritrea,' eds. Basil Davidson, et. al., *Behind the War in Eritrea* (Nottingham, Spokesman, 1980) p. 109.
50. Firebrace, 'Never Kneel Down,' p. 73.
51. Richard A. Joseph, 'Affluence and Underdevelopment: the Nigerian Experience,' *Journal of Modern African Studies*, 12, 3 (1978) p. 223.
52. Barbara Stallings, 'External Finance and the Transition to Socialism in Small Peripheral Societies,' eds. Richard Fagen, et. al., *Transition and Development: Problems of Third World Socialism* (New York, Monthly Review Press, 1986) p. 67.
53. Stallings, 'External Finance,' p. 55.
54. Mesfin Wolde-Mariam, 'The Socioeconomic Consequences of Famine,' ed. Fassil G. Kiros, *Challenging Rural Poverty* (Trenton NJ, Africa World Press, 1985) p. 15.
55. G.K.N. Trevaskis, *Eritrea-A Colony in Transition: 1941-52* (London, Oxford University Press, 1960) p. 33.

56. Araia Tseggai, 'Historical Analysis of Infrastructural Development in Italian-Eritrea: 1885-1941,' *Journal of Eritrean Studies*, 1, 2 (1987) p. 11.
57. Trevaskis, 'Eritrea,' p. 129.
58. Eritrean Relief Association, *Education in Eritrea* (Khartoum, 1983) pp. 4-5.
59. Eritrean Relief Association, 'Education in Eritrea,' pp. 16-22.
60. Eritrean Relief Association, *Annual Report* (1985) p. 12.
61. Eritrean Relief Association, *Informational Bulletin*, 31 (1987).
62. *Eritrean Information*, 9, 1 (1987).
63. *Adulis*, IV, 1-2 (1988).
64. Yonas Debassai, *Interview with Author*, August 29 (1983).
65. Eritrean People's Liberation Front, 'Political Report,' p. 88.
66. Eritrean Relief Association, *Informational Bulletin*, 30 (1987).
67. Eritrean Relief Association, *Informational Bulletin*, 35 (1987).
68. Eritrean People's Liberation Front, 'Political Report,' p. 101.
69. Eritrean People's Liberation Front, 'Political Report,' p. 96.
70. Glenys Kinnock, *Eritrea: Images of War and Peace* (London, Chatto and Windus, 1988) p. 32.
71. *Eritrea in Relief*, March (1987).
72. Eritrean Relief Association, *Health Service Delivery in Eritrea* (Khartoum, 1983) p. 38.
73. *Adulis*, IV, 1 (1987).
74. Doris Burgess et. al., *Eritrean Journey* (London, War on Want, 1985).
75. *Adulis*, IV, 9-10 (1987).
76. Kassahun Checole, 'An Interview with Dr. Assefaw Tekeste,' *Horn of Africa*, VI, 1 (1983) p. 31.
77. Burgess, 'Eritrean Journey.'
78. Michael Johnson and Trish Johnson, 'Eritrea: the National Question and the Logic of Protracted Struggle,' *African Affairs*, 80, 319 (1981) p. 191.
79. *Eritrea in Relief*, March (1987).
80. Research and Information Centre on Eritrea, *Revolution in Eritrea: Eyewitness Reports* (Rome, 1979).
81. Gerard Chaliand, *The Struggle for Africa: Conflict of the Great Powers*, trans. A.M. Berret (London, Macmillan, 1982) p. 100.
82. Amilcar Cabral, *Return to the Source* (New York, Monthly Review Press, 1973) p. 63.
83. Johnson, 'Eritrea,' p. 194.
84. Basil Davidson, 'On Revolutionary Nationalism: the Legacy of Cabral,' *Race and Class*, XXVII, 3 (1986) p. 22.
85. Bereket Habte Selassie, *Conflict and Intervention in the Horn of Africa* (New York, Monthly Review Press, 1980) p. 187.
86. Richard Leonard, 'Popular Participation in Liberation and Revolution,' eds. Lionel Cliffe and Basil Davidson, *The Long Struggle of Eritrea for Independence and Constructive Peace* (Nottingham, Spokesman, 1988) p. 129.
87. National Union of Eritrean Women, *Women of Eritrea* (1986).
88. Theda Skocpol, *States and Social Revolutions: A Comparative Analysis of France, Russia and China* (Cambridge, Cambridge University Press, 1979) p. xiii.

89. Barrington Moore Jr.. *Social Origins of Dictatorship and Democracy: Lord and Peasant in the Making of the Modern World* (Boston. Beacon. 1969) p. 474.

90. Peter With, *Politics and Liberation: the Eritrea Struggle. 1961-1986* (Denmark. University of Aarhus. 1987) p. 123.

91. I.M. Lewis, ed. 'Introduction.' *Nationalism and Self-Determination in the Horn of Africa* (London, Ithaca, 1983) p. 7.

92. Charles Humana ed., *The World Human Rights Guide* (London. Economist. 1986) p. xiv.

III

Eritrea: Development of a Nation

11

Free At Last

Seldom do we find that a whole People can be said to have any Faith at all; except in things which it can eat and handle. Whensoever it gets any Faith, its history becomes spirit-stirring, noteworthy.

—Thomas Carlyle, *The French Revolution: A History*[i]

The whole of Eritrea came under the effective control of the EPLF in May 1991 after the successful completion of the thirty-year-long, armed struggle for independence.[2] Massawa was liberated in February 1990 through Operation *Fenkil*, which overwhelmed the Ethiopians in a three-day campaign. In the assault, most of the Ethiopian naval fleet was captured or sunk; the Dergue was left with just one operational frigate. The EPLF naval units were then free to attack the enemy as far down the coast as Tio. The EPLF and the civilian population suffered severe casualties, both in the battle, and during the Ethiopian air-raids that persisted for several months. My personal observations confirmed that US-made cluster bombs were used by the Ethiopians. As a result of this experience, the EPLF revised its strategy and determined to try and take Asmara without a bloody last battle.[3]

Most of the rest of Southern Eritrea, including the towns of Adi Keih, Senafé, and Segeneiti, was freed in that year; most of the Ethiopian-trained "wheat militias" deserted to the EPLF as soon as the fighting started. Some of the pressure was taken off the EPLA by the continuing successes of the Ethiopian People's Revolutionary Democratic Front (EPRDF) which had liberated all of Tigray and started to take towns in Wollo, Gojam, Shoa, and Gondar Provinces. The OLF also gained ground in Wollega Province. The Dergue was forced to fight on many fronts.

Before the winter of 1990, a new front line was established by the EPLF at Ghinda, only twenty miles away from Asmara airport. The airport could no longer be used as a base for Ethiopian sorties and, because of increased defections of skilled personnel as well as attrition, the air force was down to forty operational fighters. Four of Ethiopia's "elite" divisions faced the Eritreans, but as Isaias told me at the time "the war is finished for the Ethiopian 2nd Army." The Eighteenth, Nineteenth, Twenty-first, and Twenty-second Divisions all contained more than ninety percent poorly armed and virtually untrained conscripts.[4]

However, in the fighting of 1991, the EPLF took very heavy casualties, as the Dergue could readily supply its own front line around Decamere and poured down fire on the EPLA below them. The Soviet Union made three significant shipments of arms supplies to Ethiopia in 1990 and some two hundred Israeli military advisers came to support Mengistu. Many EPLA battalions (five hundred personnel at full strength) that were serving at the front were left with only fifty members each at the end of the campaign.

This proved to be the most crucial period of the war. As Eritrean Chief of Staff Haile Samuel said later, "if the enemy had succeeded in the offensives mounted, we might have been forced to retreat for the second time, and the very existence of the movement might have been doubtful."[5]

The Ghinda front was defended for sixteen months, but in spite of continual attempts, the Ethiopians never breached it. This was a truly epic struggle; as the Commander of the 81st Brigade of Eritrea's 61st Division said, "this is not a battle field. It is hell. No living creature is expected to resist it."[6]

On May 21st, 1991, Decamare fell to the EPLF; the Ethiopian troops were demoralized further by the knowledge that Mengistu had already fled Ethiopia, and that EPRDF troops were closing in on Addis Ababa. Sebhat Efrem had said over ten years before that the liberation of Asmara might come through the gates of Addis Ababa and so partly it did. But EPLA training, logistical support, intelligence, and heavy weapons, were also of vital importance to the EPRDF and OLF victories. The Dergue's commanders requested safe conduct out of Eritrea for the 100,000 Ethiopian troops besieged in the towns of Asmara and Keren. The EPLF refused to make any concessions, but the Ethiopians surrendered with hardly a shot being fired.

On May 24th, the EPLF entered Asmara to a universal and delirious welcome. Assab fell the same day, Keren the day after. All Ethiopian soldiers, senior members of the WPE, and medium and high-level Ethiopian functionaries who did not leave voluntarily were expelled from Eritrea. These are the bare facts of one of the most extraordinarily successful sustained feats of warfare in history!

The EPLF took over the administration of Asmara and the other cities; the transition was smooth, and normal life was resumed in a remarkably short space of time. One factor that facilitated the transition was the guidance given by the secret EPLF members who had been in Asmara throughout the war. For instance, of the 100 personnel in the Dergue's Public Administration Department, three were secret EPLF members.[7]

Just three months after liberation, I could observe for myself that very few armed men were to be seen on the streets of Asmara. I interviewed Isaias Afwerki at that time. He told me that the

EPLF was fortunate in not having any political problems to worry about; they could concentrate on pressing economic concerns.[8]

Immediately after the fall of Addis Ababa to the forces of the EPRDF on May 28, 1991 and Mengistu's precipitous flight out of the country to a bolt hole in Zimbabwe (Ethiopia had given some support to Mugabe's ZANU during his independence struggle), peace talks were held in London, and later in Addis Ababa. The Eritrean delegation was persuaded by the EPRDF, and the United States government, to delay a referendum on sovereignty for two years; in return the Ethiopians guaranteed Eritrea a budget. The Eritreans were also affected by the consideration that Ethiopia should be stabilized before they conducted their referendum. Many Ethiopians (and their dwindling band of academic camp followers) were almost hysterical with anger and grief over the "loss of Eritrea." A cooling-off period of two years might reconcile Ethiopians to their loss.

Eritrea's acceptance by world bodies—overdue as it was— was facilitated by the excellent contacts Meles Zenawi and Isaias Afwerki had made with American statesmen in recent years and the positive impact their visits had made. In the latter part of the war, US Secretary for Africa Herman Cohen made the welcome (if belated) statement that Eritrea had the right to self-determination. Isaias was also on good terms with Salim Ahmed Salim, Secretary General of the OAU.[9]

On October 8, 1991 Ethiopia's Ambassador to the United Nations addressed the General Assembly, saying that Ethiopia "respects the right of the Eritrean people to freely determine their future in an internationally supervised referendum."[10] The Ethiopian President, Meles Zenawi, wrote a memorandum asking the UN to send observers to Eritrea to monitor the referendum. The Eritreans made their position very clear; they pressed for a referendum, but saw it as "merely bringing a formal conclusion to the wishes [of the people] confirmed in a relentless struggle; not because it harbors any doubts about the choice of the Eritrean people."[11]

The 1993 referendum was organized by a Commission appointed by Isaias Afwerki, the Secretary General of the Provisional Government of Eritrea (PGE.) It became an outstanding exercise in public democratic participation, even though the people, none of whom had voted before, had been schooled into the appropriate actions for some months beforehand, and some were apprehensive of their fate should they vote No by accident or choice.[12]

Eritrea was formally recognized as an independent nation by the UN, the OAU, Ethiopia and most other states, in the weeks following the completion of the referendum. Possibly eighty-five percent of eligible Eritreans, living in Eritrea, and some forty other countries, registered to vote. It is claimed that over ninety-eight percent of registered voters voted for independence. The Eritrean minorities, such as the Afar and the Kunama, voted in a similar fashion to the Tigrinya/Tigré majority, and in the percentage voting yes there were no significant differences between Eritreans living abroad and those in Eritrea.[13] No one could challenge the validity of the process, or question the accuracy of the result. Such a decisive vote went some way to justifying the sacrifices of generations of Eritreans.

The new nation received many expressions of good will, and a number of state visits by greater or lesser luminaries from a remarkable variety of nations. Many countries, agencies, individuals, and institutions promised aid and developmental assistance (and a few have actually delivered it.) Eritrea will, however, have to find its own place in the increasingly anarchic world of international politics and business. It will be a tough struggle.

The EPLF changed its name to The People's Front for Democracy and Justice (PFDJ) at its third congress in February 1994; for the present, it is the only political movement allowed to exist in Eritrea. All members of the Government of Eritrea belong to the PFDJ.

The major purpose of this chapter is to analyze the priorities of the Eritrean leadership under five broad headings: economic;

political; social; nationalism, religion, and language; military, diplomatic, and strategic. Many priorities and policies of course straddle these boundaries. And as government officials often say "in Eritrea, everything is a priority."

ECONOMIC

Eritrea is one of the world's poorest countries with an estimated Gross Domestic Product (GDP) per head for 1994 of $70-150; however, the GDP is growing at a rate of between seven to ten percent a year and, given good harvests and continued overseas investment, should be able to maintain this upward trend.[14] Eritrea is an undeveloped country, but its leaders have ambitious dreams of turning it into an economic power "on the verge of take-off", within twenty years. It started off its independent existence with one great asset—no debt was owed to any foreign government, bank, or multilateral institution.

For the present, about half of the Eritrean state's income comes from private transfers from Eritreans living outside the country; the Eritrean government is therefore bound to follow policies that encourage this capital inflow.[15] There is a liberal investment code—possibly the most liberal in Africa—and donor nations were moved by this, and other liberal economic moves by the Eritrean government, to pledge $250 million in late 1994. These loans are administered by the World Bank on highly concessionary and favorable terms.

There is no doubting Eritrea's commitment to a mixed economy. In December 1987, Isaias Afwerki was already talking to me about the need for an independent Eritrea to have a mixed economy.[16] In August 1990, Isaias singled this out to me as the most important priority of the future independent Eritrea.[17] Some of the senior former-EPLF cadres still believe in socialism, or at least in the superiority and desirability of social democratic rather than conservative or "liberal" political and economic doctrines (as do I). They are being swamped at the moment by exiles and officials of the World Bank, IMF, USAID, etc., many of whom push whatever are the current market nostrums.

Eritrea is firmly committed to an efficient, private-sector-led, market economy with very liberal trade policies and an economy restructured in line with current World Bank doctrine. There is always the danger that World Bank policies may fail in Eritrea as they have in other parts of Africa, unless the government can keep a tight hold on expenditures, control labor organizations, raise prices, control macro-economic policy, and rigorously avert corruption.

Eritrea is one place where this could work—but probably at some considerable cost to the poorest levels of society, and diminished freedom to organize and express dissident views.

The EPLF began to develop its commercial skills early on. They ran cooperative shops in liberated areas, and, beginning in 1984, used the profits to buy goods from abroad to sell in Eritrea. The Red Sea Trading Corporation (RSTC) was established and prospered extremely well. With liberation it has become the most successful enterprise in Eritrea. With the dissolution of the EPLF, control of the RSTC fell to the government and talks on dividing assets between the PFDJ and the government began in 1994.[18] The Nacfa Corporation, which was launched by the EPLF in early 1991, is also prospering.

The PFDJ possesses unknown funds that it intends to invest in Eritrea's future. These funds are clearly substantial, as its transitional charter states that it will play a major investment role in the Eritrean economy.[19] A conference of the PDFJ, held in August 1995, was designed to plot the future strategy of the party.

As the PFDJ will also be the largest political party in Eritrea for the conceivable future, it will inevitably dominate Eritrean economy and politics. The government is aware of the dangers of a one-party state, where party and government are so inextricably intertwined. It has started to separate party from state. Some of the leading party officials do not now have government posts, and some Ministers do not hold party positions. However, the President of Eritrea, Isaias Afwerki, is also Chairman of the PFDJ.

The Eritrean Government declares ceaselessly that economic growth is its most important policy. The main areas of priority seem to be:

Agriculture

Since the war started, over thirty years ago, the country has never been able to meet more than half its cereal food needs. In 1994-1995, even with an extremely commendable, twenty-five percent increase in land use, and a massive mobilization of fighters and peasants to reap the extra harvest, Eritrea was still dependent on food imports (much of it in the form of aid) for at least one-third of its needs.

Agriculture must be expanded to build a strong subsistence sector; "food security" is a favorite catchword of the government. It cannot expect to reach a situation where Eritrea is self-sufficient, merely one where Eritrea has generated enough revenue to be able to import the balance of its food needs without affecting other sectors of the economy.

To kick this expansion off, land reform has been instituted. The land remains under governmental ownership, but under a system of life-time (or 99-year) leases the (wealthiest) Eritrean (and non-Eritrean) investors will be allowed to invest in, or farm, as much land as they can handle. Vast infrastructural investment is envisaged, particularly in water conservation and irrigation. In the long run, cash crops will be produced on large, mechanized commercial farms with the aid of modern fertilizers, etc. If experience elsewhere in the developing world is any guide, substantial environmental degradation will occur—a price the present Eritrean government seems resigned to pay in the interest of short-and-medium term profits.

At the moment, Eritrea is suffering from acute land degradation, shortage of the basic inputs, little or no financial and institutional support, and poorly developed markets. A great deal of assistance will be required before Eritrea can hope to obtain any degree of food security. However, the drive and motivation of the Eritreans should not be underestimated. After all, they fought an enemy ten times their size for thirty years, and eventually beat them.

Extractive Industry

Attempts are being made to interest non-Eritrean investors in oil and natural gas, and commercially proven deposits of copper, coal, salt, iron ore, etc. Western Mining has already taken out leases.

Infrastructure

Considerable improvement in water conservation and supply, roads, electricity, telecommunications, railways and ports is necessary. Many public works programs are under way and are primarily funded by the government. How the programs are to be financed adequately on a continuing basis has not been revealed. At the moment, most of the work is being done by fighters (who receive little pay), the national service draft (who receive none), and civilians on food-for-work programs, who are funded by the UN and other agencies.

Manufacturing Industry

The government has said many times that it wishes as a matter of urgency to divest itself very quickly of most of the forty or so highly unprofitable, and increasingly obsolescent, nationalized industries it inherited from the former regime. The two exceptions seem to be the cement- and glass-producing firms, which are already productive. In 1997, the Red Sea Soap and the Eritrean Shoe Factories were privatized. So far, no other serious buyers have been found. The industries employ several thousand workers who would mostly find it hard to find other employment if the factories were closed down. They also produce basic necessities such as soap, cooking oils, drinking water, etc., which would otherwise have to be imported. The privatization may take some years to achieve.

The most successful new enterprise is the Fred Hollows intraocular lens factory, which employs 20 workers. It manufactures lenses of such high quality that a major US company expressed a wish to be the representative in Africa. The factory already exports to South Africa, Saudi Arabia, and Vietnam.

There are some joint projects to assemble textiles, shoes, etc., begun with South Korean entrepreneurs. Wage levels in Eritrea are among the lowest in the world, and although there is a Labor Law, there are few effective government regulations to protect the work force, in particular, women workers. As the labor unions are small, and were, for a long time, largely an arm of the ruling party, Eritrea is a particularly favorable area for businessmen interested in a disciplined, stable, cheap and willing labor force. This is an area where Taiwanese, Indonesian, and Malaysian investors and manufacturers in particular may well become interested in the future.

The private manufacturing sector is showing some commendable rises in productivity; however, there is a shortage of raw materials and skilled managerial and technical labor. These companies cannot yet compete in international markets without government subsidy. Training is another priority but, as the then editor of *Eritrea Profile* commented, the numerous training courses conducted in Asmara are mainly by "people who didn't have a clue about the specific needs of the country."[20] The programs are often inadequate and inappropriate.

The government has a vision of an industry policy "that will focus on development of capital and/or knowledge intensive industries."[21] This must be a long-term objective, as the country not only lacks the necessary foreign capital, but also has one of the least-educated populations in the world. A great deal of hope must be placed in the Eritreans in the diaspora, many of whom have acquired very impressive educational and professional qualifications.

Tourism
 The PFDJ is developing the tourist industry, and beach hotels and facilities on the Red Sea coast and islands are taking priority. An airport to take international jets is under construction at Massawa. There is an urgent need for training of staff who were used to working rather leisurely for the previous regime (many of the largest hotels in Eritrea remain under government control). At the moment, the great bulk of tourists are aid workers from other parts of the Horn—and they are not the most affluent tourists one would wish for.
 Package tours from Europe will grow. The authorities will have to be on the alert for the increase in corruption, social disturbance, and sexually transmitted diseases (STDs) that invariably accompany them.

Service Industries
 Until July 1997, Eritrea used Ethiopian currency, and therefore had limited control over its foreign exchange and currency policies. The government then announced that an Eritrean currency—the Nakfa—will be introduced and will be legal tender side-by-side with the Birr for an unspecified conversion period. In time, the Nakfa will be the only legal currency in Eritrea.
 Banking and insurance are under government control; one of the priorities is to make credit more accessible to Eritreans. Some of the best brains in Eritrea are involved with banking policy, and there is every hope that the new currency will prove to be one of the most stable in Africa.
 The media is under tight control, and although there are already laws on the statute books, and others being drafted, to allow for press freedom, the past six years have not been very encouraging. Paulos Tesfagiorgis' Human Rights Commission, partly funded by Norway, was closed down on government order

before the referendum, and has not been allowed to reopen. Newsprint is in very short supply and very expensive. Books are extremely expensive and out of the reach of most Eritreans.

Prospective media investors are scrutinized carefully; there is, for example, Saudi interest in establishing a TV network. Understandably, this is viewed with scepticism by the PFDJ. In a speech to the Freedom Forum in Washington, in 1995, Isaias indicated that "the Government must... retain partial ownership of the mediums of the free press."[22] The PFDJ clearly means to run a very tight ship for the foreseeable future.

POLITICS

For the past two years or more, much energy has been devoted to the work of the Constitutional Commission under the leadership of Dr. Bereket Habte Selassie, the distinguished lawyer and academic. It was scheduled to report by March 1996 but received its finishing touches a year later.

There was some disquiet (even in the PFDJ) about the time the committee took over its deliberations, and the expense. For example, a great deal of money and energy was spent on organizing an international conference in Eritrea. Most of those professors invited knew nothing about the country (with the honorable exception of my friends and colleagues, Ed Keller and the late Mohammed Babu) and some of the others had been active opponents of Eritrean independence until after the referendum, when the die had been cast decisively for an independent Eritrea! At the same time, the commission was short of funds for its civic education programs, which were designed to show the public how the constitution would work.

What kind of political system to adopt engaged the minds of all contributors to the lengthy debate. The commission eventually recommended a unitary government with separation of powers among the Legislative, Executive, and Judicial bodies. A unicameral assembly would elect a President from among its ranks.[23] Bereket is very familiar with the British and American systems and it is clear that "his" Constitution reflects his varied background.

In the constitutional proposals, it was declared that it was not necessary to determine the choice of electoral system in the constitution.[24] The draft constitution was debated at further length by an elected constituent assembly in May 1997 and proclaimed by the President at the Independence Day Celebrations of that year. A transitional national council was formed, comprising the 75 members of the PFDJ Central Council, and an equal number of members of the various regional assemblies and representatives of Eritreans living abroad. Three places are reserved for Eritreans living in the Sudan; the Sudanese government is unlikely to let them out to take part in the Council.

Three or four years from now, a multi-party system will (in PFDJ words) emerge and all adult Eritreans will elect a National Assembly. The Assembly will obviously have to be multi-party, at least nominally, if for no other reason than Eritrea's need to retain its international legitimacy in the eyes of important liberal democracies, such as the USA and the countries of the European Union. In 1991, Isaias Afwerki expressed his desire for a multi-party system, but stated that Eritreans did not then have the necessary background for a fully functioning liberal democracy.[25]

In 1994 the PFDJ leadership affirmed that a "periodic change of leadership, and infusion of new blood into leadership are important for a smooth transition and for a healthy political life."[26]

An independent judiciary is very important, but at the moment there are not enough trained Eritrean lawyers. Moreover, much of the law is still in the process of being drafted, has been grafted uneasily on to existing Ethiopian Law, or is traditional (Christian or Muslim) law. It is proving hard not only to codify, but even to reconcile with the needs of a modern, democratic, and non-discriminatory society. A modern judiciary will take a number of years to train and establish, but the Law School at the University of Asmara has begun this daunting task.

In a deposition to the Constitutional Commission, I expressed the view that there should be some provision, either in the constitution or in Eritrean law, for measures of direct democracy in addition to representational democracy. For example, the possibility of initiatives from local people being put on future ballots, the recall of unpopular, inefficient, brutal or corrupt elected officials, and referendums. However, for direct democracy to work to the optimum extent, a federal system is required, and Dr. Bereket ruled this out at a public meeting in Asmara, on the grounds of the small size of the country and the need to keep harmony among its people.[27]

For the next few years, it is difficult to see any opposition emerging (or being allowed to emerge) that could beat the present leadership in the polls. President Isaias Afwerki, unlike many of his predecessors as head of state of so many countries in Africa and elsewhere, does not seem set to remain in power as long as he lives, or want to remain there. The constitution imposes a two term limit on the President. His hand-picked Ministers may have a somewhat longer period in office. But, however alluring the pleasures of power (and power rejuvenates the most jaded of men and women), many among the leadership, including Isaias, had a very grueling time in the field, and many suffer from poor health. The transfer of power to a younger generation, which has not been tested in the field, may occur sooner than we expect. And that generation will not necessarily act in the same manner as the present veteran fighters.

How to form competing parties—which might have a realistic chance of taking power, when the offices of President of Eritrea, Leader of the Armed Forces and the Chairman of the one and only party are, at the moment, held by the same man—is a very difficult task. There were, of course, parties in the old Eritrea from 1947 to 1957, but these were largely based on nationality/religion. The Eritrean leadership regards this form of party alignment as divisive and will prevent such parties from operating. Parties founded on religious, ethnic, regional, or tribal basis will not be allowed.

If the transitional National Council eventually recommends a "first-past-the-post" election system, which favors a two party system (as in the USA and the United Kingdom), the only solution to Eritrea's problem of creating a "loyal opposition," seems to be to encourage the eventual break up of the PFDJ on ideological grounds—or to split it up as a deliberate policy. Isaias told me in 1990, "that not all EPLF members agree on all political and economic matters."[28] It seems that some twenty-five percent of EPLF membership did not immediately join the PFDJ when the latter body was formed in 1994, while many non-EPLF members did. It is possible that two ideological camps are emerging. One faction, not necessarily (or hopefully) the largest, is an advocate of the liberal free market; the other includes social democrats who want to keep a social security welfare net in a country whose people have suffered so much.

My personal view is that, in the long term, regionally based parties should be allowed to form and agitate peacefully, but in order to gain seats in the national assembly must demonstrate some activity and support in other regions. In other words, some form of proportional representation is vital. I would also favor (in time) a coalition government—if not formally, at least informally. Such an arrangement is allowed for and occurs in many situations, for example in some multi-ethnic countries around the world in peace-time, and in the United Kingdom and Israel under crisis conditions.

There is some opposition to the dominant role of the PFDJ, most notably among some sections of the Eritrean diaspora who live overseas in Sudan, Europe, the USA, and the Middle East, and who in former days supported—and in some cases fought for—the ELF. The ELF has split many times since 1970; the only significant sector to oppose (so far, peacefully) the PFDJ, is the self-exiled group of Ahmed Mohammed Nasser, the Eritrean Liberation Front-Revolutionary Council (ELF-RC); its numbers are unknown.

The Eritrean *Jihad* funded by Sudan is outside the country. It wishes to turn Eritrea into a state based on Islamic sharia laws.

Some sections of traditional Afar leadership are opposed to rule from Asmara, but most have accepted positions in the Danakil (since November 1995 known as Debubawi Keyih Bahri) provincial assembly, which has given *de facto* autonomy to the Eritrean Afars.

SOCIAL

Civil Society

The institutions of civil society are poorly developed. The Unions (or Mass Organizations) of Women, Labor, Youth, and Professionals which were established in the field by the EPLF are still closely allied to the Party. After the 1987 Congress, and following a period of expansion into many new areas, the EPLF reconsidered the role of the Mass Organizations. From 1990, it emphasized the dominant role of the popularly elected village and town assemblies. The EPLF cadres were being trained to act as a professional public service whose main task was to advise and service the assemblies.[29]

The EPLF kept a tight control on all its institutions and satellites during the struggle. The Eritrean Relief Association (ERA) (of which I was a very active member) could not have operated so effectively without subordinating its role at times to the strategic plans of the EPLF.

With peace, the government has demonstrated that it intends to retain a controlling hand in an area which is a vital conduit for attracting foreign money and expertise into the country. In its policies toward non-government organizations (NGOs), strict controls are in place over how they operate in Eritrea, what they can pay locally recruited staff, and what they do.[30]

Health

Eritrea is faced with totally inadequate health facilities inherited from its former colonial masters. There are very few trained Eritrean professionals, and little help coming from overseas.

In the field, a decentralized primary health care system was devised that gave a free basic service throughout the liberated and semi-liberated areas. Since independence, the majority of the resources and trained personnel are concentrated in Asmara and many key people are overseas on training courses. After liberation, health care was free throughout the country, and to all classes of society; the government introduced charges in 1994 in an effort to meet its other financial requirements.

The provision of clean and constant drinking water and sewage facilities remain important health priorities.

Education

Probably eighty percent of the male population and ninety percent of females are illiterate. To remedy this there is considerable tolerance of outside, private, and religious foundations and institutions. Some have returned to the country and are picking up the reins dropped some fifty years ago when they were forced to leave Eritrea. The government is facing problems in developing a national curriculum. That inherited from the Italian, British and Ethiopian colonial administrations is totally unsuited to the present-day. In 1983, Berakki Ghebreselassie, who was then director of Zero School, and who later became Eritrea's Minister of Education, told me that one of Eritrea's main priorities post-liberation would be the integration of the curricula.[31]

Even though Eritreans educated at Zero School to the fifth grade, were found to be equivalent to twelfth-graders in the Ethiopian system, the curriculum used in the field is now inappropriate for a country that is embracing the principles of the completely free market.[32] The University of Asmara is rapidly developing its infrastructure and preparing to play a major role in the development of the country.

The expectations of all Eritreans are particularly high in the areas of education and health, and the government must deliver improvements or face a severe drop in popularity. Any visitor to the country can testify to the great progress already made.

Employment

Some fifty per cent of the urban labor force is unemployed. Many of those who are "employed" are either working part-time or are under-employed in government service, often not through their own fault since materials of the most basic sort are often lacking. Some 10,000 (or one-third) of government employees were "streamlined," i.e., dismissed, with some severance compensation in 1995. At all levels, much of the work force lacks the skills, experience, and education to do the job adequately. There are few incentives and pay is low. However, there is still a dearth of employment opportunities for many students who have completed a less-than-satisfactory secondary education under the trying conditions of war, deprivation, and reconstruction.

Housing

This is in short supply throughout Eritrea's urban areas; new accommodation is not keeping up with the demand and there are complicated and long-standing problems of ownership that have not yet been sorted out. Some absentee Eritrean landlords—many living in Ethiopia—have become relatively rich from soaring rents. This has caused considerable resentment in those sectors of Eritrean society which suffered most in the war. Rural housing is invariably of a lower standard than that in the towns. In some respects, Eritrea is being moved rapidly into an in egalitarian society, which is a marked departure from the equality that existed in the field.

Refugees

Although tens of thousands of Eritrean refugees have returned voluntary and some others have been repatriated (mainly from Sudan), some 700,000 are still in the diaspora (500,000 being in Sudan).

In the case of those refugees living in the Middle East, and particularly Sudan, most want to come home and would do so if given the chance. Many Eritreans in Europe and the USA prefer to remain in their new homes; and some are fighting expulsion orders, when they have been found to lack the correct papers, in the USA, Canada, and Australia--three countries where I have been contacted in recent years by immigration lawyers and officials.

There is a large problem about relocating the returnees. Eritrea is a country with virtually no forests, a largely barren soil, uncertain rainfall, and where little water conservation has been practiced in the past. Most of the countryside is in fact very inhospitable. The returnees' former livelihoods and their homes have been destroyed and all resources have disappeared. In many cases, their former land is now occupied by new settlers—often as a result of fluctuating fortunes during thirty years of war, but in some cases after liberation, where resettlement of demobilized fighters has been sponsored or encouraged by the PFDJ.

When the majority of the refugees return, they move into camps very like those they left in Sudan, with little hope of the old, handicapped, and women ever getting out. But at least they are now no longer at the mercy of their fickle Sudanese hosts. Enormous sums from UN and the West are needed to rehabilitate the refugees, but less than ten percent of that pledged had been delivered by the end of 1995. While the camps in the Sudan remain they form a fertile breeding ground for resentment against the Eritrean government and one of the major source of recruits for the Eritrean *Jihad*. For the latter reason, we may expect that the bulk of those who want to return will be allowed back within five years. When they are safely back in Eritrea, they will be under the eye of the PFDJ and its efficient security police.

The Position of Women

Although women formed a third of the fighters of the EPLF, sustained higher levels of casualties than males, and were in many respects superior in combat to most of the men, they now face a great problem. Their families, and the bulk of the Eritreans who did not fight the Dergue, because they were living in Asmara, Addis, or Los Angeles, now expect them to resume the traditional Eritrean women's roles of wife, cook, household drudge, and mother. Many women who married in the field have now been divorced by their husbands—some under pressure from traditional families. There is little employment for them. Some, having no other means of livelihood, have turned to prostitution. Some of the female fighters have resigned from the National Union of Eritrean Women (NUEW) as they feel that the leadership is too concerned with following government policy and not pushing women's issues energetically enough. This verdict may be too harsh; one lone and under-funded organization cannot be expected to shoulder the burden of caring for one-half of the population.

The government has passed laws giving women the right to land, a minimum age of 18 to marry, and banned female genital mutilation (euphemistically called circumcision.) However, these laws are not always being enforced in rural areas.

The government has made a number of attempts to increase the representation of women on public bodies. One senior government minister, with the Justice Portfolio is a woman from a Muslim family, and a large proportion of the membership of the Constitutional Committee were women. This is a welcome improvement on the Referendum Commission of Amare Tekle, in which none of the five senior officials was a woman. Some twenty percent of the members of the National Assembly were women; a very favorable record compared to most Western countries. In the zonal elections of 1996-1997 some thirty percent of seats were reserved for women, and women also stood—successfully in Asmara—for the open seats. There are also women in senior positions throughout the country. In 1991, the mayors of the towns of Adi Keih, Segeneiti, and Tessenai, were women, as was the senior EPLF official in Barka province.[33]

Eritrean women are concerned that if the government pursues the goals of a free market economy too rigorously, public expenditure in the fields of adult literacy, health and agriculture will decline. This development would have a particularly deleterious affect on women.

Fighters

In 1990, Isaias Afwerki told me that with liberation the mission of the EPLA would be fulfilled. It would be restructured as a new body with a majority of new personnel. It would be a professional, non-political body serving the nation as a whole.[34]

Demobilization of two thirds of the 100,000 men and women who were under arms in mid-1991 began. It was relatively easy to demobilize the 20,000 who joined the struggle in the last year of the war. What to do with the remainder has been a very difficult problem. Many were veterans with twenty years of service; most have known no other life since they joined the Front as young men and women at the age of sixteen or seventeen. The law grants them a pension of 10,000 Birr (about 1,500 $US); but some have not yet received it. On the positive side, both the UN and the USA are keen on the demobilization and demilitarization of armies (in Africa at least) as a start towards democratization. It can be expected that some funds will be available for this measure.

Many fighters and ex-fighters are doing essential jobs such as infrastructural work and picking crops. Cotton grown on the Ali Ghidir plantation, mostly by ex-fighters, is a vital export earner. But many men as well as women ex-fighters face severe problems. Few possess marketable skills, and most do not have the educational background to enable them to benefit quickly from higher education.

Some fighters have protested at their changed circumstances. Some of the elite commandos staged a demonstration in Asmara in 1993 over working conditions and lack of pay. Many were disciplined severely.[35] In 1995, disabled ex-fighters at Mai Habar held another demonstration—over lack of any progress towards their rehabilitation and compensation—which only resulted in several deaths and numerous courts martial. The harsh treatment meted out to men and women who have suffered so grievously for a free country is, to some, a somber message that an intolerant, uncaring state is being created.

Other veterans often give voice to a feeling that they are despised by the better dressed and richer Eritreans in the towns, and those who come from overseas on brief holidays. The growing discontent felt by some ex-fighters, and present-day rank-and-file soldiers, could have serious implications for the future of the country. The very high morale and dedication the fighters sustained over thirty years was the main reason for the defeat of the Ethiopian regime. If this wonderful camaraderie is to be dissipated, what will take its place and sustain Eritreans for the even greater struggles that lie ahead?

Although the Eritrean government has demobilized many of the veteran EPLA fighters, in 1994 it introduced national service for the rest of the community. As I said in Chapter Seven, experience in other multi-ethnic countries (such as Switzerland), and in new countries trying to build an homogenous nation out of immigrants from diverse backgrounds (such as Israel), have proven the immense value of universal conscription for building in the young a sense of belonging and commitment to service.

Uniquely, the Eritreans included women on the same basis as men. There were two intakes in that year of national service draftees; a third round was completed in 1995, and others have followed. The first draft came from the Asmara area: there were no exceptions, every male and female from the age of eighteen to forty (raised in 1995 to fifty) years of age had to register. However, those in employment or qualified for university, are exempt, for the time being, from the six months of military training, and the year's community service that follows it. Pregnant women and those nursing babies receive temporary exemption. It is envisaged that everyone in this age group will at some time complete the national service requirement.[36]

There was a second draft in late 1994. This time, draftees were taken from every province. The government claims that national service is popular both with the draftees and with the general public.

One of the worrying features of the first draft, in my eyes at least, was the persecution of the few hundred Jehovah's Witnesses, all of whom stood by their religious convictions and refused to register. They had made themselves extremely unpopular in 1993 by refusing to register to vote in the referendum. Some of them were subjected to violence at the time. The whole community has now been stripped of citizenship, sacked from government posts however menial, and denied licences to trade.

Crime and Punishment

Crime is still a very minor irritant in Eritrea, but there are signs that fraud, corruption, and violence are increasing to some extent. In the first months after liberation, the streets of Asmara were plagued by young boy beggars. These were mainly orphans and disabled victims of the war. They had picked up, 'bad cultural habits from the Ethiopian occupation.'[37] On later visits, it was clear that the government had found more productive occupations for them.

A police force has been trained. And, for the first time, there are also parking inspectors on the main streets of Asmara—a job for some at least, and providing more money for government expenditure.

National Service is also a good way of controlling that sector of any population which is most likely to commit serious crime (males from eighteen to forty years of age.)

There have been a number of reports of arrests and disappearances of Eritreans (in Eritrea, Ethiopia, and elsewhere) who might be oppositionists (or war criminals). The Eritrean Government refuses to answer questions from Amnesty International, or allow human rights activists access to those held; there is no way of knowing whether the reports can be substantiated.

However, it is clear that the Eritreans have shown remarkable tolerance to most Eritreans who collaborated with the Ethiopian occupation regime. In 1985, the EPLF gave an amnesty to members of the Kunama militia who had assisted the Ethiopian army in defending Barentu against attacks by the ELF and EPLF over the previous twenty years. In 1990, Senafé, was liberated by the EPLF for the first time in its history. At that time, I was told by an EPLF Central Committee member that only four Eritreans out of a population of 4,000 were required to undergo "rehabilitation" in custody; the rest were integrated smoothly into the EPLF administration.[38]

NATIONALISM, RELIGION, LANGUAGE
Ethnicity and Nationality

Boris Yeltsin has said: "You can judge how democratic a state is by the way it treats national minorities."[39] This remark highlights the most imponderable problem facing the new Eritrea. Even while Eritreans fought for self-determination within the boundaries of the colonial state and this struggle generated a strong sense of nationhood, there were conflicting trends in EPLF ideology.

EPLF doctrine was that there were nine nationalities in Eritrea.[40] To affirm that there are "nine nationalities in Eritrea" has become something of a declaration of faith. However, to be Devil's Advocate, I could argue, for example, that Jiberti Muslims, whose first language is Tigrinya, could be classified (or indeed regard themselves) as an additional nationality. Just as the Tigré-speaking Christian members of the Mensa clan and the Christian Irob, Saho speakers, might be regarded as separate nationalities. As Tekle Woldemikael has observed "Eritrean society shows a great deal of fluidity in its ethic composition and boundaries" as a result of "ethnic mixing, religious conversion, migration, conquest, and wars."[41]

During the struggle, a main plank of EPLF policy was to favor self-determination for the nationalities, holding out a promise that, once independence had been achieved, real self-determination—up to and including secession—would be allowed for those nationalities that chose this path.

Immediately after the EPLF took over Eritrea, ten provinces were established—based on the eight regions existing under the long-running Italian administrative model, but with Gash/Setit separated from Barka and Asmara split from Hamasien. Governors were appointed who belonged to the dominant nationality in the region. Wide powers were promised amounting to a form of federalism, with the central government limiting its control to defense, foreign affairs and international trade. Elections were held in many of these provinces, starting with villages and working up through sub-districts and districts. After some elections had been held that resulted in no women or fighters being elected, a minimum number of seats were reserved for women and fighters. In granting wide powers to the provinces, the government ran the risk of training them for secession. And independence of smaller multi-ethnic entities, it could be argued, might cause the same problems as accompanied the independence of Bosnia and some other former communist entities.

Provincial boundaries were changed radically in 1995; there are now six provinces, with only Asmara (now Maakel) and Danakil (Debubawi Keyih Bahri) retaining their approximate former dimension. It is important to note that in a number of provinces—notably Gash-Barka, Semenawi Keyih Bahri, and Anseba, as well as Maakel—there are at least two nationalities. The provincial administrations now have much less power than they were promised in earlier EPLF declarations.[42]

It is worth recording the fact that, although the government's Referendum Commission collected data on nationality when registering Eritreans for the 1993 Referendum, the data has not been published, nor, to my knowledge, made available to researchers.

The constitutional proposals contain no mention of nationalities in Eritrea. If such issues were to be included in the Constitution, the stage could be set for the minorities to organize themselves on the basis of nationality/religion/ethnicity/language. This (as we have recently witnessed in the break up of Yugoslavia and the Soviet Union) could cause endless trouble. On the other hand, given that minorities exist in Eritrea, differences between them cannot be ignored; rather should the issues be addressed fully and frankly. The proposals say that Eritrea should accept, "diversity but without unduly laying stress on it."[43] This might be the optimum approach.

Religion

Eritrea is a secular state, with religion separated from the state. The draft constitutional proposals mentioned "rights to belief," under the heading of "fundamental human rights and duties."[44]

For lack of any reliable published data, we will accept the often-stated claim that Eritrea is fifty percent Christian/Animist and fifty percent Muslim. My guess is that if most of the refugees in the Sudan came home, the country would soon have a Muslim majority—a consideration which may affect the government's policy on refugees. The largest Christian denomination is the Eritrean Orthodox Church, which is in the process of splitting away from the Ethiopian Orthodox Church, with the active support of the Coptic Pope in Egypt. This represents a further assertion of nationhood by a young state.

The government takes a great deal of trouble to give at least the appearance of a fifty-fifty balance in government and in senior posts between Muslims and non-Muslims. Lower down, it is very noticeable how highland Christians dominate many areas. For instance, seventy-five percent of entrants to the only university in Eritrea come from Asmara, and most of these are Christians of various denominations. Most of the first 10,000 national service draftees came from Asmara and surrounding areas; the bulk of these were from Christian backgrounds, not Muslim.

The intolerance toward the Jehovah's Witnesses may be due to the PFDJ's fear that, if the Jehovah's Witnesses were to succeed in defying the government, Muslim fundamentalists might take heart (and action). Some traditional Muslim fathers already have strenuously objected to their daughters being drafted. The Eritrean government defended its attack on what one might have thought should be one of the cornerstones of any democratic constitution—the right to practice one's religion—in self-righteous terms such as "extreme fundamentalists who...arrogate to themselves the status of angels can be tolerated only to a certain limit."[45]

This is an unfortunate throw-back to the 1977 National Democratic Program of the EPLF, which said, in "Objective 7 Respect Freedom of Religion and Faith," that it would "strictly oppose all the imperialist-created new counter-revolutionary faiths such as Jehovahs' Witness, Pentecostal, Bahai etc...[and] legally punish those who try to sow discord in the struggle and undermine the progress of the Eritrean people on the basis of religion."[46]

The Government plans to settle nomadic areas—the present inhabitants of which are mostly Muslims—with Christian settlers could prove an explosive point. Providing that the economy can grow quickly enough to provide jobs and improved living standards, Muslim and Animist communities may escape marginalization and religious differences may prove less relevant. Industry is overwhelmingly clustered in Asmara, with only four of the largest enterprises operating outside of the capital—in Massawa, Assab, Keren and Decamare. The government has an avowed policy of decentralization, which, if successful, will help the peripheral Muslim and Animist communities. Concentration on agricultural development will also help marginal rural groups.

Language Policy

Under the British, there were in effect (if not in law) two official languages, Tigrinya and Arabic. The Ethiopian administration tried to enforce a ban on Tigrinya and replace it with Amharic.

In the field, senior commanders and leaders of the EPLF were required to become bilingual in Tigrinya and Arabic. This was of immeasurable value in forming a cohesive political and military organization, and smoothed relations with the Arab world during the struggle. (A number of Arab countries were of some help to the EPLF, and more so in the case of the ELF. See Chapter Six.)

English is now the language of instruction in the secondary schools (most of which are in the highlands) and in the university of Asmara. This is a very far-sighted choice. English is the *lingua franca* of the world's business, technical, and professional elites. Proficiency in English will be of immeasurable help to Eritreans.

What of the seven other Eritrean national languages? The policy of the PFDJ is for all elementary education to be carried out in the language of the area. Two of the languages identified in Eritrea (i.e., Nara and Bedawyet) have not yet been written down. There are few books in most of the other Eritrean languages, and even fewer competent instructors. Understandably, there have been some complaints from, for example, members of the Saho nationality, whose children have to learn three scripts—Latin for Saho, adapted Gee'ez for Tigrinya, and Arabic. They complain that their children will inevitably learn at a slower pace than others and they will be disadvantaged when they try to get a job in another area of the country or want to progress in school beyond the first few grades.

The constitutional proposals recommended "the equality of all Eritrean languages," and argued against "the designation of any official or working language."[47] Nevertheless, it seems possible that, in time, Tigrinya will become "the language of success" and that the downgrading of some of the other languages will follow.

Arabic is the first tongue of only a minority of the population. Making Arabic an official language would ensure its survival, and facilitate the future coalition of all non Tigrinya speakers into an opposition. The PFDJ government is seen (unjustly) by some Muslims as an Habasha (foreign Christian) dominance. But Arabic cannot be "un-made" as a useful working language for many Eritreans. There is a remote possibility of a Quebec-style secessionist movement developing at some stage in the future, if the development in Arabic, non-Tigrinya speaking areas lags behind that of Asmara, or if discrimination against non-highlanders increases.

MILITARY PROBLEMS

There is nothing like the presence of an external threat—real or imaginary—for diverting a people's attention away from domestic discontents. While Eritrea is very safe for the foreseeable future, the potential threats seem to be from the following quarters.

Sudan

The threat from the Sudanese quarter is mainly from Islamic extremists, in a word, *Jihad*. There have been many incursions across the Sudanese border, and one or two from Djibouti and across the Red Sea. All were easily contained, and the threat will remain, at most, a minor irritant. In April 1997, the extremely efficient Eritrean security services uncovered a plot by the Sudanese government to assassinate President Isaias.

The implementation of border pioneer settlements, protected by armed units, of the kind practiced by Israel throughout its history, will probably suffice along the border with Sudan to contain the incursions.

If Sudan persists in arming the extremists, Eritrean "preemptive" attacks are possible, like those the Israelis have mounted on many occasions, in Gaza, Lebanon, Jordan, and further afield. And if Eritrea remains on excellent terms with the USA, the government might also be able to mount attacks on another sovereign state without being subjected to sanctions from the UN or the West. The Eritrean army could be in Khartoum by breakfast time should they wish to move.

Ethiopia

There are no military threats from Ethiopia while the Tigrayan dominated EPRDF government remains in power in Addis Ababa. Eritrea is now a sovereign state, and its territorial integrity would be the key issue in any incursion by Ethiopia. If the EPRDF loses power, and Shoan Amharas regain control—a remote possibility as they are a disunited minority of Ethiopia's population, lack military experience, and cannot bring the Oromo majority with them—then Tigray would secede from Ethiopia, giving the Eritreans an invaluable buffer from attack.

Eritrea could prevent a hostile Ethiopia from importing heavy weapons (aircraft, ships, tanks, etc.) through the ports of Eritrea, and could easily blockade the route from Djibouti. And if weapons are airlifted in, Eritrean intelligence would find some way of neutralizing them. As far as infantry attacks from Ethiopia are concerned, Eritrea is fully capable of dealing with them.

Afars and Other Threats

There is no significant armed threat from Afars in Eritrea, Ethiopia, or Djibouti. However, in April 1996, Eritrean forces made a lightning strike inside Djibouti. Conflicting reports came from the President's Office and the Foreign Minister as to the purpose of this short-lived operation.[48] I assume that it was aimed at bands of Eritrean *Jihad* that had infiltrated Djibouti, who were preparing to attack targets within Eritrea. Eritrea had earlier successfully blocked their attacks from Sudan and across the Red Sea from Yemen.

There are no other threats, with the possible exception of Yemen. Yemen's harassment of Eritrean fishermen and an attempt at occupying an Eritrean island in the Hanish Archipelago led to a brief military skirmish between the two nations in 1995. Eritrea expelled the invaders. It is expected that the dispute will, in the end, be settled peacefully through legal means, with the aid of French and other international mediation.

Diplomacy

Eritrea is building up a core of experienced and able men (and a few women) diplomats. The Eritrean leadership also now has a lot more diplomatic skill, contacts, and experience than it did during 1970-1991.

A number of embassies and consulates exist, strategically placed in countries that supported Eritrea to some extent during its struggles, as well as the key ones: USA, Russia, China, Europe, and Ethiopia. Eritrea has cordial relations with most countries, barring Sudan. Relations with Sudan were severed in December 1994, after *Jihad* incursions into Eritrea, and the assassination of an Eritrean diplomat at the consulate in Kassala in April 1994. Sudan was also incensed that Isaias had received medical treatment (for a potentially fatal condition) in Israel. The Sudanese government is also annoyed at Saudi, Kuwaiti, and Abu Dhabi financing of a major energy project in Eritrea, and at IMF support for Eritrea at a time when Sudan itself has been suspended from the IMF.

Relations could be reopened at any time the Sudanese government reins in its support for Eritrean *Jihad*. The EPLF enjoyed good relations with the Sudan throughout most of the years of struggle. Both countries have a mutual objective in ensuring an orderly return of the 500,000 Eritrean refugees still living in the Sudan.

Israel and Saudi Arabia are equally well disposed toward Eritrea, although both still have hidden agendas. Israel's is to keep the Red Sea from turning into an "Arab Lake," and Saudi Arabia's is to increase conservative Islamic influence in the country.

Eritrea has some diplomatic posts in the rest of Africa. Egypt is important, and Eritrea attends OAU meetings—without much expectation of these meetings ever achieving any concrete results. Eritrea has already played some role in peace-making and peace-keeping in the region. During the Somalia crisis, Eritrea suggested that a US contingent of 50,000 troops be sent to the country and remain for twelve months, during which time they would "totally disarm" the warring factions.[49] However, actions with regard to Djibouti and Southern Sudan have met with greater success. The President of Eritrea has taken an active role in the peace committee of the Inter-Governmental Authority on Drought and Development (IGADD) along with the Presidents of Ethiopia, Kenya and Uganda. The third meeting of the group in September 1994 called for a secular Sudan, or, failing this, for a referendum on independence in the South. In 1995, Eritrea convened a meeting of most Sudanese oppositionist forces in Asmara. The Headquarters of the opposition are in Eritrea, and SPLA troops on leave are a common sight in Asmara.

Eritrea has not supported the claim of the secessionist Somaliland Republic for international recognition, even though the two countries have a very similar claim to statehood. There are obviously unofficial contacts and informal trade links between the two nations.

Strategic Considerations

Eritrea is strategically situated at a choke point; the straits of Aden are still very important shipping lanes. 300 islands in the Red Sea give ample opportunity for listening posts. The two ports of Massawa and Assab are not suitable for the bulk of US Fleet to land and requisition supplies, but goodwill visits have taken place.

Eritrea possesses a number of strategic minerals and resources. Oil and natural reserves are present and the commercial exploitation of them is possible.

Eritrea is not a member of any military pact, although there is clearly a secret agreement with the EPRDF, and some Eritrean armed units are on duty in Ethiopia. Article 11 of the *Joint Com-*

munique Between the States of Eritrea and Ethiopia issued in July 1993, says: "the two parties agree to co-operate in the area of security and to work closely on mutual defense interests."[50]

Eritrea is not a member of the Arab League. Both Egyptian and Israeli trainers were recruited for the first national service intake.

There is considerable economic interdependence with Ethiopia. (After a thirty years union during which time many Eritrean industries and tens of thousands of Eritreans were relocated in Ethiopia, this is hardly surprising.) For the first seven years of Eritrean independence Ethiopia controlled the printing and distribution of the shared currency, this gave it a considerable leverage over Eritrea.

More formal economic links with other Horn countries, as well as Kenya and Yemen, involving a customs union, leading to a free trade area, economic union, and then monetary union, have been suggested by a few scholars, but such ties are many years in the future. (After all, it has taken fifty years to get much of Europe as far as it has on its way towards union.) After the tragic experience of the Ethiopian/Eritrean federation, political confederation is many generations away, if ever.

CONCLUSION

Eritrea is now a stable country with good prospects of its economy taking off, and in time proving one of the most vigorous in Africa. The Eritreans may follow the path, charted first by Japan, then by the dragons of East Asia, and now by China. Centralized state controls and industrial policy can be combined with a free-market sector. Jack Snyder has indicated some of the factors that could make for success of such a policy. Eritrea has few vested interests, no concentrated industries that can realistically expect to lobby for continued state protection, labor that is not politically strong, and above all (at the moment) a superb *esprit de corps* among the bureaucrats who will make the policy work.[51]

A fully competitive, multi-party political system seems further away. The Eritreans will have noticed that mass-suffrage democracy is a very fragile plant in any new country that is attempting to absorb the shock therapy of *laissez-faire* economics. If some ethnic groups benefit while others suffer, the pressures on the new state will surely be exacerbated and may become intolerable. The PFDJ will move as slowly as it can towards the unpredictability of a democratic state.

A genuinely independent media and tolerance of dissent seem even further in the future. The leaders of the PFDJ spent most of their formative years in an organization that worked on the principle of democratic centralism. Matters were discussed at great length before the leadership took decisions, but once decisions were made, everyone was expected to toe the line. It will take many years before the leadership learns to deal with dissent in an easy and fair fashion.

In the meantime, Eritrea remains an oasis of peace and energy. It continues to be a place of hope for all fair-minded men and women. The sacrifice of hundreds of thousands of Eritreans down the generations has not been in vain.

Notes

1. Thomas Carlyle, *The French Revolution: A History*, 3 (London: Folio Society, 1989) (first published 1837) p. 111.
2. For some of my most significant publications on Eritrea since 1990, see Roy Pateman, ed., *Africa Today: (Special Issue) Eritrea, An Emerging New Nation in Africa's Troubled Horn?*, 38, 2. (1991); Roy Pateman, "Eritrea: Takes the World Stage", *Current History*, 93, 583 (1994):228-231; Roy Pateman, "The Legacy of Eritrea's National Question". *Society*, 33, 6 (1996):37-42.
3. Isaias Afwerki, *Interview with Author*, Afabet, August 17, 1990.
4. *Ibid.*
5. *Eritrea Profile*, 2, 15 (1995):6.
6. Daniel Mebrahtu, "Ghinda", *Eritrea Profile*, 2, 14, (1995):6.
7. Habteab, *Interview with Author*, Asmara, September 18, 1991.
8. Isaias Afwerki, *Interview with Author*, Asmara, September 21, 1991.
9. *Ibid.*

10. Gebre Hiwet Tesfagiorgis. "Referendum for a Lasting Peace Following Eritrean Military Victory", *Paper Presented* at African Studies Association Meeting, St. Louis, M.O. (1991), pp. 33-34.

11. Provisional Government of Eritrea, *Clarification on Misconceptions About the Referendum*, Asmara, October 16, 1991 pp. 3-4.

12. Kjetil Tronvoll, *Personal Communications* (1993).

13. According to Iyob, 1.8 million voters had been registered by October 1992 (a third of whom lived abroad), but only 1.1 million voted in the April 1993 referendum—this would mean that at most only sixty-one percent of eligible voters cast a ballot. In a personal communication she admits that she has made an error. Ruth Iyob, *The Eritrean Struggle for Independence: Domination, Resistance, Nationalism 1941-1993* (Cambridge: Cambridge University Press, 1995), pp. 138-9; p. 178, fn. 27; Personal communication, August 10, 1996.

14. Economist Intelligence Unit, *Eritrea: Country Report* (London, 1994, Third Quarter).

15. World Bank, *Eritrea: Options and Strategies for Growth* (1994).

16. Isaias Afwerki, *Interview with Author*, She'ab, Eritrea, December 12, 1987.

17. Isaias Afwerki, *Interview with Author*, Afabet, August 17, 1990.

18. Jacky Sutton. "Better Red than Rampant", *Eritrea Profile*, 1, 13(1994):5.

19. Abdella Jabr, *Interview*, Columbus, Ohio, November 8, 1994.

20. Aynalem Marcus. "Training for What?", *Eritrea Profile*, 1, 29 (1994):2.

21. Government of Eritrea, *Partnership in Development and Development Letter* (1994).

22. "President's Speech on Freedom of Expression", *Eritrea Profile*, 1, 47 (1995):6-7.

23. "Constitutional Proposals for Public Debate", *Eritrea Profile*, 2, 32 (1995):2.

24. Constitutional Commission of Eritrea, *Constitutional Proposals for Public Debate*, August, 1995.

25. Isaias Afwerki, *Interview with Author*, Asmara, September 21, 1991.

26. *A National Charter for Eritrea*, (EPLF: Nacfa, February 1994): p.19.

27. "Constitution-making: A People's Project", *Eritrea Profile*, 2, 34 (1995):3.

28. Isaias Afwerki, *Interview with Author*, Afabet, August 17, 1990.

29. *Ibid.*

30. Government of Eritrea, *Partnership in Development and Development Letter* (1994).

31. Berakki Ghebreselassie, *Interview with Author*, Zero School, Eritrea, August 30, 1983.

32. Habteab, *Interview with Author*, Asmara, September 18, 1991.

33. Askalu Menkerios, *Interview with Author*, Asmara, September 18, 1991.

34. Isaias Afwerki, *Interview with Author*, Afabet, August 17, 1990.

35. "The President Replies", *Eritrea Profile*, 1, 27 (1994):4-5.

36. "The Law of the Land", *Eritrea Profile*, 1, 46 (1995):5.

37. Askalu Menkerios, *Interview with Author*, Asmara, September 18, 1991.

38. Osman, *Interview with Author*, Senaf, August 13, 1990.

39. Cited, Jack Snyder, "Nationalism and the Crisis of the Post-Soviet State", in Michael E. Brown, ed., *Ethnic Conflict and International Security* (Princeton: Princeton University Press, 1993):92.
40. Eritrean People's Liberation Front, *Memorandum*, (The Field, 1978.)
41. Tekle M. Woldemikael, "The Cultural Construction of Eritrean Nationalist Movements", in Crawford Young, ed., *The Rising Tide of Cultural Pluralism: The Nation-State at Bay?* (Madison: The University of Wisconsin Press, 1993):182.
42. For a fuller account of the relationship between central and regional government, see Gazette of Eritrean Laws, *Proclamation for the Establishment of Regional Administrations*, (Asmara: Government of Eritrea, 1996).
43. *Constitutional Proposals*, p.8.
44. *Ibid.*, p.24.
45. "Statement on Jehovah's Witnesses", *Eritrea Profile*, 1, 51 (1995):3.
46. Cited in Basil Davidson, Lionel Cliffe and Bereket Habte Selassie, eds., *Behind the War in Eritrea*, (Nottingham: Spokesman, 1980):149.
47. *Eritrea Profile*, 2, 33 (1995):2.
48. Craig Calhoun, *Personal Communication*, April, 1996.
49. Embassy of Eritrea, *Statement of the Government of Eritrea on the Situation in Somalia*, July 28, 1993 (Washington, D.C.).
50. State of Eritrea, *Joint Communique*, July 31, 1993.
51. Snyder, "Nationalism" p. 93.

Index

Eritreans and Ethiopians are listed under their first names.